PROGRAMS and PRACTICES

Writing Across the Secondary School Curriculum

Edited by

Pamela Farrell-Childers

•

Anne Ruggles Gere

•

Art Young

Boynton/Cook Publishers
Heinemann

Portsmouth, NH

Boynton/Cook Publishers, Inc.
A Subsidiary of
Reed Publishing (USA) Inc.
361 Hanover Street, Portsmouth, NH 03801−3912
Offices and agents throughout the world

Editor: Peter Stillman
Production: J. B. Tranchemontagne
Cover design: Julie Hahn

Every effort has been made to contact the copyright holders for
permission to reprint borrowed material. We regret any oversights
that may have occurred and would be happy to rectify them in the future
printings of this work.

Library of Congress Cataloging-in-Publication Data
Programs and practices: writing across the secondary school
    curriculum/edited by Pamela B. Farrell-Childers, Anne Ruggles
    Gere, Art Young.
        p.   cm.
    Includes bibliographical references.
    ISBN 0−86709−334-X
    1. English language−Composition and exercises−Study and
teaching (Secondary)−United States. 2. Interdisciplinary approach
in education−United States. I. Farrell-Childers, Pamela B., 1943−
II. Gere, Anne Ruggles, 1944−   . III. Young, Art, 1943−   .
LB1631.P698   1994
808′042′0712−dc20   93−5996
                                                             CIP

Printed in the United States of America
98 97 96 95 94 PC 10 9 8 7 6 5 4 3 2 1

Contents

Introduction
Pamela Farrell-Childers, Anne Ruggles Gere, and Art Young

Writing across the curriculum (WAC) has been an important initiative for educational reform in the nation's schools for more than a decade. We have heard teachers report on WAC efforts at annual conventions of the National Council of Teachers of English as well as at various regional and affiliate NCTE meetings, at local sites of the National Writing Project, at the Bread Loaf School of English summer sessions, in classrooms and school districts, and in informal conversations in the corridors of school buildings and convention centers. Numerous articles and several books have been published recently that provide theoretical perspectives and classroom strategies for incorporating WAC into all kinds of courses and that report the results of innovative collaborations by teachers in different disciplines. Most of these conference presentations and published works have focused on small groups of teachers working together to improve their students' learning and communication abilities through curricular projects and classroom innovations. Thanks to these teacher-scholars, we have a good deal of information about how individual teachers employ WAC strategies in their classes. We know a great deal less about how groups of teachers and administrators work together to develop WAC programs that extend across schools or districts.

In diverse locations across the nation, in rural, urban, and suburban schools, efforts are now emerging to institutionalize WAC programs or to sustain WAC initiatives by integrating them into other programs such as statewide assessment. The major purpose of this book, then, is to describe and critique some ways WAC has been incorporated into schoolwide, districtwide, and statewide programs. WAC efforts, which most often begin with small groups of teachers working in a limited number of classrooms, can and often do expand to become the catalyst for systemic change. In these pages readers will find the philosophical foundations for WAC programs and numerous specific classroom applications that provide the explanatory power of practical experience. In addition, teachers and administrators will discover ways others are nurturing WAC by creating environments in which WAC becomes central to an institution's educational mission. The goals of WAC—improved learning and communication—are supported by many educational constituencies. Yet, for many reasons, ranging from lack of funding to lack of models for sustaining in schools what is fundamentally interdisciplinary and collaborative, successfully institutionalizing WAC presents challenges. As individual schools, school districts, and state agencies begin to undertake this task, we believe that the nineteen cases presented here offer workable possibilities, imaginative solutions, and honest doubts about the problems of bringing the WAC movement to the nation's children.

Writing across the curriculum has its beginnings, for the three of us, in the late 1970s. As we and others in the United States were worrying about declining test scores and the lack of value our society and our educational system seemed to place on written communication, we became aware of the important work of James Britton, Nancy Martin, and their colleagues at the University of London's Schools Council Project. Theirs was a major effort to integrate and then study "language across the curriculum" in English schools in the 1960s and 1970s. Their work demonstrated in theory and practice that language was integral to *learning* as well as to *communication* in all disciplines. Many supporters who began WAC projects in the U.S. at that time were motivated by a desire to enhance student abilities in these two areas. First, they were concerned with students' ability to communicate, what was often called student literacy—functional literacy, critical literacy, academic literacy. Teachers, administrators, and funding agencies wanted students to read and write better. Second, supporters were concerned with students' abilities as learners—they wanted students to become more active and engaged learners, critical thinkers, and problem solvers. They believed that providing students with increased opportunities to use writing as a tool for learning would help achieve these goals. We might say that first-generation WAC programs founded on these premises focused on the cognitive development of individual students. They encouraged writing in all disciplines to enable students to become astute learners, critical thinkers, and effective communicators.

In the 1980s, teachers and scholars explored the social dimensions of written communication, an exploration that gradually shifted WAC theory and practice away from the purely cognitive to a more socially based perspective. This shift paralleled WAC's move from the individual classroom into the wider social arena of school, district, and state. Thus, to the first two premises for WAC programs (learning and communication), a third and fourth were added. The third premise is that writing is a *social process*; it takes place in a social context. If we want students to be effective communicators, to be successful engineers and historians, then we cannot separate form from content, writing from knowledge, action from context. We should not teach writing generically, in a vacuum, as if it were a skill unconnected to purpose or context. Student writers need to join a community of learners engaged in generating knowledge and solving problems, to join, even as novices, disciplinary conversations and public-policy discussions. WAC programs, therefore, began to stress the role of collaboration in learning, the role of audience in communication, and the role of social context in learning to write and writing to learn. Each new context makes different demands on a writer and requires different understandings about what expressions of knowledge are valued in particular communities. Teachers began to change the social environments of their individual classrooms to nurture and challenge student writers. They began to advocate change in the way individual classrooms are connected to other classrooms within schools and in the way schools are connected to larger social units of community, district, and state. They began to lobby for the institutionalization of WAC within school systems.

A fourth premise, then, is that writing is *social action*; writers are advocates who write to further personal and social goals. If we want students to be effective communicators, we cannot continually ask them to practice writing separate from any community of shared knowledge and interests. Writers write to change their perceptions of the world and to change others' perceptions of the world. Thus WAC programs have added advocacy writing to their repertoire: students writing to audiences beyond the classroom; writing to audiences who want to hear what they know and what they think about what they know; writing on electronic networks to understand, monitor, and solve global as well as local problems; writing to change their world.

As we move toward the twenty-first century, WAC proponents understand more and more what is to be done. We do not replace the cognitive dimension of writing with the social dimension, but rather we continue to build on the knowledge and experience of others. Today, mature WAC programs attempt to use all four underlying premises as a way of empowering students as active learners and effective communicators: writing to learn, writing to communicate, writing as social process, writing as social action. Certainly, there are tensions and conflicts between teachers and scholars who prefer either cognitively or socially based instructional strategies, just as there are tensions and conflicts in each attempt to institutionalize WAC. The stance of most programs is to welcome competing viewpoints on such matters, to see WAC as an inclusive and evolving movement, one that seeks to encourage conversations about significant educational issues, and then to listen for opportunities that may lead to educational renewal based on consensus.

From one perspective, WAC is the individual teacher in all disciplines, supported and rewarded by a network of peers, administrators, and community leaders. To introduce the four premises of WAC in meaningful ways into a mathematics classroom is a difficult and risky enterprise for a teacher. New ways of designing writing assignments, responding to students and their writing, and integrating writing into the essential learning of the course must be discovered and understood in practice. Few models are available to today's teachers from their experiences in college, where most classes were taught in lectures and writing was used to test knowledge rather than to generate it. Institutionalizing WAC will help create viable models for teaching and learning accessible to teachers in all disciplines. The traditional model has created educational systems in which most teachers are rewarded when they do not attend to the language abilities of their students. WAC seeks to change this unfortunate situation, but meaningful change must be a joint effort between teachers and the systems in which they spend their professional lives.

At the level of the individual school, WAC programs have emerged from a variety of sources. Beginning with interested faculty, they have been administered and sustained in school writing centers, multimedia centers, and computer centers. They have been integrated into innovative programs in the sciences, social sciences, humanities, mathematics, and performing arts — programs often funded by state, federal, corporate, or foundation grants. School WAC programs need to be embedded in the essential values of the various communities that support them and to which they are accountable: school boards, parents, students, and taxpayers. In practice, they often establish mutual support systems with local colleges, community colleges, and businesses. With government and industry's recent interest in Total Quality Management, a management strategy that is based on empowering workers to work in teams and become involved in corporate decision making, has come a renewed interest in collaboration and workplace literacy. Thus liaisons with numerous constituencies to advance WAC goals appear more possible than they did even a few years ago.

At the district and state levels there is much that can be done to foster successful WAC programs throughout the system. In particular, administrators can often generate supplemental funding to demonstrate that WAC is a priority, use such funding combined with shifts in scheduling to allow teachers time to plan and to collaborate, develop institutional structures that encourage collaboration in teaching, develop institutional reward systems for both individual teachers and schools that demonstrate excellence in WAC initiatives, and develop connections to important statewide programs, such as assessments of student, teacher, and school performance. In one example of activities to be encountered in the pages that follow, a school district creates the structures necessary for teachers to visit classrooms across schools to give instructional demonstrations, to facilitate understanding of WAC among teachers, to collaborate as teacher-researchers assessing the impact of WAC in local classrooms, and to address thorny issues of curriculum and community involvement. In another example, a state department of education creates direct connections between successful WAC curricula in individual schools and statewide assessment of student performance. Students might demonstrate proficiency in science by presenting a portfolio of written work in science courses. Mathematics students might solve a problem by calculating the solution and then speculating in writing about the relevance of the process they used. Such concepts reinforce the connections between educational goals at the classroom, the school, the district, and the state levels.

While there is no formula for implementing and sustaining a WAC program in every conceivable context, there are patterns that emerge from a review of the successful programs described in this book. These patterns do not lessen the difficulty often associated with institutionalizing WAC, but they provide us with a clearer understanding of the issues involved and alternative strategies for initiating change at both local and state levels. Change consistent with WAC principles can begin at any point in the system with the building of a supportive educational environment by administrators in the district office, by a school principal, or by an interdisciplinary group of teachers. Often it begins with teachers who introduce WAC concepts to their classes and form a support group of professionals to offer encouragement and advice. The most successful programs are those that have attained support at all levels of the system, support that encourages and rewards innovative teaching practices associated with WAC. If a system and a school praise a science teacher who believes that her students' poor writing in science is someone else's responsibility, then WAC will be perceived as essentially a skills based, remedial program unrelated to generating and communicating knowledge in science. When the faculty reward system is structured around such assumptions, many teachers will not risk experimenting with instructional reform that may not be valued by the system or respected by their peers.

This book tells nineteen stories narrated by teachers in different disciplines and by administrators with differing responsibilities. Although there are many common threads in these stories, they have many different settings. They describe experiences in numerous states across our nation, in small, rural schools and in large, urban school districts, in public and private institutions; they describe programs created to serve ethnically and culturally diverse students and their communities, from Baltimore to Arizona, Brooklyn to Iowa, Detroit to Florida, Seattle to Appalachia; they describe collaborative networks of teachers and students that move from classroom to classroom across narrow hallways in a single school, or that move from school to school across a school district or a state, or that connect through telecommunications writers and readers in one classroom with others across the nation and the world. Each chapter locates a WAC program in a specific context, a program that emerged in response to local needs, educational structures, and site-specific opportunities. Readers will learn how various collaborations were formed to work within local educational contexts to institutionalize reforms based on WAC principles. They will learn about structures and strategies that might well apply to their own educational environments. And they will learn the potential of WAC to improve education in individual classrooms and in educational systems across the nation.

We have organized this book into three sections, each prefaced with a brief description. Part One describes pitfalls as well as possibilities for WAC in schools. This section takes an honest look at several programs, demonstrating that while educational reform is never simple or easy, we can benefit from the experience of others who have faced similar challenges. Part Two focuses on collaboration as an integral component of successful WAC programs. This section explores various possibilities for collaboration in educational settings, suggesting why collaboration is a WAC prerequisite and how such collaborations come into being. Part Three describes how particular programs were implemented, have changed, and are being sustained. The institutionalization of WAC, its integration into educational goals and structures, is undoubtedly the most difficult problem faced by its many proponents. This book is dedicated to all the pioneers represented in its pages who are tackling this challenge so that others may learn and follow.

Contexts for Change: Problems and Possibilities

As the introduction suggests, Writing Across the Curriculum has begun to be institutionalized. Rather than depending entirely upon initiatives of individual teachers in their classrooms, it has emerged in school and district-wide programs. Administrative support, funding, and collaboration with colleges frequently accompany this program development, and possibilities for faculty development, new equipment, and alternative assessment can emerge. At the same time, the euphoria that accompanies the development of new programs can obscure the complicated issues that emerge with innovation. These issues include faculty resistance, politics, externally imposed evaluation, difficulties with technology, clarity of goals and agreements, and the role of students. The chapters in this section explore these issues and offer both cautions and encouragements to individuals thinking about developing a WAC program.

In Chapter 1, Bernadette Glaze and Chris Thaiss explore the nature of teacher resistance, demonstrating how it can both facilitate and prevent change. They also discuss how students resist the regular writing and more open-ended learning of WAC. Marcella Emberger, Clare Kruft, Sally McNelis, and Sharon Robbins outline the successes and failures of a district-wide WAC program by examining its background, training model, coaching partnerships, assessment, and public relations. In Chapter 3, Lois Easton and Roger Shanley exchange letters to discuss the relationship between assessment and WAC, demonstrating how a school district can foster the development of a WAC program by emphasizing assessment of student writing. Brenda Greene and Lorraine Kuziw draw on their own experience to offer recommendations on what to avoid in developing a collaborative high school-college WAC program. Nancy Linvill and Chris Peters close this section with a consideration of the relationship between WAC and technology, showing how so-called underachievers can use HyperCard to learn through writing.

1

Resistance as Inspiration in a Language and Learning Program

Bernadette Glaze and Christopher Thaiss

"There's not enough time to read all their writing."

"I can't give time to writing because I have too much material to cover."

"They need to know the material before they can write about it."

"I don't want to take the risk to try something new. It might not work and I might look bad."

"Writing uncovers ambiguity, and the students I teach don't want to hear that questions don't have easy answers. They don't respect me if I tell them that history is all questions and points of view. They think that I'm either holding out on them or that I just don't know the right answer."

"I've never had confidence in my own writing. How can I evaluate someone else's?"

"Many of the students don't like to write. None like admitting that they don't know something. That's a sign of weakness."

"Some of the brightest students see writing as a waste of time. They want me to teach them the facts."

Judy Grumbacher teaches high school physics; Barbara Larson teaches computer science; Rachel Thompson teaches history. All three teach at Thomas Jefferson High School in Fairfax County, Virginia, and all three have come to believe in the power of writing to spark thought and learning in their classes. All three are eloquent speakers about a philosophy and a method that have transformed their teaching; yet

9

they frequently find themselves lonely voices among colleagues who resist, as the quotes above attest, to putting writing into their teaching. Indeed, they had been there themselves, until inspiring colleagues and participation in the Northern Virginia Writing Project (NVWP) encouraged them to change their understanding. Moreover, they continue to work in school environments economically and theoretically opposed to the dynamic, elusive learning that writing inspires. They have no trouble talking about the resistance of students, nurtured in such school environments, to the writing they assign. Resistances to writing are a fact of life for these teachers, and each day offers challenges to the will and to the imagination.

An In-service Program Inspired by Resistances

These same resistances, we have come to realize, have shaped and continue to shape the Language and Learning Program of the NVWP, which for fourteen years has been trying to cope optimistically and creatively. It would have been temptingly easy to write a chronological "milestones" report on the growth of what we see as a successful effort—to take pride in and some of the credit for the achievements of teachers such as Grumbacher, Larson, and Thompson. To write from the angle of the resistances we face may be to reveal the flaws in the program, undercutting our notions of success by admitting the problems that continue to drag at our momentum. But as we began to look at our NVWP history through the lens of resistance, we came to realize that resistance, rather than dragging down our program, has been our creative force. We also came to see that the resistance has been within us and our colleagues as well as in those circumstances and attitudes that resist our schemes. We began to think of "resistance" in positive terms, akin to the electrical resistance that transforms the smooth flow of electrons into heat, light, and the power to run our minds and machines. It wasn't a stretch to realize that without resistance, nothing happens.

What we'll do in this essay is describe in brief the resistances that led to each phase of our program; then, using interviews with teachers Thompson, Larson, and Grumbacher, identify the resistances that continue to inspire our thinking.

Milestones of the Language and Learning Program

1978—The first Summer Institute of the NVWP is held, inspired in part by teacher resistance to curricula dominated by rote memorization and multiple choice testing. The National Writing Project as a whole receives federal funding in response to media attacks on declining writing proficiency by students. Twenty-five teachers, K-University, come to George Mason University for five weeks of reading, writing, presentations, and talk about the teaching of writing. Elementary teachers raise the issue of finding the time to include more writing in a curriculum already packed with such varied subjects as math, science, and history. Elementary teachers explore a novel idea for combatting the resistance posed by lack of time: writing about diverse subjects as a way to blend language arts objectives into the rest of the curriculum.

A literacy report later in 1978 from the Faculty Senate at George Mason attacks the English department for having failed to instill good writing skills in students across the majors. Resisting a proposed junior-year writing proficiency test and a structure of remedial courses, English faculty in the NVWP successfully counterpropose a series of workshops for faculty across the disciplines as a way to improve the understanding of and response to student writing. Faculty members from English and eight other departments attend the first series of monthly workshops.

1979 — In response to the national "writing crises," the superintendent of Fairfax County (VA) schools requires high school social studies departments to teach students how to write "perfect" (error-free) research papers. The NVWP is hired to teach an in-service course for social studies teachers, and we encounter intense resistance to our "writing as process" philosophy from teachers, under the gun to produce mechanically errorless writing. Resisting the pressure to abandon what they consider to be sound philosophy, the NVWP directors establish goals: to recruit and train as consultants teachers of social studies; and to influence public education policy through information to administrators. Responding to the needs of teachers outside English departments, the NVWP begins to place strong emphasis on writing as a means to help students learn and think about diverse subjects.

1980-83 — The NVWP invites high school and middle school teachers of social studies, math, and science to take part in the five-week summer institutes toward becoming teacher-consultants. However, even with active recruitment, we are able to attract fewer than ten teachers in our region who see writing as more than a product to test knowledge of content. Subject-area specialists in local counties still regard writing as the responsibility of the English department. The NVWP receives state funding for writing across the curriculum (WAC) summer institutes for George Mason University faculty, but the program attracts only a small proportion of senior faculty.

1983 — Though NVWP philosophy had broadened several years earlier, the project had continued to advertise its basic in-service course as "The Teaching of Writing" until it had credentialed enough teachers from across the curriculum to justify a more cross-curricular name. (A founding principle of the National Writing Project had been "teachers teaching teachers" — not college faculty teaching K–12 faculty nor English teachers giving courses to history teachers.) Now, the project renames the in-service course "Writing and Learning" and for the first time sets up courses to be taken by teachers from across the departments within single schools.

1987 — Whenever possible, the NVWP had also resisted the pressure to give the "quick fix," one-shot workshop. Though employers, whether school principals or business managers, often see the here-and-gone workshop as a cheap substitute (sometimes not so cheap!) for the in-service course, it had been (and continues to be) our policy to emphasize the long-term benefits of continuity and reinforcement over several weeks or months.

But we, of course, had run up against very powerful resistance: teachers' lack of time to take enrichment courses. By 1987 the "Writing and Learning" courses plus other influences had kindled significant interest in WAC in the twelve school districts in northern Virginia — much more interest than could have been handled by our in-service structure. Moreover, through our network of teacher-consultants throughout the region, we knew of many teachers, both within and outside the project, who were doing innovative things with writing in their classes, but who had no forum for demonstrating their techniques for teachers in other schools and school districts. (Hence there was a need for us to overcome the resistance of distance!) In response, we organize for November 1987 what would become the annual Language and Learning Conference, a full Saturday of concurrent presentations given by teachers from across the curriculum, K–12, plus a keynote address by a well-known writer. (As of 1992, our guests have included Bob Tierney, Denny Wolfe, Toby Fulwiler, Nancy Martin, and Miles Myers.) Attendance at the conferences has averaged over 300 (in three years we had to turn away applicants). For many of the people who come to these Saturdays, this is their only contact with the NVWP, but for many others it has become an annual experience.

1993 — In the midst of hard times, as layoffs and salary cuts sour morale and send teachers in search of second jobs instead of in-service credit — while panicked pundits, bemoaning lack of U.S. competitiveness, clamor for more subjects and longer school days — the Language and Learning Program is challenged once again to turn resistance into inspiration.

Turning Resistance into Energy

Our in-service experience has taught us that regardless of the strength and variety of efforts to propagate WAC, certain resistances will never go away because of factors endemic to public schools and to the student population. We feel that we have avoided becoming burned out on WAC by accepting the need to work with these resistances rather than seeing them as problems we have failed to solve.

Some Common Resistances and the Strategies They Inspire

We gave a brief overview of writing to learn at a county social studies in-service recently and were amazed at the number of teachers who had never heard of writing to learn; who didn't know what free writing was; who had never seen a learning log. At a meeting of social studies chairs recently, one announced the beginning of a WAC program at her school. Each month all departments would emphasize a different punctuation, spelling, or grammatical error. Out of either deference or ignorance, no one challenged her definition of WAC. These two brief examples indicate to us resistances to WAC. What were the factors that kept these teachers so distant from what we know about WAC and writing to learn? How can such an experience help us to design appropriate programs?

Presented below are some of the more common causes of the resistance we face and some strategies we have developed for dealing with them in our in-service programs.

Teacher Preparation: Many of the teachers at the county in-service were new to the profession. Teachers teach the way they have been taught, no matter what they might be told in methods classes. One major source of resistance comes from the college and university faculty in whose classes teachers have sat. Even in methods courses, prospective teachers often find that professors lecture about "interactive teaching styles" but don't exemplify them.

Our in-service courses are designed to break this cycle: they reflect key elements of effective teaching—writing to learn, small- and large-group interactions, teachers teaching other teachers, high standards and expectations. Our courses have the reputation of being "tough" and "a lot of work, but worth it." As history teacher Rachel Thompson says, "People are less resistant the more they know, whether from their personal experience or from enriched academic experience."

Class Size and Time: The first question we are asked at presentations is usually about time: time to read and comment on learning logs and time out of the curriculum for students to write. Budget cuts are driving class sizes up. The class size for English is limited to twenty-four in the state of Virginia, because curriculum planners expect English teachers to devote some time to response to student writing. But social studies classes run upwards of thirty to thirty-five. Even the most conscientious of teachers would have a difficult time with the paper load. What does this say about how learning is supposed to occur in such environments? An Advanced Placement Government teacher told us that he would have to cut back on the amount of writing he currently assigns because of projected class sizes for next year.

There is no easy solution to this dilemma, which is one of the reasons we make sure that all of our in-service efforts are centered in teachers talking with other teachers. Our Language and Learning Conference brings together teachers who deal with this dilemma daily and who eagerly share strategies dealing with time and numbers. For example, at a recent conference, social studies teacher Jan Valone described the weekly letters that students write to her about what they've learned in their government class. To ease the paper load, Valone responds to the letters of only one of her five classes each week.

Learning Theory and Time: Writing to learn changes a classroom. An educational system that values "covering" material and standardized testing imposes a rigid schedule that restricts flexibility and time needed for exploratory thinking and writing. Computer science teacher Barbara Larson put it this way: "Using writing process and other things we've done which have focused on thinking rather than just presenting content . . . takes more time than if you just whipped out an explanation. The students might not know the material, but you can at least be sure you've covered it." Larson relates the story of a team meeting she had with other computer science teachers about the varied writing and learning activities they had recently tried. They all agreed that "what they had done . . . had slowed them down, but they thought they had done a better job of teaching the material." Rachel Thompson agrees: "Structuring learning around writing opportunities is a lot more difficult than saying, 'You've got to know the Stamp Act for the test.' And if you really are going to involve kids in learning, you can't repeat things from year to year—develop this little program which you throw out to them. Some teachers see themselves as technicians who go out and deliver information each day. Writing to learn demands interaction. It changes the teacher as well as the student."

Teachers who use writing to learn with their students understand the crucial role that time for reflection plays in education. The major dilemma is how to make writing to learn fit into a school *system* that equates reflection with idleness, that admires the orderly march through "material," and that doesn't know how to "count" the strange, unpredictable—albeit interesting—turns that genuine thinking and writing require. Writing to learn changes all the rules. Or as physics teacher Judy Grumbacher says, "Students are used to jumping through hoops. With writing, students make and hold their own hoops." Writing blows apart traditional constructs about how we learn and challenges us to examine what Jane Emig (1983) called the "magical thinking" that influences the decisions and choices we make as teachers:

> Most North American schools are temples to magical thinking, with the focus not only on explicit teaching but on a specific form of explicit teaching—adults performing before large groups of learners. As evidence: I recently heard of a note an evaluating administrator slipped a teacher who was helping small groups of writers actively construct their reality through imaginative sequences of experiences and activities. The note read: "I'll come back when you're teaching."
> (135)

This conflict continues to be the biggest challenge in our courses. We address it directly; we discuss it in class and we make it the topic of presentations by teacher-consultants and of assigned readings (e.g., Janet Emig's "Non-Magical Thinking" and teacher essays from Toby Fulwiler's 1987 collection, *The Journal Book*). Moreover, in assigning the participants to keep learning logs, we trust that practice of exploratory writing will lead the teachers to appreciate its value for their students' learning. We have seen again and again that teachers' experiencing the freedom to ask questions, go off on tangents, and try out new connections in their "thinkwriting" brings an exhilaration that they want their students to share.

Writing Experience: It's difficult or impossible to teach what we don't know or haven't experienced. As Barbara Larson puts it: "I grew up in an era when there were those who could and those who couldn't write and I was one who couldn't. I felt totally inadequate when I collected writing." This feeling of inadequacy is true for many teachers across the curriculum. Many of us went through elementary and high school when writing instruction was equated with grammar and editing lessons. The leap to understanding both writing process and the role of writing in the learning process is especially enormous for those who experienced writing in school as something to be feared, avoided, or, at best, memorized.

Teachers need ongoing support in making this leap of understanding. The Writing Project offers a strong in-service course that provides teachers with much writing to learn practice, which makes it possible for them to incorporate these strategies into their classrooms. Many of the teachers who take our courses say that for the first time they feel that they are writers. Still, the resistance imposed by demands on teachers' time has limited the numbers who have taken our courses, or other writing courses, and therefore limits the number who can achieve this new understanding.

The Pressure to Evaluate "Everything":   What does one do with the writing? How does the writing count in the grade book? How does one evaluate writing to learn? The idea that the student can learn through the writing itself, without its being evaluated, conflicts head-on with the widespread assumption that the teacher must be responsible for whatever learning occurs. The idea, as expressed by James Britton (1970) in *Language and Learning*, that premature evaluation of writing by a reader can even hinder a student's writing development, occasions even more resistance. Barbara Larson reflected on a writing project her students had just completed in a computer science class:

> [Because the students had used the writing in order to think], the important stuff had already happened. But I still *felt* that I had to do something with it. And there are two sides to the quandary: volume (the amount of writing to read) and my competence to even look at the writing. How do you grade something like this if you want to do something other than the normal grading for mistakes in content or mechanics and usage?

We find that the way the instructor of the in-service course handles response and evaluation of the teachers' many writings can show teachers answers to some of these questions. These methods then become the focus of class discussions. Also, a standard component of all teacher-consultant presentations is evaluation of students' writing. Further, the Language and Learning Conferences always devote time to this concern. Indeed, in 1991 "Evaluation of Student Writing" was the theme of the conference, with Miles Myers, author of *A Procedure for Writing Assessment and Holistic Scoring* (1980), the keynote speaker.

Risk Taking Perceived as Weakness: All through the interviews, the teachers mentioned "risk taking" and "being a learner along with the students." When teachers use writing to learn, "[they] have to be willing to learn from what happens. . . . In this business of writing, you really have to be a learner. I'm always making connections between what my students say and what I've read in books. . . . When teachers use writing to learn, they've got to keep growing right along with their students." How do school systems support or reward risk taking and an openness to learn from what happens? The perception among many teachers is that trying new ideas and being open and flexible to what is happening in the classroom — as opposed to following a set plan — is considered a weakness, a sign that there is no plan. One teacher said that she would be hesitant to try anything too creative during an evaluation year.

We believe that the success of our Language and Learning Conference and other in-service efforts comes from teachers seeking the support they need to "grow right along with their students." It's one thing for an in-service course to preach flexibility and imagination; it's another for teachers to take part in presentations by other teachers that exemplify how those teachers have grown through taking risks. We have also come to realize over the years that often project activities provide a safe community and validation of imagination for teachers who do not feel these in their schools.

Resistance by Students: There is one more type of resistance to be considered: the attitudes students bring to our classrooms. Writing to learn is hard work for students. It takes time and the willingness to try it and take risks. We have found that all students, no matter what their prior experience in school, are challenged by writing to learn and are often resistant. One student from an "average" class told us "it was hard to respond to a fact." A student from an advanced class said he was worried about how his writing to learn would sound to other students. He was afraid of sounding dumb or of "getting it wrong." High school students know how to play school, and writing to learn hasn't been part of the game so far. Multiple choice tests and quizzes and short answer questions and worksheets are far more comforting than writing what you understand and don't understand about a history chapter, computer program, or physics problem. Many bright students are used to "being right quickly," and writing to learn challenges and stretches them "to think about what it all means" in ways they often resist. Judy Grumbacher cites the student who said, "I don't have time to understand; I just want to get it done."

Moreover, writing to learn exposes the subjective and often ambiguous nature of knowledge, even in a computer science or history or physics class. Students are used to getting definite answers in content-based courses; years of taking multiple choice tests have reinforced this notion that knowledge is definite and not debatable. Writing to learn can lead to more questions than answers — a scary proposition! — and can open up various points of view not only about the causes of the Civil War, but also about something so seemingly obvious as how to write a computer program. Students need to learn that using their own language to figure things out is not just allowed, but is essential for lasting learning. Students need support in shifting their understanding of the teaching-learning model just as teachers do. Because we are requiring a level of thinking that they are not comfortable with, "we have to keep working with them to be more comfortable. ... It's a real challenge to think about what it all means."

Again, student resistance is a topic we address directly in courses and conferences, and that we encourage teachers to write about in their logs and to bring to discussions. Teacher-consultant presentations always feature large samplings of student work, which demonstrate the range of enthusiasm and success, and presenters invariably are asked to address how they contend with diverse forms of resistance. We assign readings about the learning paradigms that students bring to classes, such as excerpts from Paolo Freire's *The Pedagogy of the Oppressed* (1970), in which he explains the "banking" model of education: teachers pouring information into empty heads, with information — knowledge — existing outside the student in either the teacher or the text.

For the past three years, the NVWP has taken an even more direct approach to student resistance: we have held four-week Student Writing Institutes in the summers, to which upwards of one hundred children, from fifth grade through high school, have come each July. These young writers keep logs, write on topics and in forms of their own choosing, share their work in small groups, and hear presentations by guest writers.

Without Resistance, Nothing Happens

With all these resistances, why do committed teachers persist in using writing to learn in history, in computer science, in physics? The following excerpts highlight what these teachers see as the main reasons to work with the resistances:

> The students learn the content better, and they know it in qualitatively different ways than if they didn't write. ... When teachers emphasize writing, students are willing to take up pen and paper at a moment's notice. They are not afraid of it. They are prepared to write for different audiences and purposes. (Rachel Thompson)

> Learning in the real world is going to have to be independent learning. You won't always have a teacher up there explaining things; you'll have to figure it out on your own. What we had the students do was look in various texts and try to figure out a topic and write on it. Taking books and reading them and trying to learn from them ... that's how they are going to learn. (Barbara Larson)

> When the students finally buy into writing, it works better than anything I've seen. There is real excitement in the writing itself, in the class discussions based on reading their writing, and in their general approach to physics. They're becoming real scientists — problem solvers. (Judy Grumbacher)

Teachers are willing to work with resistances because writing to learn helps their students become independent thinkers and learners. Students become more self-confident when they realize that writing can help them figure things out, not only in school but in their personal lives. The teachers we interviewed, exemplifying so many of the teachers we work with in the NVWP, continue to engage the resistances because what *they* resist is processing students through the system without enabling them to learn those skills and attitudes that are taught by writing to learn. We who have been privileged to have had a leading role in the Language and Learning Program will continue to engage the resistances not only because they will persist, but also because the resistances give our program its shape, its variety, and its sense of purpose.

References

Britton, James. 1970. *Language and Learning*. Harmondsworth, England: Penguin.

Emig, Janet. 1983. "Non-Magical Thinking: Presenting Writing Developmentally in Schools." Chap. 8 in *The Web of Meaning*. Portsmouth, NH: Heinemann.

Freire, Paolo. 1970. *The Pedagogy of the Oppressed*. New York: Herder and Herder.

Fulwiler, Toby, ed. 1987. *The Journal Book*. Portsmouth, NH: Boynton/ Cook.

Myers, Miles. 1980. *A Procedure for Writing Assessment and Holistic Scoring*. Urbana, IL: National Council of Teachers of English.

2

Teachers as Decision Makers:
Creating Classroom, School, and Systemwide Changes

Marcella Emberger and Clare Kruft, with Sally McNelis and Sharon Robbins

The Baltimore County Public Schools rank as the twenty-eighth largest school system in the United States, with 150 schools and over 93,000 students in grades K–12. Our system is divided into five geographic areas, serving a region covering 610 square miles of urban, suburban, and rural communities with families of diverse socioeconomic and cultural backgrounds: farmers and 4-Hers, middle- and upper-income professionals, the unemployed from our once successful steel and manufacturing sectors, and thousands of immigrants speaking over thirty-five languages.

In 1984 our school system began its writing across the curriculum (WAC) project, which received the Center of Excellence Award from the National Council of Teachers of English in 1989. This chapter describes how and why our WAC staff development process works, the problems encountered along the way, and some methods to overcome the problems. Most important, we will show how teachers, when they are given sufficient time, can be empowered to develop their students' thinking and writing processes and through this empowerment can make positive changes in their schools, school system, and state.

Beginning the Project

In 1984 our county formed a WAC Steering Committee with representatives from across grade and curricular areas. Our superintendent asked this group to study WAC research and present recommendations to the superintendent's staff for the development of a WAC project. This committee became the base of the WAC network that has grown to include hundreds of educators in our system.

Many of us walked into our first meeting wondering why we were serving on this committee. Vocational education teachers did not usually collaborate with English supervisors within the traditional, content-specific committees our county formed to produce curriculum. We knew that this committee was designed to promote innovation.

While we began as a group of strangers, the collegiality that developed among this group became a model for school teams as the WAC staff development project began. This core group acted as spokespersons for seminars and training sessions and developed the WAC philosophy:

- Writing fosters the development of clear thinking. The writing process is important to the thinking process.

- English teachers teach writing; other teachers use writing as one method to teach their content.

- Writing to learn activities produce first drafts, not edited final copy.

- Writing to learn activities provide an opportunity for individualized instruction.

- Writing to learn activities can be used either in place of or in addition to existing activities.

This philosophy represented a shift in perspective from a product-oriented approach to one that emphasized writing as a thinking process for all teachers across the curriculum. Once the philosophical foundation was in place, our next step was to bring the philosophy to the county. Our staff development began with a "top-down and bottom-up" approach, since successful programs need support both from those in charge of funds and from those responsible for implementation. In May 1985, we held an all-day conference, "An Introduction to WAC," for all administrators, supervisors, and board members. This program provided an overview of the research and practices as well as such workshops as "WAC in the Elementary Classroom" to address specific needs.

At the end of this conference principals were asked to apply to be part of a pilot program by submitting letters of interest. These letters included a guarantee that they had faculty members who were interested in participating and a supportive community ready to accept an inno-vative program. From the forty-two letters submitted, the superin-tendent's staff selected twelve schools to begin the project, representing each of the five geographic areas and different types of cluster partnerships: elementary/elementary; elementary/middle; elementary/

middle/high; middle/high; and elementary/middle/high/vocational. Because schools were specially selected each year to join these clusters, the project maintained a deliberate pace, providing time for the development of experts within the system. This selectivity also fostered an interest in the program. People are naturally curious about something new; a program that wasn't mandated for everyone was new.

The two of us, Marcella and Clare, were designated as project resource teachers. We were classroom teachers who had expertise in the writing process, in coaching, and in demonstrating for other teachers.

Funding issues, which are a constant problem for any staff development project, were alleviated in 1985 when our school system received a three-year grant for seventy-five thousand dollars per year from the Conrad Hilton Foundation. This money was used for salaries for one of the two project resource teachers, substitute release time for the training sessions, funds for a Teacher Trainer Institute, and supplies and materials. Because of the program's success in its first three years, our funding was continued through federal block grants and staff development funds within the school budget.

The Training Model

A well-documented model to design effective staff development programs is the Concerns-Based Adoption Model (CBAM) created by Loucks and Zigarmi (1981). In this model, participants progress from a level of awareness or interest in the innovation all the way through collaboration and refocusing (see Figure 2–1).

Our training model meets the needs at each level by offering choices at each step, giving participants a significant role in the overall process. School involvement begins with one year of intensive staff development for school teams. These teams of three to seven people attend four full-day sessions, one each academic quarter. During each session participants are involved in a number of writing to learn activities that help them understand how the strategies work. We follow up each training day by visiting schools, demonstrating lessons, coaching team members, and holding conferences to discuss applications of writing to learn strategies within each teacher's content area. At the end of this initial year of training we help the school teams create their own three-to-five year staff development plans to introduce and reinforce WAC with their faculties. (See Appendix A for training timeline.)

Choice 1: Entering the Program

"Attending these sessions helped me remember what it's like to be back in the classroom. I heard a lot from my team that helped me — I'm a better administrator." *Mr. B., a secondary school principal*

Figure 2-1
Concerns-based Adoption Model

**Stages of Concern: Typical Expressions
of Concern About the Innovation**

Stages of Concern	Expression of Concern
6 Refocusing	• I have some ideas about something that would work even better.
5 Collaboration	• I am concerned about relating what I am doing with what other instructors are doing.
4 Consequence	• How is my use affecting kids?
3 Management	• I seem to be spending all my time getting material ready.
2 Personal	• How will using it affect me?
1 Informational	• I would like to know more about it.
0 Awareness	• I am not concerned about it (the innovation).

(left margin vertical labels: I M P A C T   T A S K   S E L F)

Source: S. M. Hord, W. L. Rutherford, L. Huling-Austin, and G. E. Hall, Taking
Charge of Change *(Alexandria, Va.: Association for Supervision and Curriculum
Development, 1987), 31.*

At the earliest stages of awareness and interest in WAC, principals
choose to enter our program by writing a letter to the superintendent's
staff. In doing so, they also choose to take on new roles: participating
in all staff development training with their school teams, selecting team
members who are outstanding teachers and who will become school
leaders, creating an atmosphere for risk taking, and observing classrooms
to support the change process. These new roles create a different
school climate: teachers are empowered as decision makers and staff
developers. They are now partners with the principal in this innovation.

PROBLEM AND SOLUTION

"I put that teacher on the team because I thought it would be a growth
experience and help her teaching." *Mrs. M., an elementary principal*

While most teachers can benefit from participation in WAC training,
some principals selected teachers who were having classroom management problems. Implementing effective WAC activities can help to
minimize management problems, but the WAC staff development
program is not expressly designed to help these teachers. When discussing potential team members with principals, we needed to emphasize

that every team member should be capable of becoming a "teacher of teachers."

Choice 2: Changing Attitudes and Perceptions

"I appreciate the fact that I had a whole year to try these strategies, and I really appreciated your willingness to model some of the strategies in my room." *Mrs. C., a math teacher*

As teachers become involved in the WAC program, they experience the next stage of CBAM, personal concerns about their own roles in the innovation. Teachers accept new responsibilities as team members: participating in training sessions, selecting new writing to learn strategies to try in their classrooms, coaching with us and each other, and designing and leading staff development projects with their faculties. The first training session begins with clarifying attitudes and perceptions about writing. We use a personal writing history to have participants record their past experiences, especially the feelings associated with learning to write. We discuss how these experiences and feelings influence how they use writing in their classrooms. Teachers learn how past experiences have an impact on their classroom practices.

PROBLEM AND SOLUTION

"Why do you think I became a math teacher? I hate writing." *Mrs. M., a math teacher*
"Why should I teach writing? That's the English teacher's responsibility." *Mr. P., a science teacher*

While the discussion of personal writing history usually takes a great deal of time, the time is well spent because it sets the stage for clarifying concepts, including the damage done by using writing as a punishment and understanding the differences between writing as a product and writing as thinking. Sometimes teachers' past experiences have been so negative and are so ingrained that it is difficult to change their attitudes and perceptions. However, during these initial discussions we note which teachers seem the most negative and direct our attention to trying to change their attitudes during on-site support visits. For example, during a visit to a math teacher's room, Marcella had students record their personal math histories. As the math teacher listened to and read the students' responses, she was able to identify many feelings she had expressed about writing during the personal writing history activity. This recognition helped her see how writing can be used to tap into students' thinking and open opportunities for creating more positive experiences for students.

A science teacher who had complained that his students were unable to answer essay questions ("English teachers are not doing their job") reevaluated his attitude after a lesson with his students. The demonstration lesson illustrated that one of his essay questions, "Compare and contrast diffusion, osmosis, and active transport in terms of molecular movement, energy expenditure, and types of molecules moved," required multiple levels of response. Because he was participating with his students, he had the uncomfortable task of trying to answer the question in ten minutes. He not only changed his attitude but also learned the value of writing with his students: "I think I need to write some of these myself."

After the discussion of our personal experiences with writing, we share the "Writing Process Pie" that was created to illustrate the differences between steps in the writing process and the recursiveness of these steps (see Figure 2–2).

Choice 3: Selecting New Strategies

"I was so excited when the strategies booklet came out. My creativity was recognized. I felt like a kid again." *Mr. C., a physical education teacher*

Initially we used a list of alternative teaching activities (see Appendix B for "Taking the First Step"). Once empowered, teachers moved beyond these simple strategies to more sophisticated and integrated applications such as learning logs, student-generated graphic organizers, and metacognitive reflections. Teachers decide which strategies they want to try with their students, create classroom applications, and share ideas. In all four sessions participants have time to examine research in writing within specific content areas and to examine different applications. After the ideas are submitted, they are compiled into sharing strategies booklets, including student samples, and are reproduced for the teams. By allowing teachers the freedom to select strategies that they feel fit their teaching styles, we are acknowledging that individual differences are natural, and there is no one right way to use WAC. By providing these ideas in published booklets, we demonstrate the power of publishing. This sharing across grades and content areas stimulates creativity and allows participants to discover commonalities in thinking and writing — concepts that are the beginning of interdisciplinary teaching. In addition, these booklets are used as staff development tools as teachers who were not part of the training sessions read and discover writing to learn activities they can use with their own students.

Figure 2-2
Writing Process Pie

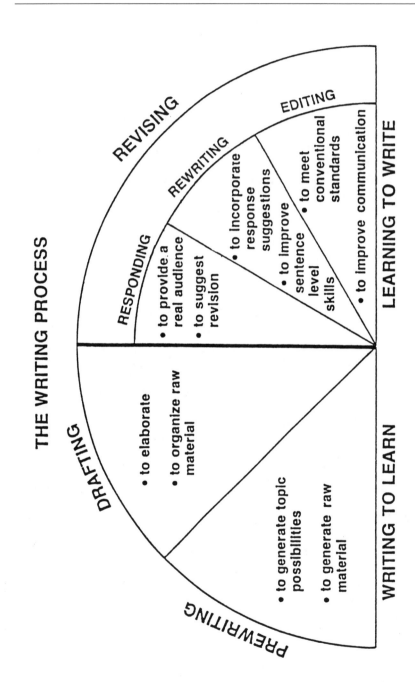

PROBLEM AND SOLUTION

"Why are these elementary teachers here?" *secondary teachers*
"Why are these secondary people here?" *elementary teachers*

Our training days include teams from elementary, middle, and high schools. After they got to know each other, most participants found the cross-curricular and cross-grade level sessions an enriching experience. But we had to overcome the stereotypes of elementary and secondary educators that are often unspoken, yet underlie much of our thinking about each group: "Elementary teachers only care about the kids and secondary teachers only care about their content." Developing a respect for the work done by teachers at all levels and in all content areas was a welcome by-product of the WAC staff development sessions. This respect grew naturally as the teachers shared their ideas. For example, Joanne, a third-grade teacher, created many applications for cognitive maps, and when she shared her ideas the secondary participants copied them down. Her comment at the end of the session was, "I didn't believe that I had ideas high school people could use."

Choice 4: Selecting Appropriate Support

"I'd like you to watch me teach this. I'm not sure if I'm giving them enough time during think-pair-share activities." *Mrs. M., an elementary teacher*

Team members at this stage are concerned with managing the innovation in their classrooms and seeing how WAC will affect student learning. They select the type of support they want from the two resource teachers: a conference to discuss an application, demonstration of a technique, or team teaching and coaching. Teachers are introduced to the concept of coaching on the second staff development day (see Appendix A for training timeline). We use a diagram that is designed to show the steps from sharing ideas informally to collegial coaching. Our diagram uses a picture of an alligator to mark the step of inviting someone in to watch a lesson, as this always connotes being observed and evaluated. In this project it is particularly frightening because teachers are using the writing to learn strategies for the first time. However, they quickly develop a trust in the strategies and themselves as they experience the power of increased thinking and communication skills that the WAC activities unlock. As team members gain trust, they begin coaching us and each other on the WAC strategies. This successful coaching builds the self-confidence that allows teachers to become effective staff developers for others in their schools.

PROBLEM AND SOLUTION

"This will never work with my basic or special education students."
Mr. K., a secondary teacher

We work in special education classrooms where teachers have created multiple adaptations for their students. The expertise and energy of the special educators helped the project throughout the school system. After one team-teaching session, we keyed in on an extremely effective strategy that one teacher of learning disabled adolescents was using to help her reluctant writers. She just stamped each blank paper with the word "DRAFT" before asking the students to do any writing on the paper. The risk-free environment that this simple strategy created worked wonders, and we shared this and other adaptations with elementary and secondary teachers.

Choice 5: Creating a School Plan

"You mean that we can create our own plan for our school?" "What if we decide to just keep coaching each other?" "Do we have to have a faculty meeting?" *team members*

On the fourth staff development day teams begin to develop long-range plans for their schools. Team members discuss a range of possible directions: continuing coaching partnerships with fellow team members, forming new coaching partnerships with faculty members who had not been team members but had expressed interest in learning about WAC, or planning open house demonstrations so that members of their faculties could watch WAC applications. After the first year of staff development we were able to use the experience of first-year team members to help our new teams. Although school teams share ideas, all school plans are unique.

PROBLEM AND SOLUTION

"I'm sorry to tell you that half our team members won't be in our school next year." *Mr. D., a team leader*

Once teams have their plans in place by the end of each school year, we are faced with the "network nightmare." Transfers, illness, promotions, and retirements of administrators and WAC team members put a strain on the long-range plans of every school. We are still struggling with this problem and have begun a computer network system that we hope will help us keep track of the expertise people take with them when they move to new positions.

Choice 6: Creating Content-Based Staff Development

"What are people who are the experts in my subject area thinking about WAC?" *Mr. S., a foreign language teacher*

As teachers trained in WAC move throughout the county, they need a stronger network, especially within their own disciplines. Therefore, we plan WAC conferences with a team of teachers from the curricular office and the curricular supervisors. Offices reflect the individuality of the subject just as each school plan reflects the individual needs of each faculty. The Office of Foreign Language held a conference on April 21, 1988, that featured June Phillips of the Tennessee Foreign Language Institute as a keynote speaker. Her keynote speech, "Critical Thinking or Trivial Pursuits," was followed by small-group sessions led by foreign language teachers who were WAC team members at their schools.

The English office selected coaching as its theme and has held coaching conferences every year for five years in order to institutionalize the concept. Each year participants receive information on coaching, and coaching partners attend demonstrations selected from a variety of sessions, each focusing on a different aspect of writing. These content-specific conferences have a rippling effect, influencing changes many years after they occur. The project that Sally McNelis and Sharon Robbins describe below, for example, had that kind of impact.

Sally McNelis, English department chair, and Sharon Robbins, Spanish teacher, have been coaching each other for two years at Golden Ring Middle School, a school located in a working-class neighborhood. Sally has learned that "in order for coaching to be successful, each partner must have unassigned time to enter the classroom of the other partner and be an on-the-spot observer as well as coach in the planning stage. This is a tremendous time commitment, and when matched with the departmental responsibilities and interdisciplinary team processes, it can at times be perceived as an overload."

Sally and Sharon have administrative support for their partnership, which combines coaching and the use of learning logs—a way of keeping track of what and how students are learning. Logs are marvelous tools for finding out what we know, and what we need to know. They are organizers and great morale boosts for the students who do not know what they think until they write it down:

> "I like using learning logs in English and Spanish classes because I am learning to express myself in more detail and explain what I am learning. Usually I have a real audience, either one of my classmates, or my mom, who wishes she had done things like this when she was in school." *Mike J.*

All eighth graders are part of the team, and parental involvement is a key factor, as students and parents communicate about the two subjects in the student log. The process involves Sally and Sharon coaching one another as they prepare at least one activity a week in which students use learning logs; attending the class during which the logs are used and coaching each other on clarity, purpose, and implementation; introducing various uses for learning logs in both classes; encouraging parental response to entries as well as entries originated by parents; coaching each other on responses to log entries and student-to-student responses; evaluating the use of learning logs to help students write to learn; sharing their project with Golden Ring staff, English department chairs, and foreign language department chairs to encourage duplication.

In the following samples Sharon Robbins had just given the assignment, *"una persona interesante,"* and students were to complete a log entry in which they explained in their own words what they understood about the task and began to define the steps they would take to complete it.

> *Juan (John):* Oh, no! Another long range assignment, and I am so bad at deciding what to do and getting down to it at all. By the end of the week, I need to interview a person I consider to be a role model ... and I don't have anyone like that ... and prepare an article for the next issue of an imaginary newspaper. If I know Señorita Robbins, she will want to publish this stuff. She gets too excited.
>
> First, I'll come up with some good questions. Then, I will ask my dad for an idea of some person to interview who will give me some good stuff. Maybe after I do my questions, Domingo will tell me if they are good or not. He always has good ideas. Here goes. ¿Quién es usted? ¿Cuantos años tiene usted? ¿Cuantas personas hay en su familia? ¿Quién es tu persona favorita en tu familia? ¿Cuál es tu programa favorita en la televisión? ¿Cuál es tu deporte favorito?
>
> Boring! Domingo looks like he is on a roll. I am going to trade this entry for his and see if he can help me.
>
> *Domingo's response:* Good start, buddy. I'm glad you asked me to look at your entry, cause I needed some of your stuff for my questions. Have you thought about interviewing your uncle who works at Westinghouse? I think you talk about him alot, so should be able to call him up and do this assignment. I am going to use your last two questions and think you should add one like ¿Cuál es tu grupo de música favorito? or ¿Qué estación de radio te gusta?
>
> *Juan's home assignment:* Domingo and I came up with pretty neat questions yesterday, so now I need to get started. Maybe Mom will read my entry yesterday and give me some help. I sure hope she doesn't think I am having her do my work like she said before. Here goes.
>
> Dear Mom,
>
>   When you get time before Sunday night, would you please read my entry and Domingo's response on page 17 and see if you can help me decide about other questions and tell me who to interview. Dad may have an idea, but he will be gone until Monday, won't he? Write back soon.
>
>   Your star son,
>   Juan

Juan's mother's response:

Dear John,

I just found this entry and am glad that I did before the assignment is due. Please hand these things to me so that they do not get lost on my desk.

I think your assignment is interesting, but you know, I can't read most of your questions. Read them to me. I think you should take James's [Domingo] suggestion and call Uncle Harris tonight. You can ask your questions on the telephone and may even want to use the extension with a tape recorder set up to get his full answers. You know how he is when he gets going!

Dad will be home tomorrow and will make time to help you with your writing assignment. I am glad we are able to be part of this. I think it is good that you get so much help from your classmates and adults at home. I hope your interview gets printed in the newspaper.

Mom

Sharon Robbins's response: I read all your entries to check the process you have used in completing the interview assignment. You are right, by the way. I am going to actually make a newspaper with some of the interviews.

Be careful to listen to your mother's advice and put your source-book in her hands. It would be a disaster if this got lost!

Your writing is due Tuesday, January 21. What do you need to do yet? Did you revise any of your questions as you talked to your uncle? Will Domingo assist you with your draft?

Sharon Robbins sums up how she feels about the project: "Time is a real problem. But the hook for me was the added interest students developed in studying the Spanish culture, knowing that instead of fill-in-the-blanks and true-or-false exercises, they would be working with writing, using sourcebook entries back and forth to each other, or writing about the history and culture of Spain for an adult audience at home, who would then respond with comments and questions requiring additional research."

Student Lynn L. summarizes part of the process and her perception of its value: "We got our sourcebooks out yesterday and described how we were going to study for our unit test in Spanish class. When we finish the test on Friday, we will go back to that entry and talk about how we feel about the test and how we did on it. If Miss Robbins and Miss McNelis do what they did before, we will add another entry when the test is returned. I am learning about English and Spanish and about myself."

Choice 7: Empowering Teachers Through New Roles: Teacher Trainers

"I love the fact that I can do both. As a Teacher Trainer I can still have my students but I can also work as a staff developer." *Mrs. M., a teacher trainer*

The concept of using teachers as staff developers has been effectively used to support writing instruction by the National Writing Project. Teacher-consultants from the Maryland Writing Project (MWP) are valuable as additional resources for our staff development. When our WAC program began, we hired MWP teacher-consultants to be instructors and guest presenters at in-service courses we sponsored to help teachers understand writing to learn. During 1986 we designed our own training program for teacher trainers. Teachers develop presentations based on their successful classroom practices and present material, coach, and team teach with other teachers. They design and polish their presentations during a one-week summer workshop for which they are paid. Because the teacher trainers are experts in their disciplines and in using writing to learn activities, they can convince other teachers to try the innovative practices. Teacher trainers in the field of music, Barbara Huesman and Martha McCoy share their applications of student note taking using cognitive mapping to list characteristics of operas, oratorios, or other musical performances. Content-based applications like these enable other teachers to generate their own ideas more quickly. Teacher trainer presentations are one of the options that schools and offices use as they design staff development plans.

PROBLEM AND SOLUTION

"I hate to say no, but I just can't leave my kids one more time this year." *Mrs. G., a teacher trainer*

A major problem is overuse of presenters. We hold many staff development sessions during the school day, using substitutes or closing schools early to release teachers and our teacher trainers. The computer network we designed to help us keep track of team members will also help us track information on staff development presentations: the presenter and current assignment, the types of presentations, and the dates the presenter has been scheduled to work in other schools.

Choice 8: Empowering Teachers Through New Roles: Teacher-Researchers

"By questioning, observing, documenting, and analyzing, teachers create learning communities where teacher and students are both engaging in intellectual stretching." (Copper 1991)

The teacher-researchers led the way in working through CBAM's top level of concern in refocusing the WAC innovations through the various research projects they are conducting. We held a seminar in 1986 to introduce the concept of teacher research to interested county professionals. Our speakers included a member of our county's Office of Research and Evaluation, and Sally McNelis who was working on a teacher research project with the Maryland Writing Project involving peer response groups. After the seminar participants were invited to apply to a Teacher Research Institute held that summer. Teachers submit a hypothesis, samples of students' work, or ideas from their teaching journals. The Teacher Research Institutes have been held every summer, and members have developed a collegial atmosphere that is maintained throughout the school year by after-school meetings where participants share works in progress. While publishing is not the main goal of our group, we do celebrate when members are accepted for publication in such journals as *The Reading Teacher*, *School Arts*, *TEAM Magazine*, *Principal*, *Middle Years*, *Journal of Staff Development*, and *Learning*. We have celebrated more than seventy times!

Researchers' topics are widely varied: a cosmetology teacher investigated how cognitive mapping increased student learning when it is used to record notes from a textbook, and a kindergarten teacher wired her room as a radio station, developed a "DJ Talk Show Station," and recorded the students' interaction to determine if the level of questioning increased. These innovative practices, which begin with writing to learn strategies, focus teachers on assessing their classroom practices. By experimenting with writing to learn strategies and reflecting on the student learning that they see, these teacher-researchers are engaged in constant, formative assessment to improve their teaching practices.

PROBLEM AND SOLUTION

"We need more time to work together." *Baltimore County public school teacher-researchers*

During the 1990 Summer Institute for Teacher-Researchers we discussed the problem of never having enough reflection time to sort through data and observations of student progress in writing and thinking during the school year. We designed a short-term solution, a release-time form that allows teacher-researchers to decide for themselves which full day or two half days during the school year would be best for them. They then acquire a substitute and take release time to gather and reflect on their research.

State Assessments and WAC

We have also gained recognition for WAC by drawing direct connections between success in WAC and success on accountability testing of students throughout the state of Maryland. In 1982 the Maryland State

Department of Education (MSDE) introduced functional tests to ensure that all students throughout the state could meet minimum competencies in various content areas before they graduated from high school. We trained teachers to use WAC strategies to enable students to learn the information they needed to be successful on these tests.

In 1990, MSDE introduced the Maryland School Performance Program (MSPP), which is founded on site-based management principles and outcome-based student performance. The outcome-based student performance guidelines include new tests, designed by teachers in our state, to assess students' abilities to apply integrated content knowledge in language arts, reading, math, social studies, and science. These tests, based on the Association of Supervision and Curriculum Development's framework outlined in *Dimensions of Thinking*, assess how well students can apply knowledge in various curricular areas. There are few traditional test questions: multiple choice, fill-in-the-blanks, or true and false. Most of the questions require students to write, either short, focused answers or more extended explanations and narratives, including metacognitive responses: "Explain how you figured out this math problem." The math, reading, and language arts tests, administered for the first time to students in grades three, five, and eight in May 1991 were scored by teachers who had been trained to use holistic scoring grids. Additional tests in social studies and science for these grades were given in May 1992. An eleventh-grade interdisciplinary test was given in 1993. These tests have created a renewed interest in WAC. While our system provides WAC materials, we emphasize that WAC is a philosophy, and needs to be approached as such for teachers to adopt WAC practices. To promote successful change, schools need to consider systematic models like CBAM.

To ensure that innovative practices like WAC are implemented, MSDE educators recognize the need to reevaluate how we assess student learning, and they know that they are on the cutting edge of new assessment measures. Being on the cutting edge has caused mixed reactions among educators in our state. Some fear that these new tests will drive instruction and require too much of teachers and students, while others, particularly those teachers who have been trained to use WAC, reported that their students "felt confident" and enjoyed "this new kind of test." The differences in attitudes may be attributed to the type of training educators have had in WAC.

Public Relations Issues

Developing and sustaining momentum for WAC innovations is crucial. In order to keep WAC in people's minds, we continually seek avenues for publicizing its significant contributions to education in our district.

Opportunities inside the school system include publishing an annual journal entitled *Teacher to Teacher* that contains articles about classroom strategies and is distributed to all schools and offices in our system; presenting WAC concepts at PTA meetings and curriculum nights; developing a picture display of the writing process that we circulate in our county's courthouse and various schools and offices; and creating short television and interactive video programs about WAC on our county's cable television station. Other publicity includes articles in community newspapers and in our major newspaper, *The Sun*, about WAC programs and their effects on teachers and students. Since our program was awarded the NCTE Center of Excellence award, we have had additional opportunities, hosting visitors from across the country.

Freeing Voices

Staff development can change attitudes and practices if the program is designed to allow the time for change and if it empowers teachers by providing opportunities for changing their role in the classroom, in the school, and throughout the school system. WAC is powerful because the strategies free the personal voices of students, as we saw in the sourcebooks of Sharon Robbins and Sally McNelis's students. It is these student voices that have tremendous power to change teachers' attitudes and practices.

Appendix A
Baltimore County Public Schools: Staff Development Training Timeline

1983–1984: WAC Steering Committee formed
May 1984: Spring Conference introduces WAC to county leadership
1985–1986: School Teams begin participating in Staff Development Project

Day/Participants	Purpose
Day #1	Introduce the writing process
(1st quarter)	Discuss applications (research on
Elementary (3 or more)	process and content-specific lessons)
Middle (5 or more)	Prepare for on-site support
High (7 or more)	

Following day #1: Trainers visit school and provide on-site support for team members — coaching, team teaching, conferences

Day #2	Share applications
(2nd quarter)	Introduce peer response/revision strategies
	Plan for new applications
	Introduce coaching/select coaching partners

Following day #2: Trainers visit school and provide on-site support for team members — coaching, team teaching, conferences

Day #3	Share applications
(3rd quarter)	Plan for new applications with coaching partners
	Introduce adult learning theory

Following day #3: Trainers visit school and provide on-site support for team members — coaching, team teaching, conferences

Day #4	Share applications
(4th quarter)	Plan with coaching partners
	Select and attend Teacher Trainer presentations
	Draft a School Plan for School-wide implementation

Following day #4: Trainers visit school and provide on-site support for team members — coaching, team teaching, conferences

---

Years 2, 3, 4, and 5, schools refine and develop implementation plans to inservice faculties.

Summers 1986–1992: Teacher Trainer Workshops
Summers 1989–1992: Teacher-Researcher Workshops

Appendix B
Taking the First Step: Writing to Learn

Short, focused writing activities are a good place to begin incorporating writing to learn activities. Although some of these writing pieces might be revised to produce final copy, many make use of writing as a learning tool without going beyond a first draft.

IN PLACE OF explaining the objectives for a new unit	TRY having students list all they know about the topic to involve them in establishing unit objectives.
IN PLACE OF opening class with a statement of the objective	TRY opening class with a question, to be answered in writing at the end of class.

IN PLACE OF reviewing yesterday's class by leading a discussion

TRY asking each student, in one minute, to write down a question based on yesterday's lesson. Use these questions to lead the discussion.

IN PLACE OF using a drill to begin class

TRY having each student prepare a single drill item.

IN PLACE OF asking questions about what the students have studied

TRY giving answers and asking students to create the questions.

IN PLACE OF giving students a problem to be solved

TRY giving the students a situation and asking them to create the problem.

IN PLACE OF giving directions for a project

TRY showing students the finished product and having them list the materials and procedures they think they would use to complete the project.

IN PLACE OF moving right into discussion from a film, story, article, or chapter

TRY giving students a few minutes to jot down reactions or answers to a central question.

IN PLACE OF writing guide questions or fill-in-the-blanks to guide reading

TRY reading the title, subtitle, or opening paragraph and asking students to write several questions they would expect to have answered as they read.

IN PLACE OF asking students to fill out a worksheet about the major concepts of a lesson

TRY webbing or charting with the students to create a study guide.

IN PLACE OF asking students to take factual notes

TRY asking students to write a first person account using the facts.

IN PLACE OF writing quiz or test items yourself

TRY showing students how to do it, and using their items to create the test (essay, multiple choice, true/false).

References

Copper, Linda R. 1991. "Teachers as Researchers." *Kappa Delta Pi Record* (Summer): 115–17.

Marzano, Robert et al. 1988. *Dimensions of Thinking*. Alexandria, VA: Association of Supervision and Curriculum Development.

3

Letters from the (Cutting) Edge: Promoting Writing Across the Curriculum Through Assessment

Lois E. Easton and Roger Shanley

"Hi. Neither Roger, Lisa, or Max can come to the phone but we want to hear from you. Please leave a message at the tone."

"Roger, this is Lois. It's been a long time! Have you been hearing anything about the ASAP? How are your writing across the curriculum programs going? Give me a call."

"Hello, you have reached 555-9289. Please leave a message and Mike or Lois will get back to you. Wait for the tone. Thanks."

"Lois, geez you're busy. To answer your question—this is Roger—to answer your question, I've heard bits and pieces about the ASAP and want to know much more. I've been struggling to find better ways to assess in our writing across the curriculum programs. Do you think ASAP will help? Give me a ca ..."

"Hi. Neither Roger, Lisa, or Max can come to the phone but we want to hear from you. Please leave a message at the tone."

"Roger, this is Lois. Forget this phone stuff. I think I'll try it the old-fashioned way—pen and paper."

Note: Lois Easton was working as director of curriculum and assessment planning at the Arizona Department of Education and Roger Shanley as English teacher at Rincon High School in Tucson, Arizona, during the time of these exchanges.

January 6, 1991

Dear Roger,

I *hate* those machines ... of course I have one too, as you've discovered, and I wouldn't be without it. I thought of you the other day when I first called because of what I remember you were doing with writing across the curriculum (WAC). I was talking with some graduate students in English education at Northern Arizona University (NAU) about the anticipated benefits of the ASAP (the state's assessment reform program), and they asked me if I thought the ASAP would support WAC. I told them I hoped it would, and then I decided I'd better talk to someone who would know: You!

I don't know how much you know about the ASAP in general, so let me give you a quick run-through. You know that we've been testing kids — every kid, every year, in the spring — with norm-referenced tests for eleven long years. Madaus (1988) could have used us as his prime example of "high stakes" testing!

Then came the GEE. Have you heard about the GEE? It is what really started Arizona down the road of education reform through changes in assessment. The acronym stands for Goals for Educational Excellence, and GEE was Arizona's response to the call for reform that began with *A Nation at Risk* (1983). The legislature's first move with the GEE was to set K−12 curriculum goals in the traditional subject areas. The Department of Education convinced the legislature to look at the state's curriculum framework documents, including the *Language Arts Essential Skills* (1986). When they saw the strengths of these documents, they dropped their own plans for curriculum. Whew!

Then they said, "How can we measure these goals?" and that's when the window opened for changing testing in Arizona. We responded, "You cannot measure these goals with a norm-referenced standardized test. You need to build assessments that match the curricula. Furthermore, you cannot just add a layer of testing in Arizona schools; you have to reduce current testing."

They agreed with all of this, so that's how we ended up with the Arizona Student Assessment Program (ASAP). We like that acronym, by the way, given our testing history. The ASAP reduces the impact of norm-referenced testing by moving it to the fall where it does less curricular damage. The ASAP also limits the testing to grades four, seven, and eleven, making it possible for us to consider a more authentic way to be accountable for public dollars.

So, have you seen the new assessments yet? You may have noticed that whatever is in the *Language Arts Essential Skills* (LAES) is in the assessments. So, you'll find both processes and whole products or outcomes on the assessments. The LAES requires kids to write personal experience narratives, among other genres, so there are assessments for writing personal experience narratives, and other genres, incorporating the writing processes we value. The new assessments have parallel state and district forms so that students using the district forms, or otherwise prepared according to the curriculum framework document, are ready for the final performance on the state form. Isn't that cheating or teaching to the test? you might ask, but is it bad if we are really teaching towards the standards we value in Arizona?

You probably gathered that these are performance-based tests. On the writing assessments students take three days to write, sometimes working collaboratively with other students, sometimes alone. On the reading assessments students preread and then read a single, intact piece of real literature or quality nonfiction (not something prefab for the test) and respond to it in different ways — by writing in a variety of forms, sketching, creating a diagram or model, etc.

The mathematics assessments are the most unusual. Students engage in a scenario, as lifelike as it can be, like working in a design studio with an architect. They work with real-life data and use the data to solve problems related to the scenario. Along the way, they write in a variety of forms: their own answers (instead of choosing from answers), short explanations, longer analyses, and sometimes even longer evaluations of what they have done mathematically.

Here's where I think the link to WAC occurs. Sure, the direct writing assessments will help students (and teachers) value real writing. But if writing is still valued only in English classes, we won't have made much progress.

And here's where you can help me frame an answer for the NAU graduate students. I remember your presentation in Flagstaff about five years ago. You described a grant you had received to support WAC. Refresh my memory: how did you get the grant? How did you use it? What's happening now with the WAC program you established with it? I'd like to explore what you think will happen with WAC when the ASAP hits the streets.

With pen in hand,
Lois

January 18, 1991

Dear Lois,

It was great to get your letter — it got me focused on the ASAP. Your letter also brought back a menagerie of memories (nice alliteration, eh?) about the week-long conference we attended five years ago in Flagstaff: "Improving Writing in Our Schools and Universities." I remember presenting with Marvin Diogenes from the University of Arizona about our FIPSE (Fund for the Improvement of Post-Secondary

Education) grant work on WAC. Also this was the first time I heard about and saw the Language Arts Essential Skills document. Little did I know that FIPSE and the LAES would play a major role in my life for the next half decade.

The grant, devised by Stan Witt of Pima Community College, was multidimensional. Stan's proposal was to fund a three-year project of writing and speaking across the curriculum programs at three levels — four-year college, community college, and secondary school levels. As coordinator of the writing programs for five high schools in the project, I knew we would all have many challenges in the following years.

About two hundred volunteer teachers received small stipends to attend workshops and assessment sessions, and to develop units for the classroom. The workshops ranged from informal gatherings at my house to more formal meetings at which experienced and new teachers gathered. During these meetings we discussed the types of writing students were currently doing in their programs, issues such as writing as thinking, and evaluation of writing. I was amazed at the teachers' range of views, preconceptions, and most importantly, their fears and concerns.

As the discussions continued, some interesting attitudes developed. Teachers arrived at more of an agreement about the qualities of good writing. Also, they began to describe traits that would be found in student writing for their individual content areas. Soon, we were arranging informal rubrics based on student samples and class discussions. Confidence grew as these educators realized that their own skills and intuition would enable them to work with student writing in their classrooms. (By the way, I think the same intuition will help teachers feel comfortable about the LAES and ASAP, but more on that later.) Still, they were concerned about how to grade the student writing.

Twice each semester we held holistic grading sessions. After developing prompts that we thought were fair and would encourage expressive, personal responses, we scored the samples. I was delighted to see the ease with which the teachers verbalized the strengths and weaknesses of student writing as we chose anchor papers in order to establish the one through six scores. I was equally impressed at the few papers we had to read a third time as tiebreakers. Best of all, though, were the discussions following each grading session. Teachers of physical education and industrial arts, counselors and algebra teachers elaborated on consistent traits found in the ranges of scores. We were talking standards based on performance assessments!

One challenge was asking teachers to view writing differently — not just as an alternative to multiple choice. The P.E. coach helped me on this one. He said he hated it when coaches made kids run as punishment because they hated to run after that moment. He got us thinking about a concept later captured in the phrase "writing to learn"—if only I'd thought of those words! Luckily, I came across some fine material to help me articulate the concept. One of the best was *Roots in the Sawdust*, edited by Anne Ruggles Gere (1985). Almost any teacher could read this and get ideas for writing in the classroom. More importantly though, they could also get the philosophy of WAC as a process of knowing through interactive composition. Another helpful source was the work of Stephen Tchudi (1983, 1986), both his book *Teaching Writing in the Content Areas: Senior High School* (and one for junior high/middle school) and his article in *English Journal* called "The Hidden Agendas in Writing Across the Curriculum." I used his article with teachers near the end of their official rotation in the program to help them examine changes in their teaching styles. Change they did!

Most agreed that working with writing to illustrate thinking forced them to examine the processes of their disciplines rather than to reemphasize the products. Tchudi's line, "It's time for interdisciplinary English to become a reality," forces not only content-area teachers but also English teachers to change their focus and use writing to promote learning across the curriculum.

While the high schools were struggling with their structure for the project, similar work was being done at Pima Community College and the University of Arizona. In addition, teachers at all three levels came to one another's sites to assist with holistic scoring sessions and observe class activities. I believe the contacts we all made during these collaborative efforts were the greatest benefits of the project.

Well, time to read a bedtime story to Max. Write me more about how the LAES and the ASAP will connect.

Sincerely,
Roger

February 3, 1991

Dear Roger,

Your letter brought back memories for me, too. I remember your exciting presentation and our intense thinking about both vertical (K−16) and horizontal (across the curriculum) articulation. Thanks for refreshing my memory on the FIPSE grant. I think there's great strength in what you've done.

You asked me to reflect on the relationship between the LAES and the ASAP. I think the LAES is the heart of the ASAP. The Flagstaff conference was the first time I presented on the LAES. The state board-appointed committee had just finished it, and it was so different from the old document's lists of discrete, isolated skills. We wish we could have gotten rid of the word "skills" in the title, as a matter of fact. But to suggest something so different—integrated processes and whole products or outcomes, connections within and across the curriculum—suggested criteria for evaluating outcomes! I had no idea what reaction we'd get.

If we had done the LAES any differently, I do not think we could have justified performance-based assessments. Because we asked kids to really read and really write, we had to test real reading and real writing. Also, because the State Board of Education liked the LAES, it declared that all other state curricula should emulate it (thus the mathematics assessments based on the Essential Skills in Mathematics or ESM are performance-based). And, finally, because the legislature liked the LAES, legislators abandoned their own curriculum-writing efforts and asked us to invent assessments to match the LAES and ESM. *Voilà*! The ASAP.

What did you think, back then, about the LAES?

Not About to Get Writer's Cramp This Time,
Lois

February 12, 1991

Dear Lois,

Your letter explaining the details of the LAES definitely got my mind working. Now I get the bigger picture: assessment based on curriculum that is based on sound theory and good practice. I remember wondering in Flagstaff whether there would be an integrated K–12 curriculum of reading, writing, listening, speaking, and thinking occurring in all classes if teachers followed the intent of the LAES. Imagine what this would mean! Then came the next question.

What would the LAES do to or for WAC programs? Yikes! Nearly all teachers would emphasize a more process-based approach to writing and learning. Math, social studies, science, art, and physical education teachers would examine how their content linked with the general concepts and constructs of the communication skills. Imagine the dialogue that would result when we all realized the similarity of concepts and processes among the disciplines! I was sure the result would be a collaboration of teachers, a community of communicators, all working together to integrate all skills for all students for the finest results.

Of course what also came to mind was how this vision would fit with our yearly albatross, the norm-referenced standardized tests!

You referred earlier to our standardized tests as "high stakes" testing. I'll add another description: ludicrous. As much as teachers try to defend or explain the standardized tests, students see through them.

"How come they call this section 'Usage' when we aren't using anything?" was one of the more pointed questions I have been asked. I
feel like Jekyll and Hyde during the testing period because I'm teaching
one way and the students are tested another way. Talk about losing
credibility! That's why I hope that the ASAP mirrors what and how
we're teaching (and it does if it's really based on the LAES). It seems
to me that if we teach to that kind of test, we're creating some mighty
fine lesson plans for any and all classrooms.

Here are a few gems for you to ponder and some questions to
answer. How do you actually assess the many processes and modes of
writing contained in the LAES? After stumbling through holistic grading
with participants in the WAC project—and scoring papers from only
three hundred students—I wonder how in the world you can score
papers for the entire state or the selected populations? Do the mathematics and science teachers know enough about the process approach
to prepare students for the ASAP? Can they set up a cadre of communicators in their fields to develop activities, lessons, and curriculum
to enable students to do well on the ASAP?

Write when you get that rare free moment, so we can keep this
"letterlogue" alive.

Sincerely,
Roger

March 3, 1991

Dear Roger,

Wow! That's some reaction to a state curriculum framework document. Usually we state folk are a reviled breed!

What was most frustrating, of course, in presenting the LAES
around the state, was how paralyzed the state was because of testing.
No matter how excited teachers would get during staff development on
the LAES, someone would always ask the giant-killer question: "But,
is this on the test?" And, I would have to answer, "No, it's not," and
participant enthusiasm would dwindle to nothing. "We'll do writing
process on Friday," they said.

That's why the ASAP means so much. I think it will allow teachers
to teach what they value. It will support them. I've had many whole
language teachers tell me that the LAES and the related ASAP assessments look like what they teach, as much as any curriculum document
and assessments can look like good classroom instruction.

Now for your questions. You asked about the processes. The
processes of writing are embedded into the writing assessments but not
evaluated. As much as possible, they are also embedded into the

reading and mathematics assessments and will be embedded in the science and social studies performance assessments that are in the first year of their design phase. I think teachers will notice the processes and incorporate them into their own instruction. Lauren and Daniel Resnick's (1989) famous statement, "What you test is what you get," deserves a sequitur: How you test is how you get it.

You also asked about how we'll test the various genres of writing. As you know, the LAES mandates writing proficiency in nine genres by the time students graduate from high school. Districts will have several versions of all nine genres to use as they please — or not at all — in grades nine through twelve. When the state administers the state form of the assessments, each student will be tested on one of the nine genres but will not know which one until the assessment sequence begins. Students will have to be prepared to take any of the nine.

You also asked about scoring the assessments. The district forms will be scored by districts according to how formal and reliable districts want the scoring to be. Districts can let individual teachers score their own assessments or arrange a formal scoring procedure.

The state form will be scored formally. Districts will send assessments to a central clearinghouse that will send entire sets of assessments to regional scoring sites. At the regional scoring sites, teachers (who will be paid a small stipend or have a substitute provided for them by the state) will be trained in holistic scoring, certified, and monitored as they score papers.

I think the trick is to get teachers from all content areas involved in scoring — anyone can score assessments. As you observed in your WAC program, teachers scoring the assessments determine what quality looks like and translate that to their own classroom activities. Doesn't the fighting and arguing about what a "4" is and which papers exemplify a "4" really help teachers in their own classrooms? I think the scoring procedure also gives teachers confidence that they *can* score something thought to be subjective.

So, Roger, what should I say to the NAU teachers who initiated this sequence of letters? What will be the effect of the ASAP on WAC? Do teachers in other content areas incorporate writing the way the LAES and their own state curriculum frameworks suggest? If so, their classrooms should already reflect a writing emphasis, and the ASAP will not frighten them. Perhaps it will even support them as both the LAES and the ASAP have supported whole language and process teachers.

However, if content-area teachers have not already begun to incorporate writing to learn in their subjects, the ASAP may be upsetting and intimidating. In fact, it may make them angry: "Who are these state folks anyway, telling me that I have to do writing in my math class?" Will legislated writing activities ruin the progress you have made in terms of WAC? In short, will you curse or bless the ASAP?

Courting Writer's Cramp,
Lois

March 24, 1991

Dear Lois,

Your last letter was stuffed with ASAP information, and I am swirling with comments and questions. Where to begin?

Your mention of the threat to teachers who examine the new assessments is a possibility. However, I prefer to believe that these folks will eventually see the benefits inherent in the assessments. As they use the LAES and the ASAP performance assessments, they'll discover natural crosshairs (with the vertical axis being the LAES and the horizontal axis being the ASAP) that will help them "sight in" on the target — improved and integrated curriculum and assessment for Arizona's students. (Sorry about the gun metaphor, but it seemed to work.)

I also believe all teachers will see that the ASAP is most concerned with thinking skills and showing thought through performance. Employers require thoughtful performance, and many lament the deficits they see in the thinking of current high school graduates. In fact, I predict that some of the greatest fans of the ASAP will be business and community leaders who realize that assessments stressing manipulation of real-life situations will benefit everyone.

Finally, you ask about how the new assessments will change or support WAC programs. Those who became involved are still immersed in writing in their classrooms and schools. An industrial arts teacher shows how he uses writing in his classrooms at conferences, and a P.E. teacher and I have a running conversation about writing in his classes and in his own life. A former social studies teacher, now an assistant principal, is steadily implementing a WAC program at his school.

These educators believe that both the LAES and the ASAP will be positive forces in integrating writing in all classrooms. In our ongoing discussions, we make a distinction, in fact, about this new reality of writing. The early converts to WAC needed some degree of persuasion. Current and future inductees do not seem to need the same degree of enticement. They seem more aware that students of the 1990s will need stronger communication skills.

Still, I know there are teachers out there who have not had the benefit of the learning provided by a grant. For these teachers, the ASAP may provide a miniworkshop. I can imagine them gathered in a

Figure 3–1
Language Arts Essential Skills

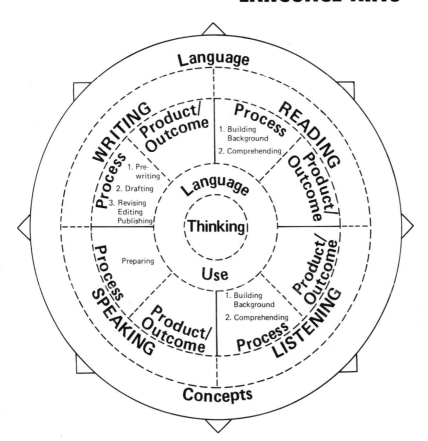

LANGUAGE ARTS

ESSENTIAL SKILLS

math department meeting, for example, speculating on how the writing on the mathematics assessments will help students learn and demonstrate one of the seven standards promulgated by the National Council of Teachers of Mathematics—communication about math (1989). I can even imagine them using one of the assessments as an instructional unit, just to try out the writing and to see how students react. I can envision them developing their own units that match the assessments.

I remember the schematic that accompanied the LAES (Figure 3–1). It was a series of concentric circles. The innermost circle was labeled "thinking." Other circles were subdivided into processes and whole products or outcomes. Points radiated from the outermost circle. The text explained that these points symbolized the cogs in the communication wheel that connected with circles representing all the other content areas. The communication wheel activated all the other subjects. I think that's true of the ASAP also.

I know, I know. This is just the rambling of an overzealous believer in performance-based assessments, but I get plenty psyched when I think of an integration of the many skills found in written communication, the collaboration of colleagues in achieving this integration, the celebration of the result by parents and community members, and the application of these new skills by today's students and tomorrow's citizens.

Sincerely,
Roger

References

Curriculum and Evaluation Standards for School Mathematics. 1989. Reston, VA: National Council of Teachers of Mathematics.

Gere, Anne Ruggles, ed. 1985. *Roots in the Sawdust: Writing to Learn Across the Disciplines*. Urbana, IL: National Council of Teachers of English.

Language Arts Essential Skills. 1986. Phoenix, AZ: The Arizona Department of Education.

Madaus, George F. 1988. "The Influence of Testing on the Curriculum." In *Critical Issues in Curriculum*. Eighty-seventh yearbook of the National Society for the Study of Education. Chicago, IL: University of Chicago Press. 83–121.

A Nation at Risk: The Imperative for Educational Reform. An Open Letter to the American People. A Report to the Nation and the Secretary of Education. 1983. Washington, DC: National Commission on Excellence in Education.

Resnick, Lauren B., and Daniel P. Resnick. 1989. "Tests as Standards of Achievement in Schools." In *The Uses of Standardized Tests in American Education*. Princeton, NJ: Educational Testing Service.

Tchudi, Stephen. 1986. "The Hidden Agendas in Writing Across the Curriculum." *English Journal* 10 (November): 22–25.

Tchudi, Stephen, and Judy Yates. 1983. *Teaching Writing in the Content Areas: Senior High School*. no. 20. Washington, DC: National Education Association.

4

A High School/College Writing Across the Curriculum Project: Successes and Constraints

Brenda Greene and Lorraine Kuziw

A colleague of ours recently noted that when he is providing school workshops he can always tell whether faculty members requested or were mandated to participate. Faculty members who have requested staff development always respond differently from faculty members who feel they have no choice about participating. Administrators often come up with creative ideas that affect curriculum; however, they also often neglect to get faculty input when it comes to implementing these ideas. Thus we have come up with a rule that should be learned by all those who wish to develop writing across the curriculum (WAC) programs: be aware of the processes that administrators have used in trying to institute curriculum reform and do not go into those territories where you have not been invited by all involved. Unfortunately, we did not formulate this rule until after we had ventured into territories unknown.

Our high school/college WAC project was developed in response to a high school administrator's desire to enrich the social studies curriculum. During the summer of 1989, the chair of the social studies department approached our college basic language skills coordinator (Brenda Greene) and asked if we could collaborate on a project that would provide students with skills that would enable them to be successful in high school and enhance their chances of going to college.

After much discussion and a series of meetings, Brenda and the social studies chair wrote a proposal that was funded by both the high school and the college. They developed a program that would use writing to reinforce what students were learning in social studies. One basic goal of this program was to create a learning environment in which tutors from the college's tutorial program would come to the high school on a daily basis and work with small groups of students.

The Social Studies Enrichment Center was scheduled to open during September of 1989; however, because funding for the center was approved after the academic year began, September and October were designated for program planning. A faculty resource person (Lorraine Kuziw) from the college was designated to coordinate the project and implement the program. Lorraine accepted this position in mid-October and immediately became aware of the absolute necessity of prior planning and preparation.

This paper provides an overview of the program that was developed, identifies its successes and constraints, and makes some recommendations for incorporating writing to learn in the social studies curriculum. It is written from the college perspective, and it also includes the voices of high school teachers and students. Its intent is to provide would-be administrators and teachers of WAC programs with our reflections on what is needed and on what works and does not work in the development of WAC programs.

Program Description

The underlying premise of our high school/college program was that the responsibility for writing instruction should not be restricted to teachers within English departments. We viewed writing instruction as the responsibility of the entire school community and we believed that teachers in all disciplines should find ways to incorporate writing into their classes. We were intent on helping our high school colleagues understand this concept, and the inclusion of writing in the social studies curriculum seemed an ideal place to start.

The program was situated in a large, inner-city high school in Brooklyn, New York. Many of the students who attend this high school do not go on to college. During the 1988–1989 academic year, only 3.8 percent received Regents diplomas; 2.9 percent passed the English Regents exams; 19.6 percent passed the Global Studies Regents exam; and 57 percent passed social studies. Students' performance is often poor because the exams require the interpretation of questions and the writing of essays. The Social Studies Enrichment Center was created to serve these students. The targeted student population consisted of students in honors classes (those reading at grade level) and students in college discovery classes (those reading two or more levels below grade). As the social studies chair stated, the goal of this WAC program was "to move students from functional literacy in an economically impoverished and culturally limited environment towards collegiate literacy."

The Enrichment Center, open during three school lunch periods, was staffed by a paraprofessional who maintained and monitored the center and often tutored students. A college tutor was assigned to assist students with writing and research. In the center were project assignment sheets (students completed three projects per semester), supplementary books, and a computer used for telecommunications.

Faculty Development

Each semester Lorraine, the faculty resource person (FRP), worked with two teachers who each had two classes that participated in the program. Lorraine held one workshop and thirteen staff meetings during the program. In addition, she provided teachers with specific recommendations for incorporating writing into their classes, for example, in the form of logs or essays. It is primarily in this area that we believe this program did not achieve all that it could have.

As we progressed through this program, it was frequently pointed out that at least one semester is needed to plan such a WAC program. Because we did not allow for adequate planning, many of the difficulties that we encountered in the program's implementation were problems that could have been overcome if meetings and workshops had been held a semester or year before the program went into effect. This situation was further complicated by the fact that the FRP did not have an opportunity to become more familiar with the content-area curriculum, the particular school setting, and the needs of the particular school population. We also realized the importance of securing teachers who were committed to the program and to the philosophical concept of WAC.

Planning meetings could have enabled the FRP to collaborate with teachers to develop materials and strategies for addressing the curriculum needs of the social studies program. Moreover, she could have also had an opportunity to observe a variety of social studies classes. In short, she could have been provided with a more comprehensive context for developing and implementing the WAC program. However, since the FRP began in October, she did not have adequate time to plan and found herself faced with a situation where writing projects were already designed and in place, where teachers were halfway through the syllabus, and where the introduction of new elements such as logs and writing instruction was difficult, if not impossible. Consequently, much of her assistance to teachers was in response to needs voiced by teachers and tutors. We believe that a WAC program should have the flexibility to respond to needs as they arise, but to run a program on this premise is problematic.

Despite the limitations discussed above, the FRP attempted to work with the faculty. Since no one had release time for this program and all had full teaching schedules, meetings were difficult to schedule and there was full attendance only once in thirteen meetings. As a result, coordination of efforts, communication, and assessment tended to be fragmentary. The above factors made it difficult to assess immediately that teachers were not incorporating writing into their social studies classes. While teachers did assign extra projects and essays, tutors were the ones who worked with students on these writing activities.

The FRP used the meetings to present instructional materials that would enable teachers to assist their students in using writing as a way of learning. For example, since one of the main objectives of the program was to improve student performance on the essay portion of the Regents Competency Test (RCT) or the Regency Exam, the FRP analyzed the test essay questions to determine the rhetorical strategies needed to answer the essay questions adequately. She then prepared materials that described the format of the questions and that illustrated ways in which teachers could adapt their social studies essay assignments, tests, and projects to that format.

Teacher response to materials prepared by the FRP varied. Because teachers were required to assign certain projects that had been determined by the department before the WAC program started, the use of the materials was fragmentary. Some teachers developed essay questions that incorporated the suggestions made by the FRP; however, many left all aspects of writing and analysis of essay exams to the tutors. Rather than provide classroom time in which students could actually engage in the process of using writing as a way to learn, teachers operated on the premise that students' writing would improve with the aid of the Enrichment Center tutors.

The major limitations to the faculty development component of our program were therefore that teachers were asked to revise their curriculum after the semester had begun; teachers had not agreed to make such curriculum changes; and teachers had not committed themselves to the philosophical concept of WAC. These limitations underline the absolute necessity of providing for prior planning meetings and workshops at least one semester before such a program begins.

Program Successes

Although faculty development was limited, the program was successful in a number of other ways. Students and teachers found the Enrichment Center quite helpful. Approximately 350 students participated in the program and student attendance was excellent. The table below indicates the improved student performance in courses and on tests after one year of participation in the WAC Program.

WAC STUDENT PERFORMANCE

Percentage of Students Passing	1989	1990
Social Studies in General	57.1%	59%
Global Studies Regents Exam	19.6%	29%
U.S. History & Government Regents	35.9%	42.2%

Unfortunately, because of financial constraints, our college could not continue its role in this collaborative effort, but the Enrichment Center at the high school is still in operation. Tutors are working three days per week and some of the materials prepared by the FRP have now been incorporated into the curriculum.

The clearest indication of student opinion about the Enrichment Center was that 40 to 45 students per day came to the center during their lunch period to work on projects or homework or to study for Regents exams. According to one of our tutors, the initial attitude of students was that they could not find enough information to write about, but after receiving tutorial assistance, they discovered how to find and use information and consequently were more confident about their writing.

In June 1990 a survey was given to the students in the four pilot classes. About 75 percent of these students felt their writing had improved. They also indicated that they had learned more. Some of their comments were, "I got a higher grade"; "I know more"; "It helps me understand what I learn about in class"; "I can write faster"; "I know how to find information"; "I improved my map skills"; "I have extra study time"; "I write better essays"; and "Before I just wrote what was in the book, and now I can write what's not in the book." These comments reveal that students appreciated and felt they benefited from the program. They had learned to synthesize information from a number of sources: class lectures, class texts, and materials from the Enrichment Center. Students' comments also indicated that they needed and appreciated individual attention. They stated: "It's a great place to go when you need help"; "I learned to express myself and be more creative"; and "They treat you with courtesy and respect and make you feel like a real human being."

All teachers whose students participated in the Enrichment Center responded to a survey. Their comments about the value of the center also corroborated the students' opinions. One teacher felt that the extra writing assignments, the tutorial assistance, and the Enrichment Center itself had a positive effect on student learning. Another teacher stated that these additional projects "reinforced the material covered in class," and that the Enrichment Center improved students' abilities "to put material into their own words and to discover information on their own." He also stated, "Students who did not do projects, did not increase knowledge the same way"; and "The center seems quite able to serve a cross-section of courses in the department. It is highly desirable that its utilization be encouraged and its continuance be made certain."

These comments reveal that teachers and students saw the program as valuable. In the words of one teacher, the help that tutors gave students with homework and projects provided "the support the students need in the learning process" and decreased "most of our students' fears of reading, answering questions, and writing essays." The words of the paraprofessional epitomize the symbolic value that the center had for students. "Many students are motivated to return, and this is an encouraging sight. They prefer to come in and do their homework rather than spend their time in the halls. They also come back and show me the high marks they have received on the projects they did in the Enrichment Center."

Finally, the social studies chair saw the center's value as follows: "Given the fact that ten to fifteen students each period report to the Enrichment Center at a time of their own choosing, this must be deemed a great success. Self-discipline is an essential element in educational success."

Program Constraints

A major problem encountered in the program was the realization that the high school personnel and the FRP did not have the same pedagogical views about the use of writing as a way of learning. For the high school teachers in the program, the writing component of the collaborative program existed outside of their classroom; their perception of the program was that their responsibility was to assign extra essays and projects for students to complete in the Enrichment Center with the assistance and guidance of tutors. The FRP, however, operated on the premise that the writing component should have been an integral part of the social studies classroom itself. According to this view, the teacher should be responsible for instructing and engaging the students in various writing activities (note taking, summarizing, research skills, essay structure and organization, learning logs, and essay questions), and the Enrichment Center, through its tutors and materials, should help the students use writing to facilitate, reinforce, and enhance their knowledge of social studies.

The conflict between teachers' and the FRP's perceptions of WAC was manifested in the way teachers responded to the kinds of assignments recommended by the FRP. In referring to logs, for example, one pilot teacher said that they were not successful with his classes. In his words, "Students were reluctant to do work that they perceived as not part of the curriculum. Perhaps I should have ridden them a little harder on this issue, but I did not want to teach them to write by negative coercion. Students did enough writing in class and they felt the logs were superfluous."

Two problems can be seen here: first, it is counterproductive if students infer that any work they are doing is superfluous or extraneous, or that it "doesn't count toward the grade"; second, it seems that the teacher himself was not convinced of the value or importance of logs. If the use of logs had been discussed and established during program planning, pilot teachers would have been both convinced of their value and committed to using them.

Although most teachers balked at the use of logs, one pilot teacher did use logs in the second semester and found them helpful to the students and herself. She explained, "The students were able to give me feedback about the lessons dealt with during the week. In many instances, I was able to respond to some of the students' comments." This teacher's response validated our wanting logs to be a significant component of the classroom. We wished to reinforce the idea that in addition to helping a teacher assess her effectiveness, logs could also be a more relaxed form of student writing, a private dialogue between teacher and student, and an indication to the teacher of the connections students make between information presented in class and their own lives and experiences.

Perhaps a good way of convincing teachers about the usefulness of logs would have been to have the teachers themselves keep logs. Logs could have been used to maintain an open line of communication between teachers and the FRP and could have also served as a way for teachers to define, analyze, and work through their successes and problems with incorporating writing into their social studies courses. Both teachers and the FRP could have then used such logs to assess the effectiveness of the program.

It would also have been helpful if the tutors had kept logs. This would have allowed us to have more immediately answered and dealt with the student needs that the tutors directly observed. For example, in March a tutor informed us that many students did not know how to use a book index, a card catalog, or a table of contents, and some could not read a map. If we had known this sooner, we could have immediately developed a lesson on the use of social studies research materials and methods.

Evaluation Constraints

The criteria used to evaluate the program and students' growth in writing were also problematic. There were difficulties with pretests and posttests, the nature and grading of such tests, and their correlation with students' performance on the RCT and Regency exams. Furthermore, we were unable to secure a consistent student pilot group, reducing the number of students whose writing growth we could assess over the full year.

Students were pretested and posttested at the beginning and end of each semester. In a forty-minute period, they were asked to summarize a newspaper article that the teachers had selected. Although the FRP had suggested that the teachers use a holistic process for grading the essays, she noticed that students who extensively copied from the article received higher grades than those who painstakingly tried to summarize the article in their own words. In view of the results of this grading process, we believe that either all graders should have been required to attend a workshop on how to grade the summary, or outside graders should have been used.

One pilot teacher gave his students an article on the 1989 revolution in Romania. The problem here was the way the teacher presented the assignment. In trying to make students feel less pressured and more at ease with their writing, and in not wanting complaints for springing extra work on his students, the teacher told students that the tests did not count toward their grade. Again, if teachers have a misconception about the relationship of writing to learning, they may convey this misconception to students, who will probably also see writing as a superfluous rather than a learning activity in their social studies classes. All of this made the validity of our pretests and posttests problematic.

One suggestion for a pretest at the beginning of the term would be to inform students that they will be given an open-notebook essay test at the end of the second week of school. During those two weeks, students would cover a social studies unit. They would be given instruction on how to take notes and would take notes in preparation for the exam. This could both provide students with a meaningful context for note taking and make them less apprehensive about taking an exam. As a follow-up, students could compare the quality of their notes with the quality of their graded essays. In such a test, students would also be responding to a question, not just paraphrasing (or copying) as they would with a summary pretest. This is not to minimize the value of learning to summarize; teachers, for example, could show students how to summarize when preparing them to do research in the Enrichment Center.

In addition to using pretests and posttests to assess the effectiveness of our program, Regents and RCT scores were also used as indicators: if test scores improved on either the objective or essay sections, or both, then we hypothesized that learning increased through the added writing component.

Finally, we found that there are often teachers in the content areas who may themselves have writing problems or inhibitions about writing. Thus it may be necessary to assess which faculty members could benefit from or are most capable of participating in a program that promotes writing as a way of learning. One way to ascertain this could be to obtain some sort of writing sample from all faculty. This information could then be used as a motivational device for teachers to explore strategies for improving their own writing as well as the writing of their students and could fully illustrate the concept of using writing as a way of learning.

Budgetary Constraints

Our budget came from two sources: the college and the high school. The college provided $6,730 for the FRP, tutors, and staff development, and the high school provided $18,950 for equipment (including a computer), supplies, and a staff person (paraprofessional). If we had continued with the program, we would have recommended that the budget be revised to allow more release time for staff development.

Since planning is a central component in the implementation of a WAC program, the need for adequate compensation prior to and during the program is critical for its success. This compensation can come in the form of money and/or release time. We found that release time was crucial, especially for the FRP, who needed time to prepare materials and consult with teachers who were often burdened with administrative responsibilities not related to instruction. Although the FRP was compensated monetarily, she also had a full teaching load (nine courses throughout the academic year). The high school teachers in our program had full teaching schedules and were paid only for their attendance at meetings and for their hours spent marking the writing samples. This demanding workload for both the FRP and the teachers greatly reduced the amount of time that could be devoted to the program.

Program Recommendations

We explored the unknown without testing the waters. We tacitly accepted the idea that teachers would buy into the concept of WAC and would be willing to accept whatever we were selling. This collaborative program needed workshops and meetings prior to its implementation for the following purposes: to create a curriculum that incorporated the teaching of writing strategies into the social studies content area; to ensure that tutor efforts and activities were not haphazard but were coordinated with teacher in-class efforts; to secure faculty members who were committed to (and capable of) incorporating the teaching of writing in their content area; and to work out scheduling problems so as to obtain a consistent student group for one year.

We believe that collaborative projects work best when faculty members are brought together as colleagues who share ideas, identify concerns, and suggest possible ways to resolve their concerns. Therefore, we recommend and view it as critical that all teachers involved in any collaborative project be brought in and consulted as soon as any initial discussion of curriculum reform begins.

We would also recommend that the participating teachers and resource person be given release time from at least one course per semester. Although this could place a strain on a school budget, the participating teachers could, for example, exchange their required hall, study, or lunch duty for tutoring duty in an enrichment center. The staffing of an enrichment center by teachers instead of tutors and a paraprofessional could serve two purposes: to decrease the amount of money needed for tutors, and to provide teachers with an opportunity to familiarize themselves with the individual needs and capacities of the students. Teachers would be able to observe their students engaged in the process of writing. As they saw their students struggling in this process, teachers might come to see their roles not only as disseminators of information, but also as guides and facilitators to help students learn ways of absorbing, using, organizing, and synthesizing different kinds of information.

Finally, we learned that there should be no outsiders in a collaborative program. The FRP was an outsider thrust in the middle of the semester into a learning environment with which she had not yet familiarized herself. Consequently, she spent the first year during the implementation of the program becoming an insider. Unless teaching strategies, projects, and assignments are agreed upon and developed by all program participants before the implementation of the program, the resource person will appear to be a taskmaster whose role is to have teachers perform superfluous activities. The resource person should have adequate time to become acclimated to the learning environment, so that he or she can move from the perspective of theory to realistic praxis. This process will also enable teachers to have time to reflect on their teaching and on the value of incorporating writing into their content-area courses.

5

Student-Developed Multimedia: An Ideal Vehicle for Writing Across the Curriculum

Nancy Linvill and Chris Peters

A volcano erupts on the computer screen. A laser disc whirls and images appear on a television screen at the command of a computer program. Handel's sarabande from Suite no. 2 is digitally recorded and put into a computer program. A human voice says, "That is correct." when a question posed by the computer is answered appropriately by a student.

The computer programs that use these sounds and visual effects are not being developed by a large curriculum-development corporation in New York or Chicago. They were produced by students in the Computer Aided Instruction Project at R.C. Edwards Junior High in Central, South Carolina. In this project students work in concert with classroom teachers to create software for almost every subject in the curriculum. This is not an example of a junior high software "sweatshop," but rather an experimental effort to explore ways of making research and writing more engaging and meaningful for students.

The Computer Aided Instruction Project had its beginnings in an attempt to find an effective way to help more students at Edwards find success in the academic environment. Nancy Linvill, the resource teacher for learning disabled students at Edwards and coauthor of this paper, wanted to identify and promote approaches to instruction that accommodated the different learning styles exhibited by Edwards's students. She had observed that many bright, capable, creative students did not seem to respond well to traditional, teacher-centered instructional approaches, and she wanted to provide a means for them to succeed on a level commensurate with their ability.

The South Carolina Department of Education was offering multiyear grants of up to $90,000 for projects that explored innovative ways of meeting specific educational needs, so financial support was potentially available. The question was, how could such money be used to develop new strategies that would genuinely benefit the target group of students?

In search of possible directions Linvill contacted Chris Peters, a Clemson University assistant professor specializing in instructional technology (and the other author of this paper). Together they decided to explore the possible benefits of involving students in designing and developing computer software related to their regular classes.

The project's guiding premise was that by combining the benefits of writing across the curriculum (WAC) with the multisensory power and appeal of computer-controlled multimedia, learning and cognitive processing could be increased in a select group of students. *Computer-controlled multimedia* refers to the use of computers to capture, create, integrate, and present textual and audiovisual material in dynamic, interactive formats. Video material might include original electronic artwork created by students, digitally scanned photographs, motion sequences and still images from videodiscs, as well as other visual images gathered from a variety of additional sources. Audio material might include human narration, digitized sound effects, computer-generated music, and any other audio material that could enhance a particular project. All these pieces of information are combined in and accessed through a single computer-controlled environment. By harnessing the enthusiasm with which most students approach computers and channeling that enthusiasm into curriculum-based multimedia projects, the Edwards computer class is demonstrating that WAC and new technologies are a potent combination.

Why Multimedia?

The commonly stated goals of education include helping students learn how to think, solve complex problems effectively, and analyze and synthesize information to construct their own knowledge and understanding. By enabling students to become active learners, writing can be an effective tool to be used in achieving these goals. Writing Across the Curriculum extends the value of writing into content areas, by promoting active engagement of students with disciplinary knowledge. Multimedia takes matters one step farther by allowing students to design and develop information *systems* rather than simply putting words on paper in written reports. In addition to being more robust than writing alone because of the additional kinds of information involved, multimedia development encourages students to probe content matter more thoroughly as they uncover and express relationships among concepts.

Writing is still central to the process, but student efforts involve much more than simply composing and polishing the written word. The work required to execute a given project includes such elements as graphic design, simple audio engineering, public speaking, and even an element of video production. Students produce software that will be seen, read, and heard by more people than just the teacher. The concept of *writing* across the curriculum is expanded to *communicating* across the curriculum. The skills needed and the effort required necessitate that students consider the delivery of their information as a multimedia package, not simply as pages to be read. In the course of completing such a presentation students must carefully consider how audiences will view the end result. Important considerations include nuances of visual design and the effect it has on user perception, the degree to which a particular graphic might enhance or detract from effective communication, and the overall effect of the integration of text, pictures, and sounds on the understanding of someone using the program.

Multimedia information systems are usually nonlinear. This means that information need not be presented in a strict, predefined sequence. Video clips, images, sounds, and written text are all potentially accessible at any point in the presentation. To construct a logical, usable multimedia system, students must evaluate the different ways people might want to access the information and then provide means for them to do so. The end result is that students analyze the content more deeply and communicate its substance meaningfully.

Allowing students to create their own software and present it to others put them in control of the learning experience and gave them self-confidence. Students do have the ability to generate knowledge and prepare high-quality presentations. Multimedia is a vehicle for students to become partners with teachers in the educational process.

How the Project Works

The Edwards computer class is made up of teacher-selected students who have previously performed below their academic potential. Some of the students have problems with attention deficit disorder; others are creative, "right-brain" students who want the freedom to chart their own course through the curriculum. In short, the class provides an alternative for students who have difficulty learning in lecture-oriented classes.

In the computer aided instruction class, students work on projects for other courses they are taking. Students confer with subject-area teachers about topics they will be studying in the future in order to select a theme for a project. Then they design a computerized, multi-media "term paper" about the topic and begin executing it using HyperCard software on Macintosh computers. HyperCard is a multi-media "authoring tool" that lets nonprogrammers create sophisticated computer software. The end result is called a HyperCard *stack*. When students complete their stacks, they use them to teach their classmates about the researched topic. They also let their teachers use the stacks for presentations to other classes.

Students begin their HyperCard projects by gathering information. They use traditional methods of doing research in the media center, such as finding books, locating periodicals, and exploring encyclopedias. Some students conduct interviews with local experts to obtain firsthand information about a particular subject. Information gathered in the interviews and from other research is combined, outlined, and laid out in a written structural plan for use in developing the HyperCard stack.

First attempts to research topics for HyperCard projects are typically a struggle for students, requiring more time and effort than expected to find the needed information and materials. Many students have never conducted this type of research and are frustrated with the process of locating what they need. Edwards media specialist Edmee Reel believes the class provides an unusual opportunity for students to sharpen their research skills. They are motivated to spend the effort necessary to become proficient researchers because projects have personal meaning and because they know their work will be used with a wider audience than most classroom assignments.

Using computers to create their projects seems to clear up the "writer's block" that frequently confronts these students when working on purely paper-based assignments. The payoff for the research is in transferring the results to the multimedia environment, and that goal keeps students motivated during the frustration of the research itself. One student in the class said, "I wanted to sit down at my computer and work rather than talk after I had the information on note cards."

Once the information is gathered and plans are written and critiqued by fellow students and teachers, students begin to construct their stacks. A typical stack consists of a number of screens or "cards" that contain pictures, boxes holding textual information, and buttons that may be activated to move from one screen to another. Buttons are also used to access video clips stored on videodiscs, to play sound effects or spoken narration, and to call hidden textual information onto the screen. While the essential building blocks (pictures, buttons, text boxes) of all stacks are similar, the arrangement of those elements and the specific information they contain are different in each project.

Figures 5–1 and 5–2 are screens from two students' stacks, *The Greenhouse Effect* by a ninth-grade boy, and *The Solar System* by an

Figure 5−1
Greenhouse Effect

WAYS WE CAN SLOW DOWN
THE GREENHOUSE EFFECT

The best way we can slow
down the effects are to
reduce the output of carbon
dioxide in the air. We can do
this by using other energy
alternatives such as
wind, solar, gas, and water
power to run our machines
instead of fuels that put
carbon dioxide in the air.
We can also reduce carbon
dioxide in the air by
planting more trees.

GO TO MENU

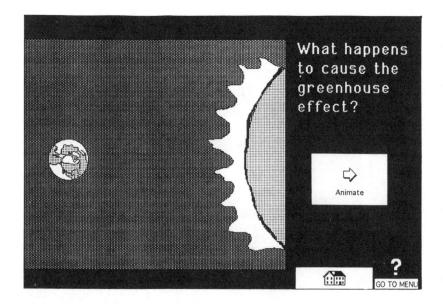

eighth-grade girl. Notice how each stack accomplishes similar goals in presenting information and allowing the user to browse through it, but the visual look and feel of each, as well as its underlying structure, are completely different and individualistic.

The designer of *The Greenhouse Effect* is a talented artist and has opted to use original electronic drawings as the graphics in his stacks. His Greenhouse Effect stack is divided into three major sections (Information About the Greenhouse Effect, Effects of the Greenhouse Effect, and How We Can Slow Down the Effect) Operators may use buttons to move easily from one section to another. The stack includes an animated sequence of sunlight approaching and striking the earth and uses sound effects with a synthesized echo added. The stack is an example of good information expressed with the help of a fertile imagination.

Laura Smith, the designer of *The Solar System* is meticulous and structured in her research. Her stack is packed with pictures and written information, and its structure reflects her systematic approach. The stack index is a view of the entire solar system. In order to get more detailed information about a particular planet, the user clicks on the image of that planet in the solar system diagram. The program then advances to that planet's section. In addition to presenting onscreen text and graphics, Laura has tied certain sections of the stack to appropriate material on a videodisc which the user can access as desired.

Figure 5–2
Solar System

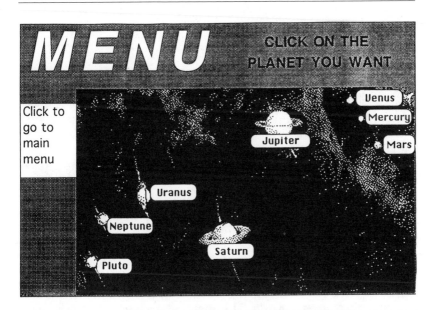

Working on the computer is fascinating for all students in the class. With HyperCard, students are able to free their imaginations and learning potential as they write. If words fail them or simply aren't sufficient to convey the ideas students wish to share with an audience, they can amplify the text with sounds, pictures, animation, and material from laser discs.

Rachel McLaurin completed a HyperCard project on atoms for her science class. "Atoms do not thrill me and I would not have enjoyed doing a typical written, research project on this topic," she explained. "If I don't like the subject, I don't like to write papers. With a paper you are just typing and the only thing you can change is the ink. I would just type dull information." She found that by using HyperCard to present her information, writing and illustrating a stack about atoms was fun and much more interesting. "I scanned a picture into my computer of a gold foil experiment by Ernest Rutherford. I also scanned a picture of an atom and used it several times in my stack. When I wrote about a positive center to an atom, I was able to change the picture and put a positive center into it. If you use a computer you take more interest in your work and learn more than if you go to the encyclopedia and do the work just for a grade. With HyperCard you have to get the information ready for a class presentation. To do that, you have to really learn what it's about. I get into it because I will show it to my classmates and I want it to be good."

Students present completed HyperCard stacks as minilessons to their classmates. An enlarged view of the computer screen is displayed with an overhead projection panel, and sound is amplified through speakers plugged into the computer. Knowing that their stacks will be shown to others encourages students to produce better work than they normally would for classroom assignments. Alton Owen said that he works differently when he knows that several of his classmates will be looking at his project. "I make it better than if only a teacher were to see it. It's a lot harder to do a halfway job when I'm going to show it to others. I need to get everything right, like the spelling."

Grades and Evaluation

Grading was as unconventional and experimental as the course itself. Students filled out a contract at the beginning of each week and wrote down project-related goals they wished to accomplish during the week. At the end of each day, they wrote a brief statement of what they did. On Fridays the teacher had a short conference with each student, discussing whether or not the goals had been accomplished and what might have been done differently to help achieve all goals. Students summarized their own views regarding the quality of their work for the week, and their assessments were taken into account in assigning the week's grades. Then students and teachers together agreed on a grade for the week. The students were also given a grade for their research and presentations, based on a simple checklist.

Edwards students take semester exams that represent one-fifth of their grade. For the semester exam in the multimedia course the students were given an incomplete HyperCard stack and asked to complete it. They were expected to make a title screen, put in a digitized sound, script "buttons" to allow users to move among screens, and use visual effects to enhance screen transitions. Work was evaluated with a checklist for each item completed on the test.

Results

Few observers will mistake the finished HyperCard stacks as the work of professional software design teams, yet the students' projects are invariably intriguing, and the students are justifiably proud of their creative work. Upon project completion students have the satisfaction of knowing that their efforts have paid off in the production of tangible products that they will share with others. The students enjoy the attention and frequent visitors the HyperCard classes receive, as well as their moments in the spotlight when they are asked to make presentations. With classes of unmotivated "underachievers," the software-development class has become a highly productive endeavor that is routinely cited by students as their favorite class and the one thing they really enjoy at school.

What is perhaps more important is that many of these students, who have been unsuccessful in regular classroom situations, and might logically be described as being "at risk" or even failures by normal standards, become effective learners. In addition they are able to generate information that is useful in teaching others. There is good chemistry among the students. Underachievers mix closely and well with high achievers. As new programming tricks or design features are discovered and shared, the students' roles switch continually from being learners to teachers to independent multimedia producers.

Edwards faculty members are equally positive in assessing the accomplishments of the software-development efforts. Many have become motivated to learn more about HyperCard so that they too can develop class materials.

Elaine Lesley, an English teacher at Edwards, observes that computer students are proud of themselves when presenting HyperCard stacks to their classmates. She believes that their self-esteem is enhanced by being able to respond accurately to their classmates' questions and that the outside reading done by the HyperCard students allows them to answer questions with assurance. Lesley plans to keep student-made HyperCard stacks and use them in future years with classes. She thinks students are pleased that the stacks will be used in the future, noting, "We all like to think we are leaving something useful behind."

Connie Stockunas, an Edwards science teacher, has had several HyperCard projects presented for her classes. She reports that Hyper-Card computer students make better grades in her class when their researched topic is being studied. She says, "The HyperCard students pay more attention during discussions and enjoy giving out information about what they already learned."

John Wade, former Edwards Junior High principal, says that the HyperCard computer class increased students' motivation and confidence. When he walked into the computer classroom, he noticed that students would push back their chairs and back up so that he could see their work. In other classes he said these same students would sometimes cover their papers with their hands so that their work would not be seen.

The community surrounding Edwards has been supportive of the HyperCard project. A committee composed of parents, teachers, and business people has acted as an advisory group and has met periodically to stay informed about the program's progress and to promote awareness of the project. Supporters at Clemson University have made many visits to Edwards, troubleshooting hardware problems, training teachers, and observing the students in action. The local Rotary Club donated money to buy an additional computer.

Attention has also spread beyond the Edwards community. Numerous newspaper articles and positive editorials about the project have appeared. The newsletter published by the South Carolina Department of Instructional Technology has run a feature on the Edwards project, and representatives of several schools have visited Edwards to explore the possibilities of adopting similar programs in their schools.

Lessons Learned

The project has functioned smoothly for the past two years, but there were many unexpected obstacles that had to be overcome. Despite being very straightforward and "user friendly," HyperCard is not something one learns immediately. The two computer class instructors had no programming experience and had never used HyperCard or Macintosh computers before the project began. A one-day training session and a box of training materials donated by Apple Computer helped get things rolling, but by themselves these were insufficient to keep the class afloat. Achieving HyperCard proficiency required much trial and error, many false starts, and occasional teeth gnashing. It helped that the students and teachers adopted the role of colearners, sharing new discoveries and techniques as they emerged. Teachers assumed guidance roles, and students had to become problem solvers, often working in tandem to tackle a particular programming issue.

It also became apparent that, as computer novices, the teachers needed to have outside help available. Frequent calls to the local computer vendor and to university faculty with multimedia expertise were necessary to survive the first year. The second year was considerably smoother and calls for help were fewer and far less frantic.

Another difficulty was a hidden partner of multimedia's appealing robustness and variety. Students were so intrigued with the technology that they could easily get off track and waste time playing with the computer's capabilities. Digitized sound effects and digital recordings of the students' own voices were frequent distractors. Some play was desirable and necessary to help students become proficient with the technology, but it could easily get out of hand. Maintaining a balance required active monitoring by the instructors and occasional intervention to nudge students back onto a project-oriented path.

Despite the added appeal of the computerized environment, students did not find all of the project's activities enjoyable. Using the computer was fun, but preparing a good multimedia presentation required a significant amount of research and planning. Many students found these processes cumbersome and preferred to sit right down at the computer and start creating without a plan or a fixed direction.

While the faculty and administration at Edwards have been highly supportive of the project and pleased with its results, there are nonetheless several internal obstacles to the project's continued success. A few teachers were not receptive to having students take over part of their planned lecture time to present a multimedia package. It was not always clear if the reluctance stemmed from the perceived difficulty of integrating students' instruction with the teacher's or from an unwillingness to relinquish control of the classroom for even a short period of time.

The length of time it took for students to execute a project also sometimes interfered with presenting multimedia projects to other classes. Whereas a typical term paper might take two to three weeks to research and write, a multimedia package could take anywhere from four to twelve weeks to develop. By the time a project was finished it was sometimes too late to be of much instructional value in another class.

Looking to the Future

The chief lesson learned from the software-development experiment has been that the intelligent use of technology can benefit the learning of every subject. Relegating multimedia to multimedia classes makes no more sense than confining writing to writing classes. If educators are to truly capitalize on the benefits of new information technologies, use of these technologies must be woven into the very substance of the curriculum. Students must have access to technology as they need it—not only within a technology-related class, but within every class.

One Edwards teacher, Tab Hughey, had all students in his eighth-grade South Carolina History class do a multimedia project about an event in the Revolutionary War. J. R. Adkins, a student in the class, said, "Doing my project about Bunker Hill helped me understand what really happened during the Revolutionary War. It will stick with me more than if I had done regular classroom activities. We didn't cover as much material while we did the multimedia project, but we went more in depth." J. R. added that he learned not only from creating his stack about Bunker Hill, but also from viewing his classmates' HyperCard stacks about other aspects of the Revolutionary War. We are hopeful that there will be more widespread use of multimedia design as a part of regular classwork at Edwards in the future.

Attempting to provide universal access to multimedia production is, unfortunately, a challenge currently beyond the means of most schools. Increased student access to computers requires purchasing a greater number of systems at a time when there is often not enough money for school essentials, much less for technology purchases. At the same time, for those who have money, choosing the right hardware is like shooting at a moving target. Each year seems to bring better computers at a lower cost. The difficulty of purchasing systems that will not seem obsolete in the near future is a serious enough dilemma that some schools put purchasing plans on hold indefinitely.

Until funding allows schools to infuse more technology into the everyday classroom, and until schools are willing to commit to the ongoing support of the use of that technology, educators are caught in an unfortunate predicament. We can't afford to obtain the facilities needed to give every student access to the technology, yet the technology is potentially so pedagogically powerful that we can't afford to wait. In the meantime, for all their successes, classes such as those taught at Edwards run the risk of remaining novelties, intriguing some and inspiring others, but not really affecting the lives of the majority of students who desperately need what the technology has to offer.

The hope is that as more schools successfully demonstrate the value of multimedia in every curriculum area, the status of multimedia (and the hardware required to support it) will change. Perhaps in the not too distant future, instead of being seen as a luxury made accessible to select groups of students, multimedia will be perceived as a school fundamental. The focus will no longer be on the technology or the hardware, but entirely on the learning taking place. Given education's track record with technology and our seeming inability to capitalize on its potential, this might seem overly optimistic. Nevertheless, the demonstrated power of multimedia to motivate students and promote learning makes pursuing that hope worthwhile.

Appendix
Logistics

Hardware

While the ability to integrate different media into a single presentation might seem futuristic, the hardware is readily available in many schools already. The Edwards computer lab houses seventeen Macintosh computers (a combination of ten SEs, four Classics, one LC, a IIcx, and a IIci file server), an Apple flatbed scanner, a laser printer, a videodisc player, and three CD-ROM drives. HyperCard comes bundled free with every Macintosh computer.

The lab setup allows whole classes of students to be involved in multimedia development at the same time and allows resources such as the lone scanner to be shared, but fewer systems integrated into regular classrooms could still be used effectively.

The cost of the lab's original twelve computers and other hardware when purchased was approximately $30,000, but prices continue to drop. To equip a similarly configured facility at this writing (Spring 1992) would cost approximately $18,000. An individual "creation station" consisting of a Mac Classic, flatbed scanner, videodisc player, and a CD-ROM drive would currently cost around $3,200.

Materials

Several good reference and training books are now on the market to help with multimedia development. Danny Goodman's *The Complete HyperCard 2.0 Handbook* (Bantam) is the single best HyperCard reference book and should be considered an essential resource in any HyperCard project. Also worth investigating are the manual that Apple includes with HyperCard and the myriad of educational HyperCard books beginning to appear on bookstore shelves.

There are at least two other widely available sources of information that would be helpful to anyone undertaking a serious project:

1. Organized training either through college classes or conference workshops can be very helpful. Single-day sessions can sometimes present more information than can be effectively absorbed by

participants, but they can still be tremendously worthwhile. College classes usually offer training that is spaced out over longer periods of time, allowing a more relaxed opportunity to master the basics in stages. At present, however, multimedia classes are not routinely offered by schools of education, and such training may be hard to find.

2. Perhaps the cheapest way to sharpen HyperCard technique is the examination of stacks created by more experienced developers. One of the nice things about HyperCard is that it is relatively simple to break into a stack to see how something is done. Stacks are routinely available for free through on-line services such as GEnie, CompuServe, and America On-Line. They can also be purchased very cheaply through companies such as EduCorp (800-843-9497) or computer user groups such as the Boston Computer Society (617-625-7080) or the Berkeley Macintosh User.

Ways of Collaborating

Frequently Writing Across the Curriculum programs develop from collaborative efforts. Teachers work together across or within disciplines to develop a new course or program of study or curriculum; instructors in different settings, such as high school and college, join forces to create new educational experiences; computers and writing centers offer new contexts for mutual projects. Whatever form it takes, collaboration brings disparate individuals and groups together and combines the strengths of several to produce more than a single person could. The chapters in this section demonstrate how various types of collaboration work to create effective WAC programs.

George Wilson opens this section by tracing the development and results of four collaborative projects, art-English, history-English, English-elementary, and an international project. Steve Pearse describes several collaborative projects aimed at integrating WAC into a student-centered thematic approach to learning. In chapter 8 Barry Gadlin, Linda Ashida, Barry Brown, Jack Elliott, Bernie Kelly, Chris Kelly, Sue Gates, Mary Beth Khoury, Robert Korahk, and Charles Widlowski explain how they worked as a team to increase student achievement by developing a WAC program. Rae Bruce and Rodney Mansfield show how English and science teachers can work together to develop an environmental science course. Mary Kollar details her collaboration with a college instructor to develop a literature program that gives prominence to WAC. In chapter 11 Eve Coleman and Jeanne Sink offer suggestions on how college and high school teachers can use computers to help students reach a wider audience with their writing. Another school-college collaboration appears in the final chapter, as Barbra Morris, George Cooper, Constance Childress, Mary Cox, and Patricia Williams describe how they moved from theory to implementation of a WAC program.

6

Four Collaborative Projects

George D. Wilson

Who put the *labor* in col*labor*ation? Once underway, collaborative projects typically reduce the labor required of any individual. More important, collaboration fosters connections among content areas and among people — connections that might not otherwise be made. Working together cooperatively across subject areas, across school buildings, and even across nations yields great benefits for the teachers and students involved. Writing across the curriculum (WAC) projects are ideal vehicles for collaboration among teachers of different grade levels and content areas. A basic skill necessary to effective learning of any subject, writing must be reinforced throughout the curriculum by all teachers. Collaborative projects that use writing as the common link — the primary mode of communication — strengthen students' writing skills. Moreover, with the English teacher as the principal player in the collaboration, these projects offer a fairly painless way for non-English teachers to use writing in their classes as a learning tool. But how do collaborations begin? Who first envisions the concept? How is that idea shared with others? What obstacles must be overcome? How can administrators foster collaboration among their staffs?

From its genesis to the revelations it finally brings, each collaborative project described here is a story of almost spiritual commitment to the idea that two minds are more than twice as creative as one. Typically, however, one person possesses the vision first and initiates action. He or she cognitively sculpts the vision into a form that others can see, then breathes life into the project by convincing others of its viability. A study of collaborative efforts reveals common themes: a vision, the sharing of the vision, the vision made real, and the outcomes (both planned and serendipitous).

The central impetus for collaboration in the Mt. Lebanon School District in Pittsburgh comes from the members of the junior and senior

75

high school English staff. Through the efforts of a number of these teachers, collaborations exist with art, social studies, science, foreign language, and home economics staff. In addition, through the use of telecommunications linkages, high school English students collaborate with elementary special education students, with students out of state and in Canada. Writing experiences lie at the base of each of these collaborations, largely because writing is a skill that transcends content-area divisions. In addition, the Mt. Lebanon School District recently completed an intensive, four-year, K–12 WAC program designed to encourage all teachers to use writing as an instructional strategy. The following four examples describe some of the collaborations that occurred over the last two years and typify the interdisciplinary writing projects in the Mt. Lebanon School District.

Visual and Verbal

Working with an art instructor, a junior high school English teacher has her students design greeting cards that are original in their visual and verbal presentation. Students design the image to illustrate their text.

In completing this project the student sees relationships between the written and visual modes of communication, identifies and addresses a specific audience (the recipient of the card), explores and selects appropriate symbols, uses color and design to enhance a feeling or idea, communicates through concise expression, and generally conveys a feeling or idea in a unified visual-verbal format. A team-teaching approach works best with this project.

In describing how she arrived at the idea of creating greeting cards, English teacher Carol Hirsch reveals the ingenuity so vital to successful teachers. As a child she had designed her own Christmas cards to send to family members, but the experience lay dormant in her memory until several years ago. At that time, as Thanksgiving approached, she asked her students to complete a writing assignment: a paragraph about their greatest blessings. Many of the children wrote tender pieces about their parents, and the writing lab clinician (the teacher in charge of the writing lab) remarked that parents would probably appreciate reading their children's sentiments. One student, a few weeks later, curled his piece into a scroll and placed it in his father's Christmas stocking. Carol synthesized these three experiences — her own childhood activity, the clinician's comment, and the student's action — into a single vision. Next, she had to bring the vision to reality, and to do so she enlisted the aid of a colleague. She had talked in the past with an art teacher, Ronald Schreiner, about developing some kind of interdisciplinary project (for example, having students illustrate their science fiction stories), but they had never acted on it. When Carol approached Ron with her idea, they decided upon the greeting card medium, which would fit well within the art curriculum as well as enhance her English instruction.

With the vision shared and accepted, Carol read in *The Saturday Evening Post Christmas Treasury* (1986) "The First Merry Christmas," an article on the origins of Christmas cards. Using the article as background, she fleshed out the assignment in an organized series of lessons. Students wrote the paragraph assignment about their greatest blessings and used those works as the basis for their cards' texts (to keep it secular, any kind of greeting card was acceptable). Once satisfied with their texts, students began designing the cards. Working with Ron, students used their knowledge of art to make design decisions. When completed, the cards were evaluated jointly by both teachers.

Only one minor impediment hindered Carol and Ron as they pursued their project. Their teaching schedules did not permit the kind of teaming they would have preferred. Ron had to come to Carol's English class while Carol worked with Ron's art students. Most students, however, became so involved in the project that they set aside time after school to meet with the teachers and to work on the cards.

The collaboration resulted in an exciting venture that enhanced students' learning in both English and art. Students enjoyed working with both teachers and having the opportunity for hands-on activity. Their pride in the final products demonstrated the success of the collaboration.

Not only the students, but also the teachers developed new understandings from the project. As an art teacher, Ron saw firsthand how writing could become an integral part of his particular content area. Carol, by modeling for Ron how effectively writing could be used, strengthened the WAC thrust in the junior high school. Furthermore, she grew by the knowledge of her success in making real her visionary project.

Poetry Illustrated

A senior high school English teacher shares with an art class the poems written by her ninth-grade students. The juniors and seniors in the art class create illustrations (pen and ink, watercolor) to enhance the written works. The resulting posters decorate the classroom and hallways, then are photographically reduced and compiled in a booklet. Through this project, art students have their knowledge of poetry reinforced as they interpret poems and design appropriate symbolic or literal drawings to amplify the written thought. The English students learn how others interpret their work.

Marilyn Bates, a high school English teacher, credits her experience as a fellow in the Western Pennsylvania Writing Project with planting the idea for this collaborative project. She saw that classroom publishing motivates students to value their writing more because others will read it, but she found the publication booklets to be somewhat drab. She asked some students to include pictures with their writings, but found them reluctant to produce the drawings. Driven by the belief that the students would have greater self-esteem and would find their writing even more valued if it had illustrations, she contacted art teacher Mark Pelusi. He saw a natural match between Marilyn's concept and one of his instructional units. Together they decided that her ninth-grade students would write poems that Marilyn would send to Mark's art class. The charge for the art students was to assume the role of publication illustrator—someone who had to design a drawing to accompany a poem. Each art student read through several poems and selected one to illustrate. Their drawing had to reflect their interpretation of the poem. Since the poems were sent anonymously, the art students did not know whose work they were illustrating. When Marilyn's students saw their illustrated works, they discussed at length the interpretation the artist had made and the extent to which it depicted the author's view or presented a different interpretation. When the booklet was compiled and ready for class distribution, Marilyn arranged for a reading complete with wine (sparkling grape juice) and cheese. The students found the experience delightful.

Marilyn points to many positive outcomes of the project. Clearly, the students exhibited greater motivation in their writing and revision. Knowing that their works would be read by audiences other than the teacher inspired them. Many extended their critical judgment skills as they identified their best poems. When they saw the illustrations, students wrestled with the multiple levels of meaning a poem can release as they reflected upon how others interpreted their work. They had a new sense of voice, and they recognized in a unique way the power of metaphor. Perhaps most important, they experienced elevated self-esteem in realizing someone could construct a picture around their poem. In fact, some of the artwork was so elaborate and elegant that the writers felt as though the art bestowed a new worthiness upon the poem. The art students also gained from the experience. Their simulation as illustrators gave them insight into one field of art-related careers. In addition, they used skills in reading, thinking, interpreting, and judging as they probed their impressions of the poems and what drawings would best depict their impressions. They also had an opportunity to demonstrate to an audience outside the art classroom what they are capable of accomplishing. As Marilyn phrased it, "We compose in many ways, and drawing is a form of composing that represents the student's version of reality. As a writer seeks words to expand on his idea, the artist tries to distill the essence of the poem in a drawing that gives off its own meaning." WAC, or what in this case might be called composing across the curriculum, clearly brings to students new opportunities to learn and to demonstrate that learning.

U.S. History Essay Program

High school English and social studies instructors team teach in social studies classes to prepare students for in-class essay exams administered four times a year in U.S. History. Linking a review of composition structures (an analysis paper and a compare-contrast paper) with specific social studies content, the teachers take students through a simulation of the upcoming essay exam. These "walk-through" experiences provide a refresher for composition skills and for test-taking strategies. English teachers assist in the holistic scoring of the papers, a step that lends credibility to the scoring process as well as provides useful staff development. Social studies teachers reinforce their knowledge of effective writing techniques.

Supervisor of secondary education Dale Cable authored this exemplary WAC program. He recounts a lengthy gestation for the program; its origins date to 1972 when the U.S. History course shifted to a concept-centered approach rather than the traditional one that stressed the memorization of facts and dates. Part of the shift included adopting the inquiry methodology. Dale felt frustration in trying to evaluate accurately students' understandings of higher cognitive concepts using objective tests. In an attempt to understand students' depth of content analysis, Dale began to experiment with essay testing. After using essay testing in his own classes and becoming convinced of its accuracy in evaluating student understanding of content, Dale began to persuade others. Although admitting that essay testing provided valid indicators of student performance, the social studies teachers found the process burdensome and time-consuming. Dale's conviction led him to propose to central-office personnel a reduction in class size for U.S. History classes in order to promote essay testing. Fueling his efforts was a belief that writing instruction had suffered as a result of an English department program shift to an all-elective format. Students, he felt, no longer opted for the challenging composition courses; they preferred to enroll in easier, high-interest literature courses. He used the argument that his proposal would provide compensatory instruction in writing, but that instruction must come from the recognized experts — the English teachers. He enlisted their support. The full proposal — it included team teaching, reduced class sizes, release time to allow for planning and scoring, and compensation for the English teacher participants— met with skepticism from other administrators and was tabled for several years. Dale continued to advance the idea and built upon the growing writing process movement to lend weight to his position. In 1984 the proposal was adopted, and after several years the program proved so successful that the National Council of Teachers of English endorsed it by recognizing the high school with a Center of Excellence Award.

Extensive review of the program reveals that it achieves the desired outcomes year after year. The English department long ago modified its total-elective program and returned to an emphasis on writing instruction; nevertheless, the U.S. History Essay Test Program continues to demonstrate that a better transfer of writing skills from English to social studies class occurs as a result of the program.

Dale's collaboration began with the single-minded determination to improve social studies instruction by changing the evaluation instruments. After enlisting the aid of English teachers, he finally won approval for the program. His unwavering conviction and ability to persuade others brought a highly effective WAC program into existence.

Telecommunications

Perhaps the most exciting collaborations are those that extend far beyond the school building. In such cases WAC takes on new meaning as the concept includes writing across *other schools'* curricula. Mt. Lebanon is involved in four such projects. First, in an extracurricular project interested high school students use a computer with modem to communicate with fifth graders at one of the district's elementary schools. Second, as an extension of the first effort, students in an eleventh-grade composition class act as writing coaches to sixth graders from another of the district's elementary buildings. Using the modem-equipped computer, the students write to each other and share their supportive criticisms of each other's works. Third, through no-cost, courtesy accounts, students in a composition class telecommunicate with a class in a rural high school in Montana. Fourth, working through Simon Frazer University in British Columbia, Mt. Lebanon's students communicate via computer with high school students in a similarly academically demanding district in Toronto.

Brendan Fitzgerald, a high school English teacher, cites an article by Jeffrey Schwartz (1990) in *English Journal* as the spark for his interest in pursuing collaborations through telecommunications networks. In addition, his motivation grew from his own computer knowledge, his awareness of the allure of technology to motivate students, his experience in telecommunicating with other educators, and his experience with one E-mail message in particular: from a homebound student in New York who poignantly portrayed his electronic link as virtually his only contact with the world outside his home.

In establishing his first telecommunications venture, Brendan collaborated with an equally enthusiastic special education teacher, Virginia Nikolich, who had recently switched from junior high school to an elementary school. They shared the belief that telecommunications would "break down the isolation of nonmainstreamed classes." Calling it the "One-Room Schoolhouse Project," they structured the activity so that the high school students focused on American Literature course content through attention to poetry, and the elementary students focused on social studies and writing skills, which were a direct part of their curriculum. Important to both teachers was making the experience more than that of just electronic pen pals. After a few "getting-to-know-you" transmissions, the students exchanged interpretations of poems that Brendan and Virginia had selected based upon their accessibility on a variety of levels of interpretation. The teachers allowed the students to interact naturally with little teacher involvement. As the individuals shared their ideas with each other via the computer, the high school students grew in their awareness of communication skills and in their knowledge of working with others. They also gained a more conscious awareness of the reality and validity of different readings of the same text. The elementary students benefited from the extra attention to their writing and ideas. At year's end the collaborating teachers arranged for these students to meet one another by having the elementary students take a field trip to the high school. Never told that the elementary students were from a special education class, the high school students, on meeting the elementary students for the first time, recognized and cherished a unique benefit afforded by telecommunications: to relate to people without regard to individual differences.

For the second project, Brendan worked with Cynthia Biery, a teacher at another elementary building. She had begun an after-school writers' group for interested students. The telecommunications linkage enabled Brendan's eleventh graders to act as writing coaches and to conference with the sixth graders about their works in progress. By writing for a broader audience, the students strengthened their writing skills.

As he became convinced that telecommunications had great potential, Brendan began to explore a wider range of possibilities. Through electronic networks he contacted like-minded teachers across the country. The third project, though still in its infancy, involves Brendan's composition class and eleventh graders from Montana. In the icebreaker stage, both groups recognize the stark contrasts of their settings:

Mt. Lebanon is a large, affluent suburban district whereas its counterpart in Montana is little more than a one-room school whose entire eleventh grade consists of six students. Both groups grow in the knowledge of regional differences and the similarities that all teenagers share. As the project continues and they share their writings, they will have an opportunity to learn more about their respective environments and lifestyles.

A similar project extends beyond our nation's boundaries into Canada. Still in the planning stages, this collaboration will involve a suburban Toronto high school that appears quite similar to Mt. Lebanon in community and school climate. Brendan believes that the students will share many similarities in lifestyle, yet will learn much from their international linkage. These students will be exchanging views on American literature — topics on which the Canadians may hold different perspectives. It promises to be an exciting collaboration and one that offers a new vision of WAC's potential. In addition to what the students will learn through the experience, Brendan and his Canadian counterpart have an opportunity to reassess their respective programs of study, their expectations for students, and their instructional techniques using each other's practices as a model. Most WAC projects focus on a single building's or, at best, a single district's curricula. In creating his interstate and international linkages, Brendan takes the WAC approach to new levels of opportunity.

Challenges for Brendan in all these projects were to obtain the necessary equipment (computers, modem, phone line connections) and to motivate others to join him in investigating meaningful telecommunications experiences. With help from the administrative staff, he received the required equipment, and with his own persuasive enthusiasm, he convinced others to collaborate. His students and the students in these other locations benefit from his and his collaborators' efforts.

Creating a Collaborative Climate

Each of the collaborations described here began with one person's vision. Through personal initiative each visionary brought the idea to a concrete level. Each conveyed the difficulty inherent in implementing new projects — the lack of time to plan, the complications in gathering materials, the need for technical support. In most cases, strong administrative support helped bring the vision to reality.

This history leads to the following questions: How do school districts encourage teacher initiative? Are there steps administrators can take to create a climate conducive to collaborative exploration? What is most needed on the part of administrators is an openness to intrapreneurism. *Intrapreneurs*, according to *The American Heritage*

Dictionary, are people *within* an organization who take personal risks to make new ideas happen. Like their counterparts, those extra-corporate rebels called entrepreneurs, intrapreneurs may be characterized as free spirits. Admittedly, an organization comprised solely of intrapreneurs would be an administrative nightmare—one of their traits, after all, is a low tolerance for bureaucracy. Nevertheless, such people play an important role as innovators and change agents. Administrators who support and promote new initiatives help inspire teachers to become intrapreneurs. In Mt. Lebanon, for example, the administrative and board support for the WAC program fostered enthusiasm among staff members and encouraged teachers to investigate ways to integrate WAC principles in their classrooms. These collaborations stand as testament to that encouragement. In short, administrators who give support to teachers with new ideas and who encourage exploration of new territory will rarely regret those actions.

How do teachers get their ideas? By synthesizing their experiences, by acting on long-held beliefs, by expanding upon ideas from journal articles, and by embracing new opportunities such as the WAC movement and the emerging use of technology. What steps do they take to realize those ideas? The intrapreneurs convince others to join them, and they use that combined energy to make the projects work. Yes, *labor* lies at the root of collaboration, but through cooperation, synergism reduces the effort and brings increased learning opportunities to students.

Notes

For additional information about any of these projects, please contact Dr. George D. Wilson, Director of Secondary Education, Mt. Lebanon School District, 7 Horsman Drive, Pittsburgh, PA 15228.

Acknowledgments: Mrs. Marilyn Bates, Ms. Cynthia Biery, Mr. Dale Cable, Mr. Brendan Fitzgerald, Mrs. Carol Hirsch, Ms. Virginia Nikolich, Mr. Mark Pelusi, and Mr. Ronald Schreiner. These collaborators made the projects described above work. They also collaborated on this publication.

References

Anon. 1986. "The First Merry Christmas." In *Saturday Evening Post Christmas Treasury*. New York: Bonanza Books.

Schwartz, Jeffrey. 1990. "Using an Electronic Network to Play the Scales of Discourse." *English Journal* 79.3: 16–24.

7

Writing Across the Curriculum at Shorewood High: Integrative Models, Student Investments

Steve Pearse

"How can I possibly be expected to read—much less grade —more student papers? That's just too much."

"What with huge class loads, more and more at-risk and non-English speakers, and another new prep this year, I'll barely have time to grade their *tests*, never mind assign them more writing!"

"You're asking for 'another other,' and I'm not going to do it."

These and many more reactions, complaints, and declarations made over the years by non-English teachers I know are apparently timeless, if not universal. For many subject-area teachers, incorporating writing in the process of teaching has meant conducting rigorous assessments, with an emphasis upon grammatical and mechanical correctness (Fulwiler 1986). Despite assurances to the contrary, only a small minority of teachers outside the English department regularly involve their students in exploratory, expressive writing for the purpose of responding in personal ways to key concepts and content. Of course, English teachers also chafe under the rub of the ever-present paper load. Writing is, after all, a subject to be taught; all too frequently student writing is viewed as teacher burden. Thinking of writing as process and product that know no curricular bounds and are integral to class activities as well as to authentic assessment may not be a new idea, but neither is it an accepted practice in many schools.

The notion of what writing can be and do for students has contributed in significant ways to the restructuring conversation that has begun at Shorewood High School in Seattle. Like many other schools across the country, Shorewood is reassessing its effectiveness for students' present and future needs. Over the years, its population has changed, as have the social and economic conditions and expectations that confront these students. Armed with a mission statement ("Success for Every Student") and with an eye on the SCANS Report for America 2000 and other recent reports, the staff and community have been discussing what our students need, and how we might go about delivering those many and complex services to them.

One strand of that conversation has involved a number of English, social studies, and science teachers, among others. Working individually, in pairs, and/or as contributors to schoolwide projects, teachers are piloting thematic, integrative units and programs that link writing, thinking, and other learning skills; honor individual initiative and performance; and involve students more directly in determining the what and how of their own learning. How those initiatives began and how writing-related activities contribute to their thematic, integrative nature is the subject of this chapter.

Philosophical Context, Real Possibilities

Three central questions are currently driving change at Shorewood. As interrelated pieces of the same puzzle, each places teacher collaboration and a broadly defined concept of writing's nature and value *in medias res* — "into the middle of things":

- In the current Shorewood curriculum, where do our students practice and gain the identified skills and personal qualities needed for their success?

- Can Shorewood students identify, articulate, and offer proof of the skills and qualities they have mastered?

- What student learning activities can we create to enhance social and personal development?

We are beginning to develop a teaching/learning design for our students that is informed by these three questions and driven by a central goal: to deliver a curriculum that owes its design to thematic links across the disciplines (Kersh, Nielsen, and Sirotnik 1987).

Teachers involved in these projects wish to provide nothing less than a sense of unity between students and essential subject-matter knowledge and related skills. In other words, they are aiming for an *integrative* curriculum that "requires a new recognition of the interdependence of knowledge and its relevance to the life of the learner in a free society" (Tanner 1989, 11). By introducing teacher-provided structures (themes and projects) that have the potential for unifying knowledge and by encouraging students to imagine and construct models that work for them, teacher teams are designing units and programs that reflect integrative teaching and learning (Harter and Gehrke 1989).

Different Approaches for Similar Outcomes

In response to the idea of making thematic, informational, and skill-related connections happen, two schoolwide initiatives were begun two years ago at Shorewood: an integrated curriculum team and a senior project team. Excursions to workshops and conventions combined with individual and committee research led to tentative directions, and a core of five to eight teachers for each project began planning for the 1990–91 school year. To complete this schoolwide portrait, several teachers working on their own have established writing-based, integrative programs for their students as well.

Integrated Curriculum: Teacher Collaboration

Choosing "diversity" as their theme, teachers of ninth-grade English and social studies planned further discussions, established several working teams, and considered ways of connecting their respective content and concepts with thinking and writing skills. The following fall a teacher-leader team organized an all-day work session so that ten of their peers could agree upon a central theme, select essential cross-curricular skills, propose appropriate key content, and design one or more concept-driven, skill-based, student-centered units of instruction.

Honors Ninth-Grade Social Studies and English: Jack LeGore and Kathy Agather

> 9/24/92
> Dear Pat,
>
> Here's what we'd like to do. We'll combine the Honors English 9 study of the Meeting of the Minds and Jack's World Geography study of three cultures:
>
> 1.   SW Asia—North Africa
> 2.   East Africa and South Africa
> 3.   Europe/Soviet Union

Students will create and become an ethnic identity/personality of a particular culture. They will, through research and immersion, identify with the ethnocentricity of a group. They will become familiar with the group's language, music, dress, values, beliefs, religions, traditions, food.

This study will produce a research paper and a fifteen-minute videotaped presentation. Students will be in the full dress of their ethnic choice. We will then enjoy a feast of food and the music of the various ethnic cultures chosen.

We'll send the plan: Skills, objectives, content, product lists to you soon. Will this be approved?

    — Kathy and Jack

As Honors program director for Shorewood, Pat Hegarty was delighted to discover that these two teachers, neither of whom had team taught since the late sixties, were taking previously isolated units of study and transforming them into a single thematic vision, linking academic content with researching, reading, writing, thinking, cooperating, and performing skills. After a year of participating in presentations and discussions concerning student needs and curricular goals, these teachers were beginning to implement their own ideas for thematic, interdisciplinary, process-to-product units and projects.

Kathy and Jack had spent two days last August doing what teachers representing differing subject areas have rarely done at Shorewood: sharing, explaining, and reseeing their respective course outlines for the purpose of student-centered, thematic collaboration. Discovering that both of them wanted their students to muck around in the stuff of content as well as hone skills, Kathy and Jack began to consider ways of consolidating and coordinating their programs.

Yet the planning process did not come easily for them, nor for the other teachers who decided to establish collaborative teams. The previous year Pat and I had presented curricular models emphasizing skills and processes; engaged teachers in discussions of core content, key concepts, relevant skills, and possible student products; and suggested ways of proceeding. Kathy, Jack, and the other members of our ninth-grade planning team moved from the central theme, diversity, to relevant supporting themes ("home," "change," "culture"), and to key thinking skills (observing, recognizing patterns, comparing and contrasting).

Now it was up to each teacher team to choose essential content, assess student needs, and devise one or more units that would lend themselves to our goals. Honors as well as "regular" and "basic" students would be involved, and both process- and product-oriented writing experiences — along with speaking and presentation skills such as writing articles for submission to the *Seattle Times* — would anchor each project and program.

As for this Honors 9 pairing, Jack was concerned that his students be held accountable for the content of world geography, even as he was intrigued by Kathy's enthusiasm for multimedia (she also teaches Film Study and is actively involved in the Seattle Film Festival), performance-related skills, and individualized content. Combining Jack's emphasis on cultural studies with Kathy's interests came quite naturally. In English, "Meeting of the Minds" required each student to choose a historical figure (e.g., Helen Keller, Thomas Edison, Mother Teresa) as a focus of study over several weeks. Students were expected to conduct detailed research on that person's life, times, and legacy; engage in a variety of writing activities in preparation for a formal written and oral presentation; and present that character's essential nature and experience in the form of a dramatic monologue to include dressing, behaving, and speaking in character.

Meeting of the Minds had always implied the concept of diversity. The next step for Kathy and Jack was redefining essential content. For World Geography, students would be encouraged to select a region along with a time frame. Representing all three major geographic areas in the course outline, students' topics ranged from twentieth-century Brussels to 1300 B.C. Memphis (Egypt). All students would gain a sense of the themes of similarity and difference among three key regions. Both teachers were interested in helping students work through time and resource management, in addition to enhancing their speaking, listening, and critical thinking skills.

The essential content of this quarter of Honors 9 emphasized research theory and practice, including selecting and pursuing an appropriate research question; framing that research; drafting expository paragraphs; and establishing and maintaining appropriate voice and style. Creating original characters based upon ethnohistorical precedents, these students then presented highlights of their newly acquired knowledge of time, place, and society via carefully planned and researched fifteen-minute monologues.

Topics and dramatic characters reflected an eclectic, far-reaching span across time and place, as the following sampling of and excerpts from student projects suggest:

Fictional Figure	Ethnocentric Scene	Ninth-grade Student
Nalathi Moise, 17	South Africa, 1986	Lisa Dietrich
Paydro B. Salazan, 37	Madagascar, 1500s	Miriam Oh
Akidinimba	Ituri Forest (Congo), 1970s	Rachelle Cruz
Sasha Nikolayovna Cherdonikovich	Uzbekistan, C15, the present	Amy Carlson

8

Using a Team Approach in High School to Increase Student Achievement

Barry Gadlin with Linda Ashida, Barry Brown, Jack Elliott, Suellyn Gates, Bernie Kelly, Chris Kelly, Mary Beth Khoury, Robert Koralik, Marianne Rosenstein, and Charles Widlowski

SCHOOL SITE: Elk Grove High School; 500 W. Elk Grove Boulevard; Elk Grove, Illinois 60007 (part of Northwest Suburban High School District 214 in suburban Chicago)

CONTACT PERSON: Barry Gadlin, English teacher

GRADES FOR PROGRAM: Grades 9 and 10

ENROLLMENT AT HIGH SCHOOL (9–12): 1,700

PROGRAM INITIATED: September 1990, as a pilot program to attempt to raise student achievement

FUNDING: No additional funds needed besides paying for substitutes on two nonconsecutive days (winter 1989) when the team met to put the program together and for two summer workshop days when the team met to plan for the beginning of the school year (1990)

RESULT OF PROGRAM: Two years later, all incoming freshmen would join one of six teams (each team consisting of a science, English, and social studies teacher)

Background

A few years ago my older daughter's third-grade teacher asked me, "What do you think happens to some of these (sweet) third graders by the time they reach high school?" She had heard too many stories about her former students falling on their faces socially and/or educationally. I nodded my head in understanding, and, before offering her a fuller version of my world view — a diatribe about the breaking

99

1
Jeff Boschee: Mursilis Amenophis, 29. Memphis, Egypt, 1300 B.C.

It is very hard to imagine moving more than 100 fifty-ton blocks of rock. This would be a hard task today, even with cranes and pulleys. During the time the Egyptian pyramids were built, they didn't have either. Tools were also lacking, but they didn't let that intimidate them. The early Egyptians built more than eighty pyramids: smooth, perfectly shaped pyramids ...
Once the pyramid was completed, they started removing the sand around the base; at the same time, they would smooth the outside. They continued slowly down, removing brick and ramp until they reached the base and the pyramid was completed. ... It is an amazing accomplishment for these people because of their primitive tools. Seeing one of these massive buildings would be like a trip into the past. This proves that Egyptians spent much time preparing for their after-life. It also demonstrates that the Egyptians were very innovative people.

2
Miriam Oh: Paydro B. Salazan. Madagascar, 1500s

Uniqueness is what tells them apart. No one group is like the other. Classing traditions, distinct characteristics, and opposed tastes divide these societies into eighteen growing cartels. Describing the 18 ethnic groups of Madagascar distinctly allows outsiders to distinguish which one is which and informs strangers of their way of life compared to their own....
Along with the Bezanozano and the Betsileo, the *famadihana* is essential to these people. Below, a woman describes her account of this tradition:

> There was a lot of activity in and around the tomb, and soon a group of six men came out carrying our hostess's great uncle. His bones, dusty and dry, were now held together in a polythene bag, the old *lamba mena* having disintegrated long ago. They brought him to a special shelter, wrapped him in a vastly expensive, beautifully embroidered new white lamba mena (*mena* means red) and laid him in the midst of guests (Bradt 15).

... The Tsimihety (Those-who-do-not-cut-their-hair) number 700,000 [according to] Kent (184). ... Of all the tribes that I know about, the Tsimihety is my favorite. Because of the fact that a great king died, let alone from another tribe, these people show such endearing respect for him and not cut their hair. It is just impressive.

Though I have only reported on half of the eighteen ethnic tribes, I can clearly comprehend that despite meager similarities, these groups are indeed individuals of their own time and culture.

With diversity as their controlling theme, these students explored

such related concepts as home, change, and culture through careful research and observation. Kathy and Jack's emphasis upon recognizing patterns and accounting for similarities and differences is evident in learning logs as well as class discussions and presentations.

The Senior Project:
Cross-Disciplinary Process-to-Product

Belly Dancing: Its Origins and Cultural Meanings ... Fifty Years of Doll History: Porcelain Portrayals ... Designs & Possibilities: Alternative Fuel Engines ... Self-Defense for Women: Tae Kwon Do.

Nearly fifty students — representing Honors English and philosophy classes and regular program courses in creative writing and home economics, as well as some independent-study students — volunteered to present papers, products, and performances in late May, 1992, our second year of involvement in the senior project (Summers 1989). Preparing for rehearsals these seniors wrote reflective and process-related pieces that chronicled their discoveries. They revised and edited essays, original short stories, and other documents and products, even as they began to choreograph twenty-minute presentations that ranged from dramatic performances to rock-climbing demonstrations to Macintosh multimedia productions.

Process and Purpose: For the teachers and administrators who elected to research, then implement a senior project component at Shorewood, two long-term goals have driven all other considerations and activities: to provide a focus, a *showcase*, for our buildingwide efforts to establish thematic and skill-related links across the curriculum; and to work toward a truly student-centered, integrative culture of teaching and learning (Kersh, Nielsen, and Sirotnik 1987; Tanner 1989). We believe that if high school teachers are to establish a climate that supports student initiative and nurtures connection making across departments, topics, and skills, the greater community must also invest in that goal. To that end, community members — including parents, business managers, university professors, museum curators, and craftspeople — are involved in the process. Granting interviews, providing access to art collections, conducting workplace tours, reviewing students' initial ideas and findings, and serving on project committees, these adults become major contributors to student growth and accomplishment. As Deanna Chadwell (1988) has stated,

> School is for society. In order for our form of government, our form of economy, our level of prosperity to continue we must have a well-educated populace. The community contributes to this end. ...
> Parents contribute by disciplining, nurturing and encouraging their children. Teachers contribute by preparing and presenting the subject

matter and by holding students accountable for learning. Students contribute by cooperating, disciplining themselves, learning the material and skills taught. (Far West EDGE, 1988)

Working from process to product, demonstrating self-discipline, making commitments—for many Shorewood seniors, including Honors students, these performance-based concepts are daunting. Whereas class discussions, teacher-student conferences, and on-task checks have been helpful to most participants, reflective, process-oriented writing has contributed in affective as well as cognitive ways to many students' feelings of competence and confidence. To support their efforts, some senior project students have been required to complete "process writes" on a weekly basis. Combined with large-group discussions and admit slips, individual conferences, and small-group sharing, these frequently reflective pieces add up to a **process portfolio** that was submitted as partial fulfillment of project requirements. Key segments from a document providing directions for these students follows:

Your Process Portfolio: Keeping Track of that Senior Project!
Dear Seniors:

From imagining to researching, planning and preparing, writing and revising, gathering and managing, and rehearsing and presenting . . . it is time to document the process beyond Works Cited and preliminary lists. For each of these final eight weeks before you will be presenting your Senior Project, I'd like you to maintain a series of 8–10 record/responses in the form of a **Process Portfolio**.

Purpose: To guide your thinking and planning for this project, and to serve as a kind of *anecdotal model of performance* for future projects you will most certainly be initiating and completing in many forms and for a variety of purposes during your post-SW career!
Designs: Since the idea is to conform to your needs and interests as you continue to refine the *what*, the *how*, and the *why* of your Senior Project, choices matter! Consider the following ways of *thinking and responding* to your Senior Project process . . .

Reflective writing suggestions include such writing to learn strategies as metaphorical questions, soliloquies, dialectic notebook entries, biopoems (Gere 1985), as well as charts, maps and sketches, letters, and guided imagery. Some specific student examples follow.

As they research ancient Hawaiian culture (including a trip to the big island), Courtenay Brooks and Emily Ackles picture themselves in performance, replete with native costumes, authentic dance (hula), and a hint as to the planning and choreographing that remains to be done in this brief overview:

Wearing a *pa'i* (red) with a blue overskirt, I *oli* onto the stage. I sit down, beat my ipu on Teri's *pa'i* pad, and hit Emily and Pam in. I chant *o'panaewa* or another *ma'i*, and they exit. I talk for seven minutes, and end with a modern song to show the difference. Then I am done!

A week later, Courtenay considers the *how* of this team presentation. Reflecting upon the choices available to her, she completes a "questions needing answers" write:

What costume do I want to wear? Should I bring my modern costumes as an example of how hula has changed? In particular, should I show my tinsel skirt? Should I have someone dance a *hapa haule* song as an example of Hollywood's influence on the hula, or do I have time to spend on that? ... How can I enlarge a map to chart size so that I can trace the migration route of the Polynesians for the Committee to see? Will Jeri let me borrow an *epu* pad? Or, better yet, will she trust me with one of her good *epus*?

Designing interview questions, pouring over telephone directories, and conducting an ERIC search on preschool education in the Northwest, Erin Hart completes what might be called, for want of a better description, an "affective admit" slip for her third process write:

Well, I've managed to get in touch with a few people and lay a bit of groundwork. Mostly this week I've been on the telephone, going down my resource list of preschools. ... My second phone call was a little more pleasant, but yielded pretty much the same result [no help!] I really had a bad feeling when I had finally gotten to the Chelsea House preschool number. But my experience there was such a joy. My first triumph came in merely talking to a human being — as opposed to cold receptionists and answering machines. The next thrill was that the owner/head teacher was available to talk to at that very moment. By this time I was so very excited I nearly dropped over dead when she was excited at the prospect of being interviewed and insisted that I come and visit for the morning. I hung up feeling very satisfied.

Never one to be deterred by any sort of setback, Erin wrote this reflective response the following week. Clearly, she knows what she is after and why:

After having been continually frustrated by the lack of documented information on our country's preschools available, I have decided that the only way I am going to learn anything is to make contact with as many people (including children) in the field of preschool as possible. ... I have compiled documents, intended to aid me in my quest for preschool knowledge. These will help me to keep track of the people

and the information I encounter in [a] somewhat organized way. First, with the help of Mr. Pearse, I developed a questionnaire. I intend to conduct phone interviews with the teachers/directors of the various preschools I contact. ... On this questionnaire are questions dealing with affiliation (Montessori, religious, etc.), basic philosophy, curriculum, atmosphere, and other related information. ... This questionnaire will help me to keep all of my information straight (I hope).

A final example of students' use of writing to define, describe, and otherwise make sense of the process of planning and presenting is Phil's weaponry project. Dedicated to returning to his ancestral home in England and refurbishing it with the first fortune he makes in this country, Phil is also an avid, well-informed fan of English heraldry and weaponry. Shortly after having written this complaints and frustrations response Phil found the solutions to the problems he describes here, and much more. Using the Xap Shot disc camera, he took numerous slides of weaponry, spoke to professors and their graduate students, and was stunned when two students offered to stage a mock battle, complete with authentic armor and weapon replicas as a backdrop for Phil's multimedia presentation:

> I am having trouble coming up with ideas because there is only so much I can do using pictures from texts and the information from those texts. As I'm sure you know, it is rather hard to come up with authentic weapons as they are quite rare. I'm going — when I have time — to the UW [Seattle] and will try to set up an interview with a professor there. Hopefully he may know of some weapons which I may be able to film or even bring in as demonstrations, even if they are replicas.

Individual Teachers & Their Classrooms: Self-Contained Yet Integrative

ESL (English as a Second Language) at Shorewood: The Diary of Anne Frank: Shorewood is a comprehensive high school. Its students reflect the community's ethnic diversity as well as its occupational, educational, and religious multiplicity. The more than eighty Shorewood students enrolled in ESL classes learn interactively in Trudy Lothyan's class, and writing is part of nearly every lesson. Just as Pat Hegarty's ninth-grade English students explore the concept of home or culture as a focus for the theme of diversity, Trudy's students approach course content first from the meaning-making context of their own experiences and perspectives. It is fitting that, of all Shorewood courses, the ESL program strikes the clearest balance between writing as a mode of learning and writing as a means to improve the quality of students' written expression.

Even though the majority of Shorewood's ESL students are of
Asian descent, *The Diary of Anne Frank* speaks to them. Issues of
justice, complicity, persecution, sacrifice, evidence, documentation,
and atrocity have figured in many of their lives, too, if only through
stories told them by their Korean, Taiwanese, or Russian elders. (These
students are also now American teens, noted for their abiding interest
in issues of fairness in its many forms and applications.) For this unit,
Trudy has devised a series of writing activities that dovetail in cognitive
and affective ways with reading, discussion, and vocabulary study. (To
repeat a key premise for this discussion, truly integrative teaching and
learning involves teacher provided structures that unify knowledge,
and it empowers students to imagine and construct models that work
for them and are their own.)

Beginning with a presentation of the big picture, including the
historical events that frame Anne Frank's story, Trudy involves
her students in personal ways with the excerpts from *Anne Frank*
that the class has read together:

> Pretend you, like the Franks, are a German Jew whose ancestry in
> Germany dates back hundreds of years. Write a short essay describing
> your feelings about being persecuted and being labeled
> "non-German." Include such things as your reactions and questions
> related to you and your family's military service record, the law
> forbidding you to attend public schools, and the seizing of your
> property.

Soomin, a Korean girl with a clear sense of the power of dialogue,
denouement, and of the concepts of persecution and brutality, drew a
compelling word portrait, as this closing segment demonstrates:

> My child John asked me, "Mom, I want to ride my bicycle with my
> friend. I'm going to come back early, Mom."
>   Oh, I forgot to tell him that Jews couldn't use any transportation.
> I answered to John, "My dear, I'm sorry. You cannot ride your
> bicycle. Jews cannot use any transportation."
>   My child, John, asked me, "Why, Mom? Oh, I know. Because of
> the Nazis, right?"
>   I just said that I'm sorry.

Following this instructional sequence, Trudy introduces several
additional writing-speaking activities that help students articulate key
concepts and recognize important literary features (e.g., descriptive
detail, characters' roles and relationships) and devices (e.g., imagery,
narration). One such lesson calls upon students to create a chart that
reflects the connections among theme, plot, and characterization as
they pertain to their own lives:

Who are the People in the Annexe?

Make a chart showing members of your family and/or others you might wish to save in a similar circumstance. Write a short paragraph about each person, detailing their strong points and weak points that might make it difficult to live together closely for two years like the Franks.

Chun-pei's response communicates her sense of herself and of her family in a most compelling way. Clearly, Chun-pei has seen and understood some of the universal mysteries of human behavior portrayed in the *Diary* mirrored in her perceptions of her own family:

My parents would have diffent [*sic*] opinions from each other, because they are stubborn. They both think they are right, and hurt each other. And my sister would be caught in the middle between the fight, because when they become frightened my sister will say who is right, who is wrong. But it won't solve the problem, and maybe even will cause more of it. My brother and I will stand aside, not because we don't care, because in the end they will [be] peaceful and loving again. It will be like nothing happened. Even so, my parents would be like everybody's friend they have met. My brother, and sister will easily get along with other people. Especially my sister, she will talk, talk, and talk. . . . And I try to be peaceful and not let anyone be angry with me.

Ninth-Grade Geography: Process and Product: As a teacher of English and social studies at the ninth- and eleventh-grade levels, Karen Hansen brings expertise to the building goal: to deliver an integrative, student-centered curriculum that owes its design and impetus to thematic, generalizable links across the disciplines (Kersh, Nielsen, and Sirotnik 1987). Piloting the ninth-grade theme of diversity across the several required units of World Geography, Karen has combined a variety of writing activities with class readings, panel discussions, videotaped and audiotaped documentaries, assorted maps, and other resources.

Karen's students write frequently in journals, and she has begun to involve them in selecting individual pieces to be kept in their process portfolios. (Several of us hope that most members of the class of 1995 will be involved in the senior project program; therefore, the processes of learning are at least as important as the products that demonstrate learning.) Writing for Karen's students follows the general process of previewing, forecasting, and assessing the nature of their assumptions and (mis)understandings, followed by responding to new learning, especially as it informs students' own awarenesses and interests.

Recently, Karen's ninth-grade students began to consider the

extent of their knowledge about Africa. Unlike Jack LeGore and Kathy Agather's Honors classes, classroom rosters are not the same across Karen's ninth-grade social studies and English classes. Because it has not been possible this year to team in a direct way across regular classes, Karen has directed student thinking, writing, and speaking activities in response to Africa's political, economic, cultural, environmental, historical, and geographic diversity.

Before assigning her students to read "Trail of Shame," a *Time* magazine (October 16, 1989) cover story tracing the greed and devastation of the ivory trade in Kenya and Tanzania, she asks them to complete a learning log write: "What comes to your mind when you think of Africa?" Few students, it turns out, go beyond the bounds of stereotypical images perpetuated by Hollywood and television, and only a very few offer comments that relate to personal experience or interests. Jennifer's response is typical:

> Africa—I don't know much about Africa, but I think Africa has a very hot temperature. I saw something on TV that was about Africa. The people there were skinny, the adults wear long skirts and women wear veils around their heads. Jungles, forests, starvation, hot temperatures, straw or cabin-like houses, are things that come to my mind when I think of Africa.

Michelle's response, although even less informed than Jennifer's appears to be, nonetheless reflects her teacher's emphasis upon diversity as both integrating concept and viewing lens:

> I don't know a whole heck of alot about Africa. I know we took slaves from there and it's kinda safari like. When I think of Africa I think of lions and girafe [*sic*] running loose. I'm sure that's what alot of uneducated Americans think.

Students frequently share their impressions with one another in Karen's classes. As a result, issues are raised that serve as a focus for the discussions or projects to follow. Jen's entry, for example, moves environmental, economic, and social differences to the front burner, igniting a classroom discussion. In addition, her reference to comparative qualities of apparently distinct cultures anticipates her teacher's objectives even as it establishes the student-centeredness of activities to follow:

> When I think of Africa, big open spaces come to mind. Spaces of dried grass and sand, on which elephants and other wild creatures roam free. I think of half naked people, who don't give a thought to modesty, wearing little white cloths over very little of their bodies. These people strike me as friendly and naive. Maybe it's the comparison of our society to theirs. Somehow I feel we are linked, as if we're the same in more than just the obvious ways. I like their culture better, its says "home" to me. Being brought up in Brazil probably

has alot to do with the way I feel. I get lonesome when I watch African movies.

Some Closing Comments

Writing student profiles, interviewing parents about their beliefs about schools in general and this school in particular, holding faculty discussions about curricular priorities and student needs — these and other "pre-restructuring" activities occurred at Shorewood during the 1991 – 92 school year. Many teachers continue to express concerns about the pressures they are experiencing as they continue to puzzle out where we should be taking our students at the close of the twentieth century.

An apparently endless — and probably cyclical — series of questions has been raised, answered, and reviewed during these past two years: Is the stuff of content in jeopardy as we concentrate on the skills of process, the activities of reflection and metacognition with our students? Do we risk slighting a common core of content and skill if we continue to encourage students to pursue their individual interests? Should we be developing true alternative assessment measures that include but go beyond projects, portfolios, and presentations?

Yet because of the work a number of teachers and their students have done, two strands of the conversation have achieved nearly universal community support: the value of student — and teacher — teaming; and the possibilities of writing as a cross-disciplinary, reflective, integrative learning device. A core of Shorewood science, social studies, and English teachers have provided models of teaching that invest heavily in interactive, thematic learning. And, although it is true that content of various kinds is central to each of the projects and units described in this chapter, it is *connectivity* in the broadest sense, after all, that is at the heart of students' thought and action. As Robert DiYanni (1985) states in *Connections: Reading, Writing, and Thinking*:

> All learning involves making connections, linking new information and experience with what we have previously learned and, in the process, readjusting our understanding of what we know. From this standpoint, learning is less a matter of accumulating information and adding one bit to another than a way of re-envisioning and re-conceptualizing our knowledge. ... Learning proceeds by a ... revision and reconstruction of what was previously known. (Preface)

Note

p. 91 Admit slips:
brief written student responses often collected as tickets to "admission" to class. Collected and read aloud by the teacher with no indication of the

authorship of individual students. Frequently used for community building. (As noted in Gere, Anne, *Roots in the Sawdust*, 1985, p. 222.)

References

DiYanni, Robert. 1985. *Connections: Reading, Writing, and Thinking.* Upper Montclair, NJ: Boynton/Cook.

Frank, Anne. 1952. *The Diary of Anne Frank.* New York, NY: Modern Library.

Fulwiler, Toby. 1986. *The Politics of Writing Across the Curriculum.* Urbana, IL: National Council of Teachers of English.

Gere, Anne R. 1985. *Roots in the Sawdust: Writing to Learn Across the Disciplines.* Urbana, IL: National Council of Teachers of English.

Harter, Paula D., and Nathalie J. Gehrke. 1989. "Integrative Curriculum: A Kaleidoscope of Alternatives." *Educational Horizons* (Fall): 12–17.

Kersh, Mildred E., M. Elizabeth Nielsen, and Kenneth Sirotnik. 1987. "Techniques and Sources for Developing Integrative Curriculum for the Gifted." *Journal for the Education of the Gifted* 11: 56–68.

Summers, Jay. 1989. The Senior Project: A Walkabout to Excellence. *English Journal*, 78, 4: 62–64.

Tanner, Daniel. 1989. "A Brief Historical Perspective of the Struggle for an Integrative Curriculum." *Educational Horizons* (Fall): 7–11.

up of the traditional American family and about the need for elementary school districts to hire more counselors and social workers—
I uttered, "Something goes wrong, something."

Indeed "something" was happening to student attitudes and
achievement at Elk Grove High School. The teachers had seen "it";
the administration had heard about "it" and had seen "it" documented
in the form of student grades. A frightening proportion of teenagers
at the school were doing poorly—and didn't seem to care; at least,
they pretended they didn't care. Pointing the finger of blame began,
although not fruitfully: the junior high schools, the lack of at-home,
after-school supervision, the general disintegration of the American
family—all of these received some of the finger pointing.

However, no matter how far one looked for causes or how
deeply one placed the blame on one factor or another, something else
needed to start happening so that students could lead themselves
away from the direction in which they were headed—toward an adult
mindset of mediocrity and malaise.

Getting the Program Started

Dr. Jack Elliott, an assistant principal at Elk Grove, saw interdisciplinary teaming and writing across curriculum (WAC) movements as worthwhile approaches around which to structure a pilot program to improve
student achievement at the high school. During the spring of 1989
Dr. Elliott gathered six teachers—a math teacher (Marianne
Rosenstein), a social science teacher (Robert Koralik), a biology teacher
(Mary Beth Khoury), two Spanish teachers (Suellyn Gates and Linda
Ashida), and an English teacher (Barry Gadlin)—to come together to
work on a pilot program in which the group would take responsibility
for about 105 (of the 350) incoming freshmen for two years. Dr. Elliott
gave us the power to organize the program on our own as far as would
be physically feasible for the school. We began meeting a little more
than a year before initiating the program. We received release time to
meet early in the school year prior to implementation, so that any
problems that did arise in our planning could receive attention before
deadlines closed in. Given the unknown effects of this new program on
a fairly traditional building and staff, we decided not to try to mold a
pilot program too different in appearance (with regard to scheduling
and curriculum) from what was already in place. So one of the first
"givens" was that all of us would have five classes, not four as we had
considered earlier. Eventually, our wide-ranging of discussions of the
program's strengths and our questions about its structure and curriculum
helped us mold the program into one suited to and workable at Elk
Grove High School.

Structuring the Program

The Selection and Scheduling of Students

The team wanted to fill five average freshman classes to allow each teacher to focus on the program. The teacher makeup of the team would be based both on the required freshmen classes (English, math, and science) and approximately 120 students per year in previous freshman classes signing up for Spanish and social science. So one afternoon the six interdisciplinary teachers looked through the incoming freshmen's course selections to find the 105 students who could meet the criteria for entering the program. The next step would involve coordinating the teachers with the students over an eight-period schedule. We solved four problems before proceeding. First, we decided that we did not want five groups of students traveling around together. (Group A might have English first hour and math second hour while Group B might have history first hour and Spanish second hour). We wanted students to experience as normal a school day as possible. Second, we did not want to section off part of the building as our sole territory. That would mean displacing other teachers from their class-rooms—not good for PR.

The final two problems related to curriculum and school-day flexibility. Could we organize a schedule that would allow any interdisciplinary teacher the flexibility to keep a group of students an extra period or more without interfering with other teachers? And *could* we have four larger classes instead of five smaller classes to make possible visiting each other and being each others' aides? Again, our desire not to disrupt the traditional program helped us resolve these dilemmas. As mentioned above, we would have five classes, and, no, we wouldn't be able to devise a system where the six teachers could take students without affecting other teachers. (However, many of the students opted to take a business, music, journalism, or gym course, with the result that decisions of the interdisciplinary teachers did affect teachers not in the program.) We chose our class schedules, we selected a common planning time, and we decided to monitor an interdisciplinary study hall in order to help our students during the required study hall to keep them more on track.

Planning the First Weeks

Our first weeks of planning during the summer involved getting to know each other, dividing up responsibilities, and deciding how we wanted to proceed as the semester opened. With regard to the division of responsibilities, for instance, we decided on some study skills strategies to incorporate into our classes: Mary Beth would introduce methods of reading a textbook in biology, and the rest of us would reinforce these methods in our own classes; Marianne would take the responsibility for administering a learning styles survey; Barry would provide results from a reading/vocabulary inventory. Our willingness to help each other learn about our students became apparent. To ensure a good start in our individual classes, we delayed any cooperative thematic units until November. However, as the next few sections will demonstrate, the students began to sense connections among their classes when the teachers began to develop an interdisciplinary program focused not on thematic units but on integrating skills.

Implementing the Program

Adding to the Interdisciplinary Concept

During the summer, unbeknownst to the team members, Dr. Elliott had added another dimension to the program — a dimension that would greatly add to its success. Charles Widlowski and Barry Brown, two counselors, split the program's students between them (maintaining their other counselees). Elliott's rationale was simple: If one of the strengths of the program was supposed to be the improved communication among the staff, then having only two counselors for the teachers to contact not only would seem consistent with the program but also would benefit the counseling process. For example, once a week the two counselors would join the teachers at their team meetings to share information about students and to hear from the teachers about problem students. The two counselors also helped resolve scheduling problems.

Gathering Student Information

We decided to spend the first two weeks of the semester with two purposes: to get our classes off to a smooth start and to gather student information that would help paint the fullest possible picture of each student. Because only the English, math, and biology teachers saw all the students daily, their classes became the ones to introduce and gather information and to give surveys. After Barry gave the students a reading inventory and got several writing samples, he listed the consistent writing problems for each student and shared the results with other team members. After Marianne gave students a learning style survey in math class, Dr. Elliott went to their biology classes to explain to the students how to read the results. Finally, we all observed student behavior and motivation to discuss during our team meetings.

The Shift from an Interdisciplinary Model to a Student-Support Model

Team Meetings

With the above information, the teachers spent their fourth-hour team meetings during the first few weeks getting really clear pictures of the students. We looked for the following:

1. Who seems to be having trouble in all or most classes?
2. Who might be misplaced with regard to skill level?
3. Who is having attendance problems?
4. Have any parents or students spoken or written to any of the teachers giving additional information about the students (e.g., hobbies, family problems, illnesses, attitudes toward self or others)?
5. Who are the class leaders?
6. Do students have any study-habit problems that we need to focus on?

After only a couple of weeks, we had identified students needing immediate attention. One student, for example, was continuing a truancy problem that had begun years before. At one of the team meetings one teacher related that when this student returned to class after missing several days, a classmate blurted out, "Just like junior high school, eh, Joe?" Another student exhibited immature and disruptive attention-getting behavior in almost all her classes. She would screech, not take her seat when asked, and talk across the room. In both cases the counselors talked with the students, and the teachers called the parents. Only a month later, teachers, counselors, and social workers began meeting with the parents of students like the ones above if their behaviors hadn't improved. By the end of a few weeks then, we knew the program was already reaping benefits: We were helping students adjust to high school, we were able to act quickly to remedy classroom problems, we were involving parents faster when their teenager was having problems, we all felt less "picked on" — that is, we saw that a student's misbehavior was usually showing up elsewhere — and we felt that as a team we were more effective in promoting change.

With regard to study skills, Chuck Widlowski and Barry Brown helped bring parents into the program. In late September they asked teachers to tell students to bring home a flyer seeking more active parent involvement. That same month they met with their first "Parents as Partners" group to discuss how parents could help improve their teen's study habits. Chuck and Barry held two meetings — the first attended by twenty-three parents, the second attended by over sixty. By June parent responses to the program were incredibly positive; these initial study-skill meetings had made parents feel confident that the entire team wanted their teens to succeed.

The Semester Begins: The Interdisciplinary Concept and WAC

Although we had agreed not to concern ourselves with building any thematic units early in the year, we were able to support each other's classroom efforts in smaller ways. Because the entire group reviewed various writing activities, all the teachers included more writing assignments in their classes. For example, after Barry taught students how to write a biopoem in English (Gere 1985, 222), Bob reviewed this format in history and had the students write a biopoem about one of the distant cultures the class had studied. Introduced to process writing, Bob also had students produce several projects: an interview with a historical figure, and journal writings following the life of a fictitious person born at the turn of the century (to show how historical events through the 1970s could have influenced his or her life).

Barry also reviewed *admit slips* and *exit slips* (Gere 1985, 222–24) with the other teachers to illustrate a couple of ways for them not only to include more writing in their classes but also to check student learning and generate class discussion. Suellyn had her Spanish students keep spirals in which students would write reactions to stories, keep a log of lessons, list information they learned from class or their readings, and write questions about parts of a lesson or reading. Mary Beth had her students write exit slips as reactions to films: What did you learn? or What were some of the more important bits of information in the film? She also had students write up more labs so that the students could practice the scientific method informally but more frequently. She included more report writing—one assignment on part of the digestive system and another on two women's experiences bearing and delivering children. (For the second topic, students chose their interviewees and wrote up summaries of their discussions.) Team members would help each other as problems arose. For example, when Mary Beth became dissatisfied with the quality of newspaper article summaries (due every other Friday for Biology), Barry discussed with the students how to paraphrase, summarize, and use quotations for their science articles.

The teaching team had other activities to help the students see connections among their teachers. First, on the opening day of class in English, Barry had the students memorize a short poem ("We Real Cool" by Gwendolyn Brooks) for the next day. However, he told the students that if they could recite the poem for any of their other teachers before the end of the day, the students would receive extra credit. A couple of weeks later, students would be able to earn extra credit if they taught one of their teachers how to write the teacher's name in hieroglyphics. In math, Marianne reviewed some formulas to prepare students for writing a biology report. In English, Barry asked students to write a classification-division paper related to a class topic soon after the students had studied classification and division in biology. And, as mentioned earlier, we helped each other teach study skills. These examples were but a few of many that helped give the students the mind-set that their teachers were, indeed, working together and that helped create an integrated curriculum. Although we didn't put together an extended thematic unit until mid-November, in small ways we were letting the kids know that we knew what was going on in their other classes.

Beginning an Extended Thematic Unit

During the thirteenth week, one of the interdisciplinary units began. It didn't begin with any fanfare: instead it developed organically. The unofficial topic of this five-week span was "Accepting Differences and Making a Difference." Students in English received the novel *To Kill a Mockingbird*. The English teacher spent a great deal of class time talking with students about how characters in the novel prejudged others on the basis of rumor or physical appearance. Much later in the unit the students attended an all-day, activity-based workshop at school sponsored by the Anti-Defamation League of B'Nai B'Rith. All 104 students spent the school day in the library divided into small discussion groups; the workshop leaders focused the students' attention on ways people today wrongly judge each other based on the color of skin, height, physical appearance, disability, and occupation (among others). Between the beginning of the novel and this final activity, all the interdisciplinary teachers involved the students in a miniunit on homelessness. Teachers received materials from the HUD office in Chicago to use in their classes and had students look at the issue from different angles.

Activities that developed parts of the unit included the following:

1. In English, students read a couple of short stories and articles about homelessness.
2. Teachers and students sponsored a clothing drive to donate to a local shelter.
3. Teachers tried to solicit parent volunteers (via a flyer sent home) to work at a shelter.
4. Bob analyzed newspaper and magazine articles about homelessness as part of the classes' current-events discussions.

5. Marianne gathered some statistics about homelessness and shelter attendance and had students apply graphing and other math skills to see the rise in homelessness.

6. Linda and Suellyn created skits in which students used new vocabulary in their speech and writing to describe a homeless couple and to ask questions of a homeless couple newly arrived at a shelter.

7. Mary Beth talked to students and had them write about their own nutritional needs and about the proper diet a homeless person would need to stay healthy, especially during the cold Chicago winters (looking at inexpensive sources of nutrition).

8. All the students met in the school auditorium during third period to listen to Mrs. Frankie Walters, who helped organize the Public Action to Deliver Shelter (PADS) program in the suburbs, talk about what the PADS program does and about her own experiences as a homeless child.

9. A free-writing activity in the form of an interior monologue in which students described what their lives would be like as a homeless teen (later turned into a polished piece), a persuasive essay about the need for people to feel concerned about the homeless, and other class discussions centering on both understanding homelessness and accepting individual differences added to the unit.

Findings

Statistics

With regard to the program's immediate effect upon students' grades, we stepped back from comparing our grades with grades of students outside the program; we weren't sure how valid the results would be. What seemed more valid, however, was to look at each teacher's class grades before and during the program. In one case a team member had had between thirteen and sixteen failures each semester for the previous two years. As a member of the interdisciplinary team he had six failures one semester and eight failures another semester. And we're as much interested in what will happen over the next two years: How effective will these students be as learners during their junior and senior years once they leave the program?

Team Member Attitudes at the Year's End: The eight interdisciplinary teachers and counselors discussed two questions: How do the teachers involved feel about the program's success? What was the effect on teachers of having had the opportunity to share ideas and problems with other members of the team? Summaries of their responses follow.

Teachers' Opinions of the Effectiveness of the Program

Adding counselors to the team made a big difference. Often, students wouldn't respond to their teachers' concerns about achievement, and having a nonclassroom staff member talk to the student proved valuable. Additionally, the counselors could initiate staffings and parent meetings easily. In short, their presence simplified and sped up the counseling, staffing, and problem solving. The teachers felt that the counselors were keeping better track of kids with the interdisciplinary teams. Meetings three to five times each week kept each member up-to-date about student progress. Sharing across the curriculum writing ideas and teaching techniques proved valuable to the team members also.

Effects of Interdisciplinary Team Sharing

Teachers in the program felt more a part of the total school environment. First, the team was more aware of what goes on in other courses and in departments. Writing Across the Curriculum activities aided in this area. Admit and exit slips and other informal writing activities (those that help students think through an idea and generate class discussion, those that check students' understanding, and those that express what's on the students' minds) have become part of all team members' classrooms. Second, and as a result of the first, the teachers felt less cut off from other division teachers. Third, the program gave each team member a better sense of what kids do during the day. Fourth, because teachers talked about the same students and quickly identified troubled kids, each team member felt less "singled out" by a disruptive or problem student. Fewer teacher "why me's?" occurred during the year. Finally, team members became more aware of student achievement in athletics and in school organizations not only because four team members coach but also because teachers shared overheard stories about students' successes.

Parents Respond Favorably at the End of Year One: We received parent feedback in a number of ways — (generally) during phone conversations with parents, during the study-skills sessions early in the first year, during sophomore course registration with the counselors, and through comments made on a survey filled out by parents at the end of September during the second year.

Counseling sessions during October 1990 helped create positive attitudes among many parents toward the interdisciplinary program. Parents who felt helpless about guiding their teenagers in schoolwork really appreciated the study-skills and coping-skills information given to them at two separate parent meetings. During the year and during the following summer, when parents talked to counselors about course selection and schedule, parents offered thanks for the close tabs that teachers and counselors had kept on their kids.

Early during the second year, at a parent night in late September, we asked parents to help us document our successes and failures. Anonymously and voluntarily, parents filled out a survey seeking their feedback about the program. Questions related to our communication with them, the value of the homework assignments, the effect of the program upon the teen's enjoyment of school, and the effect of the program on their teen's growth. Responses are detailed below:

1. *Overall, teachers communicated as well as or better than expected.* With regard to communication, eighty-seven and a half percent felt that we communicated within or above their expectations. Comments include the following: "They were there when we needed them (the death of husband/father) and also after, when it's so important"; "Everyone was very supportive and willing to communicate and advise"; "Excellent!" In contrast, twelve and a half percent rated communication below expectations. One comment in this group was telling: "I did not completely understand the program's emphasis and goals." Looking back on the year, what we may have forgotten to do was to tell parents more about the shift in the program from an interdisciplinary one to a counseling one.

2. *Parents saw homework assignments as having a positive effect on their teen's growth.* Ninety-seven percent felt homework assignments were about right (sixty-three percent) or became a positive influence in the teenager's growth (thirty-four percent). Some parents saw specific growth in certain classes; others saw across-the-board growth. Of the six percent who felt homework came too frequently, one parent commented that the student was having adjustment problems to high school.

3. *The majority of the parents polled felt that their teen's enjoyment of school improved because of the program.* The most positive results came with the question about enjoyment of school. Ninety-four percent saw their teen's enjoyment of school remain the same or improve and fifty-five and a half percent felt their teenager's enjoyment of school increased. Positive comments included the following: "Much more self-confidence by the end of freshman year"; "[He] really was helped last year by his teachers' understanding; this year he is able to talk [about problems] and is getting it together." In contrast, six percent felt that their teens' enjoyment of school lessened, although as noted earlier, one of the parents felt his son was having general adjustment problems and saw some improvement just before responding to the survey.

4. *Parents were cautious but felt the program made a difference.* Some parents responded as the teaching team would: "In some areas it's

too soon to tell." However, other parents who responded to this question were most complimentary: "[They] being a new freshman, I think the unity was a good idea and helped them grow together as a class"; "Tremendous! It was just what he needed. The core made for an easier adjustment and more of a unified approach"; "The personal attention was an asset. Being part of a smaller group in a large school was also a plus"; "[The program] made a tremendous difference because the teachers were so caring and, he felt, 'friends.'"

How Students Felt at the End of Year One: At the end of the school year, interdisciplinary students evaluated themselves in terms of how much they had grown and in terms of perceived weaknesses students needed to pay attention to the following year. What most students said reflected the values and attitudes that the teachers had tried to convey all year:

> "[One] way I have matured is the way I feel about school. Now ... I have to take more responsibilities and be conscious of how I'm doing so I won't slip. ... Before I could have cared less."

> "Getting good grades is important to my future, and I really opened my eyes to that this year."

> "I remember the summer before starting Elk Grove. I used to hate getting involved in school [activities], but this year I've been ... enjoying a lot of clubs and sports to keep me busy. I also take my school work and my teachers very seriously, for I know that if I don't accomplish something in high school, I can forget about going to a college altogether."

> "I need to stop [making excuses] and start getting my [homework] done."

> "For homework I need to improve a lot. Homework is there to help understand the subject better, not to make my life more difficult."

> "I've learned more, not just about school but [about life in general]. I've learned all the bad things not to do, and all the things I can do. School is what made me learn these things. ... I like math; it's just that I need to be better at it if I'm going to be an architect."

> "I used to think that all my teachers hated me because they were always yelling at me. But now I know they were just there looking out for me and trying to help keep me on track."

> "Since I'm in a special program, I'm in class with the same people. This helps a lot. Being around the same people all day builds my ego also. I seem to speak out more and answer questions that the teacher asks."

> "In junior high I always liked to work alone while everybody else was working in groups. I just couldn't get along with the other people

in the groups. But in high school I tried to have a different attitude towards it. Now I really like working in groups with other people. I like to see how other people get some of their ideas."

"I used to study while watching TV. Now I study at my desk in my room without the TV and the results are better."

"When my teacher gives an assignment and gives me a time limit, let's say two weeks, I now know I should start it when he gives me it instead of putting it off till the last minute."

"School also helped out with some of the problems I was having at school and home. My grades were slipping, so my parents and I went to the school counselor who put me on a green (assignment) card that I had to (have my teachers) fill out every day. I would get it signed by my teachers, parents, then bring it back to my counselor."

"I'm in the program where the teachers care more."

Teaching Teams for the Future

All freshmen would join a team for one year beginning with the next school year. The second year of the pilot program went extremely well, but scheduling problems made teaming all freshmen and sophomores impossible in an otherwise traditionally structured high school setting. A speech instructor needed to join the team during the sophomore year to teach the required oral communications course, further complicating the schedule. What does remain, however, are the beliefs that teachers and counselors working together do make a difference and that the model described above helps to better keep track of students. Did some students fail? Yes. Did the failure rate go down significantly? Yes.

Additionally, writing has become an important activity in all classrooms across the curriculum. The sharing of ideas within teacher teams and the building leadership's commitment to provide writing ideas to teachers and writing help to students have led to acceptance of writing to learn and writing as thinking at Elk Grove High School.

References

Brooks, Gwendolyn. 1975. "We Real Cool." In *The Poetry of Black America*. New York, NY: Harper and Row.

Gere, Anne Ruggles. 1985. *Roots in the Sawdust: Writing to Learn Across the Disciplines*, 222. Urbana, IL: National Council of Teachers of English.

Lee, Harper. 1960. *To Kill a Mockingbird*. Philadelphia, PA: Lippincott.

9

Writing to Learn Science

Rae Bruce and Rodney Mansfield

In the science lab students gather around a table with two teachers and an assistant principal. They all hold in their hands computer-printed books entitled *Glimpses of Nature*. One by one, the students stand to read and share their poems. Some read with confidence, others hesitantly. These poems about photosynthesis, population density on specific natural sites, and symbiotic relationships involve looking at scientific concepts through lateral thinking. Although most students are reading the first real poem they've ever written, these poems brim with analogy and metaphor.

As the group turns the pages of *Glimpses of Nature*, Rod Mansfield, the science teacher, and Rae Bruce, the English teacher, take turns reading their own poems. Everyone smiles, for this is a celebration of publication and learning. Rod gets applause for his poem about the stately pine; students applaud not only the poem but also the risk he's taken by writing poetry with them.

The assistant principal offers enthusiastic comments and suggests other nature poems for students to read. Then slapping the book against his leg, he goes directly to a budget meeting where he will use the poems as an argument for interdisciplinary projects such as the writing center. He leaves behind a room full of students autographing each other's poems and congratulating one another on their work.

This booklet of poems attracts attention and positive comment from people outside the project. Because of the analogical thinking required, these poems are very important; however, they are only one component of a carefully constructed series of writing activities that require students to write as a way of learning and exploring new concepts. Both Rod and Rae want students not only to write to learn in this course but also to realize that writing is important outside of

English class, that it is a tool for learning and thinking, and that it is important for communication of ideas in every discipline.

The students who have taken part in these writing projects were heterogeneously grouped and at various times have included all academic levels in the school. However, when Rod and Rae started the project, most of the students were of average ability and many were not college bound. This project has shown Rod and Rae that the kind of thinking skills their projects included can be done by all levels of students. Enthusiasm for the course has encouraged more college-bound students to enroll.

At the inception of this project Merrimack High School in Merrimack, New Hampshire, had recently embraced a new philosophy as part of the reaccreditation process by the New England Association of Secondary Schools and Colleges. This philosophy, adopted enthusiastically by the faculty, included a strong interdisciplinary thrust. Using the new philosophy to support their belief in writing as a way of learning, Rae and her department head, Deborah Woelflein, developed THE WRITE ROOM, an interdisciplinary writing center that provides staff and students an opportunity to focus on writing in all disciplines.

Therefore, when Rod started to develop his new environmental science course, both the interdisciplinary emphasis of the school philosophy and the availability of THE WRITE ROOM were natural factors to incorporate in the new syllabus. Collaborative work was a natural outgrowth of the administration and faculty support for an interdisciplinary approach to learning.

Originally, the project came about informally over coffee in the teachers' room. In the spring of 1989, as Rod discussed the new course and his plans for students to adopt a natural site for study, Rae suggested that journals would provide a good way for students to record their observations, reflect on them later, and connect them with the course content. This feeling led Rae to experiment with journal keeping that summer. She soon realized that double-entry journals would provide the best format for this kind of thinking.

In the fall Rod and Rae began to implement the project, discussing ideas in both formal and informal meetings and collaborating to develop activities to fit the objectives of the course. As the course evolved, the two teachers developed six major course assignments incorporating content objectives and strategies to facilitate student learning through specific writing projects:

- a double-entry journal
- a site description
- speciation of the site
- paragraphs about relationships among various aspects of the site

- a free-verse poem
- a synthesis paper applying and relating course content to observations of the site

During the first semester, the teachers expanded their collaboration to include the computer specialist so that students could take advantage of both word processing and data bases as tools for facilitating learning.

The Double-Entry Journal

The double-entry journal provides the foundation for all writing to learn activities and helps meet course objectives:

1. Students will increase their powers of observation of natural phenomena and begin to focus on important details within the setting. Students will be able to distinguish between significant and irrelevant factors in any ecosystem.

2. Students will be able to recognize and document the unique role (niche) that each species plays within the ecosystem.

Early in the semester Rae modeled for students a brief excerpt from her double-entry journal in which she kept her observations of sunfish and their nests in a New Hampshire lake. Making the point that she is not a scientist, she shared her entries, which included observations of size, shape, and changes both in the sunfish and in their nests. Putting the entries on the overhead projector, she emphasized that her right-hand entries went beyond pure observation by hypothesizing that one fish seemed to guard each nest, that the nests consist of gravel piled like a moat around sand, and that the fish guard the nest because it probably contains eggs. She stated that further research in the school media center confirmed her assumptions.

When assigning the journal, Rod instructed students to choose a site easily accessible to their homes and of a minimum size of ten meters by ten meters. He required students to make three visits a week, recording observations and impressions in a double-entry journal. Following Rae's model, students set up journals placing their observations on the left page and their comments, questions, hypotheses, content connections, and plans for future tests and observations on the right.

In order to address the objective of having students increase their powers of observation, Rae presented material on observing and recording sensory detail. The class and two teachers discussed details that might be observed. The following interplay among Rod, Rae, and the students demonstrates how the teachers responded to the students' question, "Where do we start?":

Rod: From what perspective or point of view might you describe your site?

Student: From one corner to another.

Student: From biggest species to smallest.

Rae: Or pretend you're taking a walk through the site.

Student: Yes.

Rod: Is your site two- or three-dimensional?

Student: You mean I might describe it from bottom up or top down?

Rae: Yes, what other senses might you use to describe the site?

Students: Hearing? smell? touch?

Rod: How about focusing on time of day? Does it look different in the evening than in the morning?

Rae: Or try different weather conditions.

Thus the teachers encouraged students to explore varied ways to communicate the qualities of their sites and the value of looking at them from different perspectives. To further focus and sharpen their observations, they also suggested that on some visits, students record details about one species or attribute and make as many observations as possible.

Following this discussion and after students had made several entries and refined their observation techniques, Rae returned to the class to have them write about their feelings, questions, and concerns. After a focused free write of five minutes, students shared their writing. One difficulty they expressed was finding enough material for the right-hand side. Both teachers asked some students to read sample right-hand entries and had the class collaborate on questions that they might ask and assumptions they might make.

Samples from student journals show that in spite of their initial difficulty in making connections and forming hypotheses based on their observations, they soon became adept at these thinking skills. On the left side of his journal, Jason notes that "about six squirrels are very active collecting acorns, even though they haven't ripened."; on the right side he states that "it's [squirrel activity] very odd because some days I don't see any," and then he speculates that "maybe it's the time of day or the weather." About two weeks later on a blustery day, he observes that after a morning's rain "a huge patch of moss seems to be losing its radiant greenness." On the right side of his journal, he infers that the wind is drying out the moss and causing it to change color.

Kathy's site included a local pond where she observed that the water level had receded, probably because it hadn't rained for some time. On September 23 she notes that there is "green algae stuff on the surface and edges of the pond." On the October 9 she notes that the algae is nearly gone and wonders why. Her question illustrates the changing patterns in nature that she notices over a period of time.

As the semester progresses students become more efficient at observation and use their journals more frequently to form scientific hypotheses. Many begin to recognize that writing not only records observations but also helps connect recorded observations to the course content.

Speciation

The initial journal entries increased students' awareness of the variety of life forms in the sites that they had selected for study. To enhance their awareness of the multiplicity of life forms found in any natural site, the students were required to collect (and often return) and identify as many species as possible from their site. At the beginning students expected to identify four or five species and were amazed that their completed species lists contained between thirty and fifty entries. An auxiliary competency developed as a result of this activity was the ability to use efficiently a dichotomous key to identify the various forms of life. This also led students to the realization that mammals or other high life forms were not the only residents of their sites. The computer teacher assisted students in this endeavor by using a data base to document the various species collected and identified. In the future it is anticipated that through a telecommunications network students will be able to compare the species identified on a site in New Hampshire with those identified by other environmental science students in different regions of the United States or perhaps even in other countries. This will allow students to compare ecosystems and to recognize that different species serve similar functions (niches) in various ecosystems around the country or world.

The Site Description

The first paper of the semester is a one-page description of the student's site. Limiting the papers to one page forces students to concentrate on the most important aspects of their sites and to choose words carefully. Bringing in excerpts from Annie Dillard's *Pilgrim at Tinker's Creek* (1974) to use as models, Rae reads them with the students and points out Dillard's use of sensory detail; Rod emphasizes Dillard's scientific content and use of scientific language. Both teachers emphasize that good scientific writing need not be dull, but should include sensory detail, scientific language used in a context that makes it clear, and some sort of order.

When students ask how to start, Rae and Rod refer to the prior discussion on observing from different perspectives, utilizing various senses. They state that although many starting places would be appropriate, the perspective chosen determines to some extent the order of the piece. Students return to their journals for details to start and soon discover that limiting their description to one word-processed page means choosing details carefully.

Relationship Paragraphs

These descriptions lead directly to writing paragraphs exploring the relationship between two parts of the ecosystem. Using as a model an essay (1990) about a lake beneath Yellowstone Park, Rae asks students to write sentences showing the relationships between thermal activity in this lake and its location over a hot spot in the earth's crust. Then students turn to their journals and list relationships they might explore on their own sites; for example, the sneeze weed and the caterpillar, the Eastern gray squirrel and a tree, migrating birds and a pond. The assignment asks students to state the relationship between two parts of the ecosystem clearly in the topic sentence and to develop the paragraph using details from their journals. Writing these paragraphs sometimes involves research about a species and also helps students leap from description to the metaphor needed in the next assignment.

The Free-Verse Poetry

The poetry project aroused a good deal of positive interest from faculty and parents and also some anxiety among students. For many students these would be the first poems they had written. Some wondered how the teachers could defend composing poetry in a science class. A look at the poems shows doubters that they include real science content.

Rae acknowledges students' anxiety by admitting that she used to feel the same way. She tells them, "I know you can all write poetry because I'll show you ways into a poem, ways to tap the creativity that's in all of you. If I can do it, you can!" She gives examples of the metaphors that already exist in science, for example, *the food chain*, and a nebula's being called *a nursery for the stars*.

Because both teachers believe strongly in their objectives for students to use both linear and analogical thought, to integrate ideas by using metaphor, and to perceive the site or a species in new ways, they address all questions and continue to reassure nervous students. Three years later, this assignment has become an accepted, enjoyable part of the curriculum.

As the first class started the poetry project, Rae introduced lateral thinking by mentioning that many people had seen the apple fall from the tree before Newton did. However, he formed the law of universal gravitation because he looked at a common occurrence and related it to all motion in the universe. Only he asked why it happened and worked out the theory of gravitational attraction. Important discoveries often involve looking at phenomena in an unconventional way, making associations among previously unconnected material.

To assist students in getting started, Rae demonstrates clustering (mapping) on the overhead projector. Using a common word such as *Thanksgiving* as her nucleus, she soon fills the screen with her personal connections to Thanksgiving. Then she clusters again using *sunfish* as her nucleus, spreading her cluster by drawing circles until words like *guard*, *moat*, *sand*, and *flick* appear; soon obvious connections between parts of the cluster appear. Students quickly recognize the power of clustering to generate metaphor.

Next, students choose a nucleus word related to their site and start to cluster. Rae urges students to be free and relaxed. Rod sits at a table clustering with his students. Rae circles the room encouraging the reluctant. Soon students begin to talk, sharing their clusters and developing metaphors of their own. One girl announces, "Water is a mother, parent, transporter of nutrients, nourisher of all cells." She has started a poem. Rae asks students to construct three metaphorical sentences showing new ways of looking at some aspect of the site.

The next day, Rae passes out copies of her poem *Six Ways of Looking at a Sunfish*. Students note the scientific nomenclature and the use of elements from her cluster. Then they share the sentences they have developed from their clusters. In order to help them develop their images, Rae asks the girl with the water metaphor, "What does a mother do that water does?" The girl's answer sets her to scribbling the first draft of her poem. Moving around the room, Rae asks other students similar questions and soon nearly everyone is writing.

They go away with an assignment that reads: "Write a free-verse poem about some aspect of your site. Include concrete, sensory detail. Do not rhyme. Use scientific content and language. Use condensed language."

When Rae returns to the class, students hold up their papers and protest, "But this isn't a poem." Rae asks students to put their drafts on the overhead projector and assists them in condensing language. She suggests that students play with line breaks, pointing out the shape of the poem on the page and the difference in emphasis created by changing lineation.

Later, using a word processor helps students to play with line breaks and word arrangements. Julie's language takes on a poetic quality as she makes her leaves "swoosh in whirlwinds." More important, the poems show that many have perceived their subjects in new ways. John, who has never written a poem before, writes about the gray squirrel, "Zing! Zing! Zoom and he's gone!!" The squirrel uses that nest "as a pantry for the food!" John has internalized the motion and food-gathering habits of the squirrel.

Chrissy ends her poem with a metaphor that shows clearly her understanding of the chemical makeup of natural sugar. "Water and CO_2 combine to mother glucose."

The first stanza of David's poem, *The Floating Ecosystem*, reads

> a log on the water
> ... like a traveling barge,
> [has] passengers from all Kingdoms,
> coming from all sides.

Using a bit of humor, he personifies the animals in a twentieth-century human context.

> In daylight, a beach,
> where turtles and frogs
> use this gliding mobile home
> as a tanning salon
> warming their slimy bodies.

And his ending lines illustrate his understanding of the floating log's niche in the ecosystem:

> Remnant of a once strong tree,
> Now foundation of aquatic life.

Jason's poem illustrates that scientific writing need not be dull, but may include lovely images to communicate scientific content. Calling the falling leaves *Autumn's Orphans*, he ends his first stanza with

> Slowly leaves combust into
> blazes of orange, gold and crimson.

And his second stanza uses scientific terminology in a way that makes the term easily understood by the nonscientist:

> Trees mourn over losing their *annualities*.

He finishes by spiritualizing the annual cycle of rebirth:

> With the falling snow, the leaves pass on,
> their spirits melting into the earth.
> They find their parent tree and travel its roots
> to become the leaves of spring.

Requiring students to research a specific species to write about often helps them discover metaphors for their poems. These metaphors lead them to increased understanding of relationships among aspects of the natural world. Mark's poem illustrates the advantage of asking students to concentrate on a single species or relationship. Note that he has extended his metaphor throughout the poem to show the strangling effect the grape vine has on its host tree. He starts by describing the "Hard gripping twine amongst the ... branches" and continues in the second stanza with

> The paralyzing python grasps
> the masculine tree trunk,
> takes hold to make a strangling stand,
> expands the reach and squeezes harder,
> aggressively saps the tree's power,
> Slowly takes it down.

Mark's use of strong verbs makes the force of his language match the force of the vine on the tree. He understands both the relationship between the tree and the vine and the use of words to match his content. Thus, the writing of free-verse poems helps students to integrate science content and practice their writing skills at the same time.

The Final Synthesis

Sitting in the chairs in the teachers' room as they had the previous spring, Rod and Rae found that the final project of the semester generated itself as casually as the collaboration had begun. Rae had just reproduced copies of an assignment for her college-bound juniors. She handed it to Rod, saying, "What we need to draw the journals together is an activity like this one."

Rod read directions for a synthesis of a reading response journal on a novel. He smiled and said, "I see what you mean. I can arrange for my science students to do the same kind of thinking by writing this in terms of the course content." The assignment he worked out included writing about three major aspects of the site and relating them to five major ecological principles studied in the course. Further he asked students to predict conditions on their sites at some future time, giving an ecological rationale for their prediction.

The second year of the project, the synthesis assignment included a part in which students expressed their feelings about their adopted site. Students became very fond of their site during their semester of study and wanted to express that feeling. This need showed that they had met an important objective for both teachers, developing new attitudes toward the natural world.

One of Kim's final entries demonstrates the effect of the semester's work on her:

> At first, I would look around sometimes, not closely, and think that all I saw was green and trees. As time went by, I got closer and closer, looked at berries, leaves, moss, and other things and inspected them. I got more in touch with my site. But, at the same time, I noticed the environment as a whole. While driving, I still look around and think about it. For instance, how much I hate litter and plastic, and trying to think of ways to make people more aware. My site and journal have made a definite impact on me, both at my site and out of it.

In addition, Kim became one of the student leaders in a full-day celebration of Earth Day that spring. She had not only learned ecological principles but also believed in them strongly enough to volunteer many hours helping organize the Earth Day celebration. Kim is only one of many students who have been affected by their participation in this project. Unlike Kim, many of them will not go on to college; this course in their senior year of high school is one of the last chances the educational system has to help them develop lifelong environmental attitudes before they become citizens whose decisions will affect the future of the planet.

Authors' Note

The administration supported the project in several ways as it developed. Deborah Woelflein, chairperson of the English department, covered Rae's classes so that she could meet with Rod's science classes during their regular period. So that THE WRITE ROOM's interdisciplinary objectives might be fulfilled, she suggested that collaboration with teachers in other disciplines be one of Rae's objectives for the next year. Thus Rae's work on the collaboration had official blessing. The chairperson of the science department gave Rod complete freedom in structuring the new curriculum.

The environmental science project was among the first of the interdisciplinary projects at Merrimack High School. Other teachers developed projects soon after the philosophy was adopted. The enthusiasm of teachers involved in these projects spread rapidly and continues at the present time. An active interdisciplinary committee tracks interdisciplinary projects and will record them on a data base for teacher reference. Teachers in every department use interdisciplinary content either in collaboration with other teachers or by incorporating content from other disciplines in their curriculum. Presently a small group of teachers from nearly every department is meeting to put together a core curriculum for a ninth-grade pilot program.

References

Bruce, Rae. (Unpublished) "Six Ways to Look at a Sunfish."

Dillard, Annie. 1974. *Pilgrim at Tinker's Creek*. New York: Harper's Magazine Press.

Milstein, Michael. 1990. "Yellowstone's Underwater World." *Christian Science Monitor*. October 18.

10

The Puget Sound Literature Project: Secondary and University Instructors in a Teaching Team

Mary E. Kollar

Forces that Preclude Professional Contact Among Teachers

It has been three years since I followed a series on education that was broadcast by KUOW, our local National Public Radio station, attracting attention to crises in Washington State schools. I tuned my car radio dial to the afternoon talk show as I commuted from my Woodinville High School classroom to my home in Seattle — twenty-five minutes of debriefing time in which I listened to the commentator's prognosis for the ailing system in which I worked. Not much new nor consoling to a twenty-year veteran, and I would have tuned out the station with my Vivaldi tape had it not been for a topic he introduced that I had long known about but never acknowledged: teachers' isolation and even alienation from their colleagues. Separated by thin walls, teaching professionals might as well be working in monks' cells for the sparsity of time we have to share our successes and failures. Through the walls, we hear an occasional blossom of laughter, the soundtrack of a film — something indicating there is another classroom in session next door. I, for one, interpret the noises as coming from a classroom more successful than mine, especially if the sounds are laughing while my students are grumbling. Locked into five classes out of a six-period day, there is precious little time to seek out conversations with neighboring teachers. At the end of the day, it is all we can do to erase chalkboards, perhaps stop by to wish each other a good evening. It seems merciful to avoid talking about the classes we taught all day, so we discuss the weather or our plans for the weekend. Multiply these silent days by years, and the structure of public schools has constructed buildings of professionals who not only don't share ideas; in their muteness they begin to resent or distrust each other. Dealt the classload that most of us teach, none can feel successful, so we suspect we are not as good as the teacher next-door, and if we develop any bonds at all, they are between ourselves and students whom we see for more hours than we see our colleagues.

What about in-service classes or advanced degrees we take at universities? Certainly we work side by side with other teachers, but we rarely convene as professionals who have authority to shape education. Most district curriculum committees are hierarchical, administrators having determined the district will adopt a program or text that teacher committees have to devise the strategies to implement. Any money for the implementation often goes to a contracted "outside" professional who tells teachers "how to do it." Likewise, university and in-service classes revert the teacher to student status. It's no surprise that many experienced teachers are cynical about their postgraduate education taken at universities, for the courses too often hypothesize about ideal classroom models and are taught by professors who have little recent public school teaching experience. Summer after summer, hopeful teachers return to universities as if climbing to Delphi for the oracle. They return to crowded classrooms with prophecies that don't speak to the 150 students of various abilities and interests whom they teach. There can't be anything wrong with the prophecy—look at the research, the authority with which the professors taught. Teachers wrongly conclude that there must be something wrong with their own abilities.

Writing Project Model and Teachers' Authority in Their Profession

Enter the Puget Sound Literature Program (PSLP). After a decade of successfully involving Pacific Northwest teachers, the Puget Sound Writing Program expanded its offerings to entice alums with additional courses that focus the writing process on specific areas of the curriculum. The Puget Sound Literature Program was born from this expansion. Intended to marry theory and practice in the teaching of literature, the three-week summer workshop teams a university professor with a secondary teacher, an alum from the Puget Sound Writing Program. The implication of the teaming is that the university professor is conversant with literary theory; the secondary teacher attuned to hands-on activities that make those theories palpable for teachers and students. Although the theory-with-practice assumption holds true, now that I have successfully taught the course for two years with Kate Cummings (associate professor of English at the University of Washington), I have happily discovered additional virtues of the collaboration.

Planning the class with Kate in the winter and spring, I benefited from her suggested readings in literary theory. Public school teachers don't often have the time for or access to current research that surrounds a university instructor. Likewise, I was able to share with Kate the kinds of writing activities, games, and media a secondary teacher would use to translate some of those readings into high school curricula. I felt validated by having a university colleague. Kate received my knowledge of strategies that invite classroom participation.

The same kind of collaboration we experienced created the design of the class. Typically, a member of our class was in at least a fifth year of teaching and had enrolled in our class because of previous involvement with the Puget Sound Writing Project or because of word-of-mouth recommendations that indicated this class was led by "colleagues in the trenches." Our design fit nicely with the philosophy of the Puget Sound Writing Project (recently the Washington State Writing Project). That is, it affirmed that teachers are excellent instructors of teachers and that people learn best when they model or role-play the strategies they propose. What distinguishes our class from one designed after a lecture model is the time offered for metacognition, to debrief with each other about why we select a certain approach to literature.

Articulating Literary Theory

The cornerstone of our class: "Every teacher teaches from a theory of literature, even if that teacher has not consciously admitted it." Our job as instructors is to demonstrate ways we can engage our students with literature and to make teachers aware of existing academic critical schools. Teachers may even be teaching from theories that conflict with what they aspire to teach their students. This misfortune exists when teachers haven't taken time to explicate their own theories or to examine the practices they support in their classrooms, practices that may run counter to their own ideology. A case in point: I am one of hundreds of English teachers whose undergraduate schooling was steeped in New Criticism, where literature was the "well wrought urn," stolen from the social and historical context from which it was created and locked in a museum showcase where we stood outside, noting symbols, ironies, and intentional fallacies. In their high school class-rooms, most teachers hope to entice students to a lifelong reading habit for pleasure, information, and insight, yet they may not understand how practices, born from inappropriate theories, may repel the students from reading. It is a rare reader who delights in finding pathetic fallacies in personification. Also, when writing about literature, a bright student catches on to the motif game and skillfully maneuvers a five-paragraph touchdown without once ever feeling the literature in his hands.

Kate and I selected three schools of criticism to address formally. We wanted not only to show how these are distinct schools but also to demonstrate how they borrow freely from the tenets of each other: Reader Response, Feminism, and Deconstruction. We reproduced articles by Robert Probst (1988), James Marshall (1988), Helene Cixous (1981), J. Hillis Miller (1989), and others. Kate teaches much literature from contemporary culture, leading us to include selections featuring gender and ethnicity. In raising the question of what constitutes literature, we approached a variety of genres: short story, novel, poem, MTV, drama, paintings.

Most of all, the class wrote to learn literature. Just as in recent years teachers have tried to demystify the writing process for our students by having them write about their process of writing, so in our class we asked teachers to write about what informs their teaching of literature. The journal topic of the day: "Why do you teach literature?" It didn't take long to get beyond "It's in the curriculum" to discussions of a personal drive that each of us has to go at *Hamlet* one more time. We shared our writings daily. Some class members told of how they wanted students to revel in literature much as they themselves do, finding a kind of aesthetic garden in a concrete world. Others wanted students to think critically about motive and response, using literature as the vehicle. Many saw literature as a real-world arm into history. After sharing their journal entries in small groups, class members were asked to provide a "School of ..." name to each teacher's written reflection of why he or she teaches literature. We came up with *Literary Nutritionists, Revel-Waders, Reconstructionists*, among others. Listing our coined schools on the board beside established schools (*Formalists, New Critics*), we acknowledged that our movements were no more nor less bizarre, and we demonstrated that just like established literary critics, we too work from theories that we need time to write out and to examine. Only then can we ask, "Are the questions we ask our students and the activities we connect with their literature ones that will lead them through our theoretical schools?" If not, then one or the other must change.

Design and Syllabus for PSLP

The Puget Sound Literature Project is a three-week summer course, taught mornings from 8:00 to 12:00. Students enroll through the University of Washington Summer Quarter or through the University

Extension depending on whether they wish credits toward a degree, clock hours, or professional advancement. Our first catalog course description read as follows:

> A three-week program designed to explore a response approach to teaching literature. We ask: How can teachers help students enjoy and understand challenging literature? What literature should we teach and for what reasons? For teachers of grades 6 through 12.

We limit the class to twenty participants, a maximum classload for a workshop that allows time for each student to present a half-hour unit in the last week as well as to participate fully in the first two weeks of class.

Kate Cummings and I met periodically beginning in February to introduce ourselves, our preferences in literature, our notions about what would benefit teachers in working with literature. We agreed that most secondary teachers taught literary analysis à la New Criticism and could handle concepts of metaphor and genre. Others frequently used biographical-historical approaches, such as teaching *The Adventures of Huckleberry Finn* in the context of mid-nineteenth-century America. Therefore, we decided to select other theories of literature to feature up close the first two weeks. We chose Reader Response, Feminism, and Deconstruction for a number of reasons. We chose the first because it lends itself nicely to student involvement, recognizing that young people are experts first about their own experience. Reader Response criticism invites those connections. Feminism and Deconstruction we chose because Kate teaches with authority on both schools, and after all, that is what this collaboration is meant to do, feature our distinct authority. Also these schools often use similar vehicles in doing what they do with literature. We hoped to demonstrate that schools of thought are interdependent. After our second spring meeting, I left Kate's office with an article by Cixous (1981), tucked under my arm. Here I became the student again, for although I had heard of Feminism and Deconstruction, I could not explain their theories. I found Derrida beyond my intellectual reach. But the virtue of collaboration allowed me to be student as well as teacher, and as someone fairly representative of the people who would enroll in our class, I could ask the questions and structure activities that would clarify new trends in criticism.

The first day we spent building a sense of community in the class by structuring activities that required people to work in pairs and groups, to interview each other, to ask questions about interests and concerns. We gave students blank escutcheons with six segments that we asked them to fill in for their partners after interviewing. For each of the segments we had questions such as (1) a favorite book, (2) a time when you felt successful teaching, or (3) something you recall from childhood more from family stories than from actual memory.

Weaving in and out between the personal and teaching self, literature and literary perception, one person in the pair explained the answers for each of the six segments while the partner with crayon and pencil drew in that section a scene or symbol that typified the event. At the bottom of the coat of arms was a three-part motto ribbon that interviewers filled in with three appropriate words that summed up the way they read their partners. Following the interviewing and filling of the escutcheon, each pair introduced each other to the rest of the class, referring back to selected parts of the escutcheon. As the noon hour approached, the class was in possession of narrative and common literary, personal, and professional experiences that sealed a commonality and yet opened up concerns that we were anxious to discuss. We posted the colorful escutcheons for the remainder of the course.

Journals, learning logs, dialectic notebooks (or whatever one wishes to call them) began with the first day and continued in our thinking and sharing about the course. The first night, when Kate and I assigned the initial readings from Probst (1988) and Marshall (1988), we explained the dialectic journal. Dividing two pages into a total of four columns, the teachers took notes in the first column as they read from the selections. Notes included quotations or issues in the reading with which they agreed, disagreed, or were puzzled. In the column to the right, they took brief notes indicating why they had focused on certain sections: a specific question, a related experience, a "what if" speculation. The next day in class, the teachers exchanged notebooks and turned to the third column. Reading a partner's citations and consequent comments, the new reader could add to the dialogue in column three by providing answers, reshaping the question, or relating common experiences. Next the notebooks were returned and the original writer, reviewing all three columns, made conclusions, speculations, or observations in the fourth column that were somewhat shaped by involving another person in their thinking about the readings.

The dialectic journal proved an excellent writing across the curriculum (WAC) activity for our students, not only in helping to focus on provocative issues in the readings but also in establishing an intellectual dialogue with the peers in the class—the kind of dialogue one would like to have when reading, but reading as a silent activity often limits inner dialogue. Reading with an open journal for quoting and questioning captures the fresh insight that comes from a first exposure to a text. Then sharing the next day those questions with others who have read the same materials, the reader has a record of first impressions and a community of responders. As a matter of fact, all our journal writing established a community of thinkers as well as an audience for some talented writers, whether that writing was done in the dialectic notebook or in reflective journal entries.

The dialectic journal activity is one that teachers could use with their students, particularly when dealing with dense, difficult materials such as poems or Shakespearean plays. In our first readings, neither the Probst nor Marshall articles was too obscure; both call for the mind of the reader in a reader response approach to literature. What makes the Marshall essay so pristine for introducing our class is that its research is based on cogent observation of typical high school classes most of us have taught. These are classes where the teacher has all the answers and stages what are called class discussions to involve students in critical reading, but what are in fact quiz sections to see if students can guess the "one correct reading" the teacher possesses. Marshall's article goes on to show how that teacher-centered class contributes to students writing slick five-paragraph essays in which they are distanced and unthinking about literature. By virtually detonating the symbol-hopping, guess-the-theme game on the first two days of class, Kate and I were ready to point down different roads to teaching literature.

We hoped to address two issues in the class: literary theory and the literary canon. In choosing the selections to model Reader Response, Feminism, and Deconstruction, the latter two were most difficult to isolate. Many of the most readable feminist essays used reader response and deconstruction for their purposes; several crossed from issues of gender to ethnicity. As our class evolved, we began to think of deconstructing literature as the act of featuring what in the text keeps us from reading a certain point of view — that is, finding and holding up to scrutiny the minor voices in a text that the main voice of the text has subdued with the power of cultural-social stereotype. By enlarging the small picture in a text, one begins to acknowledge the premise from which the larger text is built. With that recognition, a reader is less a passive receiver of cultural expectations and more a participant in understanding.

For the literature with which to practice our theories we relied on fairy tales, selections teachers already use in their classes, and selections they might consider for their schools. (One of the course goals is to expand the current school canon.) Fairy tales are superb vehicles for deconstruction and feminist readings. We selected *Snow White* and *Hansel and Gretel* for both purposes. Students retold *Snow White* from the queen's point of view, exposing the fault of a society in which good fortune moves to a pubescent girl because she is young and pretty, although she has not enough common sense to avoid falling for the same thinly disguised ruse three consecutive times when offered gifts by an itinerant old woman. Even blessed with youth, the female does not determine her fate, but is swept into fortune when she is a lovely corpse, possessed by a kiss from a prince who hasn't heard one word from her and probably doesn't wish to, as long as Snow White is young, pretty, and silent. We had fun with these stories and many teachers have reported back that deconstructing works that their students thought they knew has opened up critical sensibilities to works that typically intimidate students: the official canon of our curriculum.

In applying feminist theory to fairy tales, we found Angela Carter's "The Company of Wolves," a revised telling of *Little Red Riding Hood*, from *The Bloody Chamber* (1981) enjoyable for our teachers. With this story we played "frame stop," asking our readers to stop at a climactic point, and to continue to write their own conclusions. The story, an obvious tongue-in-cheek feminist version with an assertive Little Red, led our students to finish the story with ironic twists and worried wolves, thus showing how a reading can either ride on cultural stereotypes or manipulate them in such a way that the informed reader can play along. When writing into literature as if stopping the frame and continuing the narrative on one's own, the writer perceives how an author establishes a tone that the reader implicitly accepts as the ongoing convention — an interesting way to learn about the impact of tone and point of view. Had Angela Carter's tone been less blatantly satirical, our readers might have finished off the tale with the version they knew from their childhoods. Not so. The author's tone implicitly suggested there would be another way to write the myth.

Other selections we introduced for working theory into practice included some pairings of traditional works in high school canons with ones not so well known: Maya Angelou's *I Know Why the Caged Bird Sings* with Brent Staples's *Black Men and Public Spaces*, also Hemingway's *Hills Like White Elephants* with Viramontes's "Birthday" from *Moths*. After reading the first two, we wrote in our journals any association we had with the stories. Both selections dealing with African-Americans showed their protagonists facing discrimination. Our students wrote about times they suffered or observed discrimination. Most often, the men in our class related to Staples as a misunderstood man. The women chose to write about Angelou's adolescent self. In other words, in our brief, unofficial study, we found that our readers as often identified with characters through gender as through race. Such observations led to discussions about what our current canon offers for both genders, and opportunities the canon gives for students to respond as empathizing readers.

What is Literature?

Not a day went by when teachers did not read aloud from journals to the class or in small groups. The practice circulated ideas and confirmed the use of our own writing as literature. When inspired with a writing activity, the journals took on a literary life that entertained writers and readers. Too often teachers spend all their energies creating topics on which their students write, but do not write themselves. Writing and listening to each other's works nurtured our vision of teachers as creative professionals. Our own writing is literature as is film, art, and video. So in thinking of "What is literature?" in the class, Kate and I sought opportunities to use our own writing and visual texts, texts that also required "reading." A scholar in the literature of AIDS, Kate included film clips from both dramatic and documentary depictions of the AIDS crisis. Following our preliminary work deconstructing fairy tales, our students easily "read" the cultural biases and fears operating within apparently "objective" treatments of the issue.

Allan Kollar, an art historian, presented an hour of art slides with which we connected the visual and literary treatment in masterpieces. Several poets have been inspired by van Gogh's *Starry Night* and paintings by Brueghel. Working from poem to canvas and back inspired critical discussions of point of view and reader response. That session ended with our students writing their own poems about paintings by Munch, Homer, and Dali. Inevitably, to select what one writes about a painting excludes what one sees but will not include in the literary text. One adds personal experience to the visual in order to narrate and create metaphor. The art-writing connection introduced a kind of microcosm of the literary act.

Finally, we used our small consultant budget to invite a local poet to read and discuss her own work. High school students often ask their teachers, "Well, what did the writer really mean?" We respond with educated guesses or confess that without the writer with us we can never know for sure. Unfortunately many teachers do not have among their acquaintances published writers. Our guest poet added dimension to the search for meaning when she confirmed the fluid meaning of her own work.

Bridges from the University to the School Classroom

Here I add that our poet presented at one of our two potluck dinners during the three-week course. Although our workshop provided ample time for contact, it was structured time. The potlucks allowed informal sharing of what was going on in our own classes or our own school districts, public and private; the dialogue our thin-thick walls preclude during the school year.

Our curriculum for PSLP contains two more formal bridges from course to classroom: a review of some literature to add to the teachers' canon and a lesson or unit plan that launches literary theory into practice. We did not specify that the literature be of any particular genre, nor that it be print or film. After discussing the kinds of literature we teach in our schools, we found an appalling similarity in texts: *Huckberry Finn, A Tale of Two Cities, Julius Caesar.* Yet all the teachers said they were starved for new texts that would work with their students and rejuvenate their own interests. What kept them from adopting new works? Caution about appropriate subject matter or style for their grade levels and a reverence for a fixed curriculum that needed anything new to be tied in with the traditional. When at the end of our first two weeks we allowed class time to bring in a short, written review of suggestions for the canon, the teachers surrounded each other in the way one does at any good browsing bookstore. By then they were well acquainted and respectful of their classmates, eager to hear suggestions. Since we phrased the assignment to bring a suggestion for what might be included, not what one has actually taught, teachers stretched their wish lists somewhat and wrote convincing proposals for materials they perhaps had not had the opportunity to test run. We asked that the additions to the canon be written, although orally presented, so each teacher left with a nicely annotated bibliography, one that not only reviewed the new text but also imagined the way it would be incorporated in the classroom. The writing served the teacher suggesting the material as much as the students hearing the suggestions, for in writing out how they could actually integrate a new text, teachers had to envision themselves teaching the works. Teachers brought poems, essays, films, and novels. Pat Hegarty, teacher at Shorewood High School, recommended Redmond O'Hanlon's *Into the Heart of Borneo*:

> Redmond O'Hanlon is part Monty Python, part Charles Darwin, a dash of David Attenborough, with perhaps a modest sprinkling of lakeland poet tossed in for purposes of gentler digestion. His narrative captures the natural beauty, majesty, violence, and comedy of life in a totally foreign, utterly non-Western environment.
>
> In nineteen eighty-three, Redmond O'Hanlon — writer, natural historian, Oxford fellow — accompanied by his friend and poet/journalist James Fenton, undertook an expedition into the heart of the Borneo rain forest **just for the hell of it!** Ostensibly in search of the famed white rhinoceros of Borneo . . . our two latter day explorers set out, poetry books and field guides in hand, to see what's to be seen. They are rewarded with misadventure, danger, and a general fungal, awe-inspiring rain forest vacation.
>
> This should become a part of the canon because it is a book that celebrates experience. O'Hanlon and Fenton are ideal — balding, bespectacled, and often reluctant, they struggle through their adventures, constantly adapting and growing. This spirit is one we need to see more of in the canon. Unstuffy, at times both lewd and profane, profound and beautifully poetic, *Into the Heart of Borneo* is a book that speaks to opportunity and challenge and growth and possibility — and FUN!

It is, of course, also a bridge to a multicultural canon. This book, and others like it, opens up all kinds of possible applications in the study of culture and cultural differences. Because of this, I'd like to use it with ninth-grade students. At Shorewood our freshmen study the geography of the world in social studies. I'd like to challenge and expand their map drawing with this type of literature — the literature of the traveller. This genre, a revitalized industry, takes readers out of the classroom, beyond our walls, and over the hills and far away. I can't picture an age group more open to this type of challenge than those in the ninth grade.

The final four days of PSLP, the class members each had a half hour to present a "Bridge," a projected unit for their classrooms that used the notions we introduced in our summer workshop. Our class outline describes the Bridge this way:

> A Bridge is presented orally in the last few days of class with copies made available for classmates. The Bridge is a proposed unit of study* that has evolved from the activities of this class. (Presentation time of 30 minutes.)
>
> 1. Start with an explicit pedagogical theory in approaching literature.
> 2. Direct the unit in the context of the theory.
> 3. What are the specific goals of this unit?
> 4. By which activities will you achieve your goals? Select some portion of the activities that you may role-play with the members of this class.
> 5. List any sources used in the design of your Bridge.
>
> * A unit of study could be anything from one class period to a term.

This culminating assignment extends from the Writing Project's belief that teachers have valuable knowledge to share with their peers, given a structure and theory from which they can be expressed. Ending with the Bridges demonstrated for us what the teachers carried from our class and how they rendered this learning in terms of the students they would teach. Most of the presentations used several activities we had used in class to engage our teachers with the theories we taught: activities where students took physical stances in the room according to whether they sided with heroes or villains, writing activities where each student became an "expert" by writing from a card with one question about a motif that would later show up in the literature they would study, or viewing experiences where art slides launched points of view. The Bridges demonstrated our students' comfort with new terms such as deconstruction. What pleased me was the variety of innovations teachers played around with: units centered around teaching not a specific work so much as a theme or idea. These included units on masks, roles of women, and political sensibility. Where teachers wrote about specific works they had taught for several years, the class had inspired the teacher to try a unique approach. Helen Frost, teacher of a tenth-grade Honors class at Woodinville High School introduced her Bridge:

> In the preface of *The Odyssey* (Penguin), W. H. D. Rouse explains that the story "enchants every man, lettered and unlettered, and every boy who hears it." *Man the Voyager*, another Odyssey reader, introduces the major hero adventure with "a son searches for his father, ... a wife dreams of her husband." The language used to introduce this story points to a problem for classroom reading and teaching: *The Odyssey* conspicuously portrays the male as the hero who undertakes the perilous journey, while the females, many of them powerful in evil, destructive ways, play the role of the monster and impede his journey. A conventional reading of the various myths in the story ignores the female journey, whatever it may be, in favor of the myths of "woman as temptress/seductress/witch." Despite the distorted, narrow portrayal of a woman in *The Odyssey*, there exists, using deconstructive techniques, the possibility of a fuller reading of a woman's journey in terms of the text, future texts, and the reader's life.

Helen's Bridge paired The *Odyssey* and *Circe* by Eudora Welty with the notion of the male and female hero in a journey as discussed between Bill Moyer and Joseph Campbell in the video "The Power of Myth."

Maggie King Everett designed "Bridging Value Systems" for her eighth-grade language arts class. She begins her philosophical focus:

> A large part of my job as a language arts instructor is to help students to see how language shapes and focuses our lives; to examine what is done in terms of what is said. I'd like very much to do a series of readings focusing on the question of what it means to "Do the Right Thing." Taking Spike Lee's film as a cue, I want students to read texts of various genres (including visual and musical "texts") and look at how language leads us to see things from differing points of views.

Maggie's texts included:

- *The Good Earth* by Pearl Buck
- *Rashomon* by Ryunosuke Akutagawa
- *If Ya Wanna Dance, You Gotta Pay the Band* by Stanley Gray
- *Thank you M'am* by Langston Hughes
- *Newsweek* article about Oliver North & Irangate
- *Enemy of the People* by Henrik Ibsen
- *Spare Parts* by Bruce Springsteen

The culminating Bridges helped me see how the first two weeks of writing activities served our students when it came time to design their own projects. Because we had written our way into articulating our own literary theories, the students felt prepared to articulate their own theories at the beginning of the Bridges, without feeling constrained to phrase their theories in established schools of criticism. Our coined theories had become household phrases in our classroom, so we had come to call each other "Revel-waders" or "Literary Nutritionists." Each Bridge opened with a version of those self-examinations that students had written in their journals the previous weeks.

Secondly, all Bridges included some writing-one's-way-into-litera-ture activities through which the students led us in their presentations. For instance, Helen gave each of us a card with a separate question on which we would become the expert by being the only person in class to write a solution or explanation of that question. My question was "What do you write to your spouse back home when you're delayed several weeks on your business trip and you want to affirm your spouse's loyalty to you?" I happily wrote away on my letter, thinking of my own husband. Helen had compiled a set of different questions for each student, introducing *The Odyssey* by making us feel as if we were a published expert on the epic before we had begun to study it. Sharing aloud our topics and our responses to them, we were all eager to know what exciting literary work might lie ahead of us. I had introduced a similar "expert card" approach to *Hamlet* earlier in the course. By making writing central in our instruction in literary theory, Kate and I inspired our students to employ writing in the lessons they designed to engage their own students with literature.

Evaluation

One Saturday the following January our class members met once again for a reunion to talk about how we crossed those Bridges from our summer school PSLP experience and our real-world classes. Some teachers had not yet taught their units, waiting for the appropriate place in the curriculum, available texts, and so on, but most had tried their Bridges as written. Undoubtedly, the best part of the reunion day was the chance to reunite with colleagues with whom we had written and exchanged ideas that summer. It is that room-without-walls collaboration that revitalizes our teaching. Just as we had explored in the idealism of summer, this group felt secure enough to confess what real-world circumstances they returned to that fall that might have curtailed a one hundred percent success of their applied learning. We were still applying, still adapting. The advantage of this workshop as opposed to a traditional summer class is that our adapting occurred in a community of understanding peers.

Writing together in the summer, especially when the writing is daily, exploratory, and shared, seals the community. Often teachers talk eagerly about their profession, and we did a lot of valuable talking. However, our writing cemented things. Initially, we wrote alone, allowing each one to get a complete thought expressed without being interrupted, as so often happens in discussions. But immediately after or the following day, we shared our writing, either reading aloud, passing our journal to someone else, or writing addenda to ideas started by each other. We learned to appreciate each other for our distinct written voices, which, by the way, are not necessarily the echo of our spoken voices. Within a couple of days, we knew who were the surprising, often gifted writers, and we came to encourage them to read aloud, much as we turn to gifted orators to share a few words. Finally, we took home with us our own written journals, copies of each Bridge presented, and a collection of new works to add to the canon. Back in our separate classrooms that fall, we turned to that collection as we slowly changed the ways in which we taught literature.

On behalf of the collaboration between high school and university instructor I will say that I am professionally renewed by those three weeks tacked on to my school year. I don't wish to return to school for a Ph.D., but I still want to learn what is new in English. Having to design a course for my peers, I have to articulate for them and for myself some premises that need shaking out in the fresh air every few years. Finally, the collaboration allows me to teach a different age group without leaving my area of specialty altogether. What ideal students teachers are. They come to class ready to learn, they work diligently to apply what I share, their presence dissolves the walls that separate me from colleagues between September and June.

References

Angelou, Maya. 1988. *I Know Why the Caged Bird Sings.* Chap. 23. New York: Bantam.

Carter, Angela. 1981. "The Company of Wolves." In *The Bloody Chamber.* New York: Penguin.

Cixous, Helene. 1981. "Castration or Decapitation?" *Signs,* July 1, 1981, 36–40.

Cummings, Katherine. 1991. "Of Purebreds and Hybrids: The Politics of Teaching AIDS in the United States." *Journal of the History of Sexuality* (Univ. of Chicago).

Gates, Henry Louis, ed. 1987. *Writing Race and the Difference It Makes*. Chicago: Univ. of Chicago Press.

Hemingway, Ernest. 1988. "Hills Like White Elephants." In *The Bedford Reader*. 3rd ed. Edited by X. J. Kennedy. New York: St. Martin's Press.

Hooks, Bell. 1990. "Reflections on Race and Sex." In *Yearning*. Boston: South End Press.

Marshall, James D. 1988. "Classroom Discourse and Literary Response." In *Literature in the Classroom*. Edited by Ben Nelms. Urbana, IL: National Council of Teachers of English.

Miller, J. Hillis. 1989. "What is Deconstruction?" In *Heart of Darkness: A Case Study in Contemporary Criticism*. Edited by Ross C. Murfin. New York: St. Martin's Press.

Probst, Robert E. 1988. "Readers and Literary Texts." In *Literature in the Classroom*. Edited by Ben Nelms. Urbana, IL: National Council of Teachers of English.

Staples, Brent. 1988. "Black Men and Public Spaces." In *The Bedford Reader*. 3rd ed. Edited by X. J. Kennedy. New York: St. Martin's Press.

Viramontes, Helena. 1990. "Birthday." In *Moths*. Houston: Arte Publications.

11

Technology: An Invitation for Writing and Collaboration

Eve Coleman and Jeanne C. Sink with Odessa Wilson

Some collaboration begins with careful planning and clearly defined goals. Other collaboration simply evolves. The collaboration between the two of us as individuals and between our institutions, Morningside Middle School and the College of Charleston, falls into the second category. Our collaboration as individuals has evolved over the past ten years through hours and hours of conversation; through job changes for both of us; through formal course work with one of us as teacher and the other as student; and through learning, playing, writing, and planning together. It is a unique collaboration, one that has evolved into a writing across the curriculum (WAC) program that *now* is carefully planned and has clearly defined goals. Our collaboration has evolved into a formal arrangement called a "Teacher-Scholar Collaboration" through Project REACH, a Rockefeller-funded initiative, for which one of us serves as the school project chair and the other as the college partner.

Working collaboratively through a formal teacher-scholar interaction, we have documented student work with writing and technology that we could not even imagine in our early years of collaboration. A relationship that began as a personal friendship and became a professional collaboration has evolved into an important partnership that involves a college, a middle school, teams of excited and involved teachers, college students, community members, and most importantly, the students at Morningside Middle School.

Morningside Middle School

When our formal collaboration began to evolve in spring 1990, Jeanne was teaching at Morningside Middle, a school where many students present evidence of typical barriers to learning: low socioeconomic status, single-parent homes, crime-ridden neighborhoods, and a history of school failure. Morningside serves approximately 850 students in grades six to eight. Almost half of the students are from a minority group, predominantly African-American. A team from Johns Hopkins University recently collected data on the school. The university team found that sixty percent of the students had failed at least one grade, with forty-two percent of black males having failed the previous year. According to data collected in preparation for an article published by the National Middle School Association (Dunham 1991), sixty-one percent of the students are considered to be at risk for dropping out of school. The school has a large "over-age" population of students who are two to three years behind their peers in school. Morningside is considered a Chapter I school for purposes of federal aid.

The school population presented a challenge to the administrators and teachers at Morningside, who began in spring 1990 earnestly seeking ideas and funds to tackle their biggest challenge — helping the at-risk students overcome the barriers to learning that were keeping them from realizing their potential. Jeanne led the search for the "answer," taking a Telecommunication for Educators course from Eve; enlisting the help of knowledgeable faculty members, particularly those with writing process interests and backgrounds, making a visit to the class-room of teacher Gail Morse who, according to *People* magazine (1991), was doing amazing things for at-risk students in her Charlotte, North Carolina school (Solomon 1990); and, finally, writing and receiving well over $100,000 in grants within six months. The largest grant, which Jeanne wrote to fulfill a requirement in the graduate course she was taking from Eve, enabled the school to equip a student production center. When the grant was funded, Jeanne's principal, Barbara Cohn, assigned another teacher to take over Jeanne's former teaching responsibilities, freeing her to serve as a resource for the entire school. She would be available to work with teachers and students in the Production Center, as well as in individual classrooms. We later identified this allocation of a professional teacher to assist other teachers with the use of new technology to be one of the key factors in the successes that occurred. Writing, technology, team planning, and col-laborative learning projects were part of the plan. The plan, a vision dreamed up in early 1990 by a core team of teachers and administrators at Morningside, is now a reality that far exceeds the initial team's wildest expectations.

Writing Across the Curriculum

Although the plan was multifaceted, including team planning, cooperative learning, and a strong emphasis on technology, the improvement of writing was threaded throughout. Eve, who serves as liaison between the Charleston Area Writing Project (CAWP) and the National Center for the Study of Writing, helped provide research on the importance of integrating writing throughout the curriculum. District humanities coordinator Beverly Varnado and CAWP codirector Sally Newell also assisted in planning, as well as Charleston (SC) Southern University faculty member Don Clerico.

Several of the teachers at Morningside — Ron Gibson, Peg Sordelet, and Odessa Wilson — are Teacher Consultants for CAWP, having completed the Summer Institute of the local writing project. Early on, the group reached consensus that the model for writing would be that of considering writing as a process and using it as a mode for learning. According to Fulwiler and Young (1990), "Some programs set out primarily to improve student writing, others to improve student learning — yet in the long run most programs try to do both" (3). Morningside's WAC plan fits the above description. The plan was designed to improve student learning, using as many modern technological tools as possible. The team hoped to make technology a hook to motivate students, as well as to provide students with the tools that professionals use in the real world. Technology expert Seymour Papert (1992) believes that we must change schools from places that instruct to places where students construct. In a sense, the Morningside team envisioned change in much the same way as Papert would describe it two years later. The team planned to use technology as a way to change Morningside from a place where the teachers' main purpose is to instruct to a place where the emphasis shifts to one in which students construct knowledge.

Writing, with or without technology, is one way to construct knowledge. One aspect of learning that is infused into almost every aspect of student learning at Morningside is writing. A casual look around Room 216, the Production and Communication Center, shows the plan in action, with students writing for many different purposes and audiences.

Morningside: An Overview of the Plan in Action

During the course of a week, visitors walk down the hall of traditional-looking Morningside Middle School, cross the threshold of Room 216, and enter the classroom of the future. Room 216 is a technology-intensive room, one where students have access to the most up-to-date tools for learning.

A South Carolina Target 2000 grant totaling $90,000 over a three-year period helped equip Room 216 with the kinds of writing and learning tools to which professionals have access. Two walls of the room are lined with Macintosh Classics. One Macintosh IIci, along with its color monitor, is the station for the CD-ROM player and a modem. From this station students run programs that require a great deal of memory, such as PageMaker, or are more effective in color, such as the Prodigy on-line service. This IIci computer also supports a scanner, which enables students to scan pictures into newspapers, hypermedia stacks, and reports, as well as to create their own images with the use of a video camcorder and Computer Eyes, a digitizing software package. In the middle of the room, one Macintosh is attached to a data display viewer that can project the computer image onto a large screen, thus allowing for whole-class demonstration. This is also the station for another modem where students can access data bases through DIALOG ClassMate. In addition to the computers, scanner, camcorder, and modems, the room houses three large stands that each hold a large TV, a VCR player, and a videodisc player. These three units are portable and go out to teachers' classrooms.

While high-tech in nature, Room 216 is also a writing-intensive place, one that invites students to produce writing for a wide range of audiences, purposes, and media. It is no longer the room of Jeanne Sink; rather, Room 216 has become the hub of activity for collaborative activities planned and implemented by teachers and students alike.

A Typical Day in Room 216

When visitors cross the threshold of Room 216, they are likely to witness a variety of activities going on at the same time, with groups of students working on collaborative projects that span subject disciplines and may span grade levels. Some students are there along with their teachers; others have been sent from their classes to work individually or in small groups. Some students even come on their own before or after school.

Desktop Publishing PageMaker: A team of seventh- and eighth-grade students may be putting the finishing touches on their eight-page newspaper, researched in the "field" (sometimes literally on the community football field), typed initially as word-processing files using Microsoft Works and later imported into PageMaker, one of the most powerful desktop publishing programs available. During the first semester of the 1991−92 school year, one of Eve's students, Willie Dasinger, opinions editor for the College of Charleston's *Cougar Pause*, spent a few hours each week teaching a core group to use PageMaker. By January of 1992 that core group had become experts, teaching

PageMaker to others who had a need to use it, whether they were students or teachers.

The success of the PageMaker group demonstrates the layers of collaboration that developed at Morningside. Jeanne and Eve worked together to link the school and the college; Willie worked weekly with the students and later reported back to his undergraduate Computers in Education class about how much these middle school students were capable of learning; the students collaborated with each other and with teachers, while using important real-world skills. Aside from the collaborative aspect, the students were developing the power and esteem that comes with knowledge. As the students became the experts in various aspects of technology, the teachers began to view them in a different light—with a heightened sense of respect for the learners. The students also won respect from their teachers with their developing on-line research skills using such tools as the Video Encyclopedia of the 20th Century and DIALOG ClassMate. In some cases, the students actually became research assistants for their teachers, using their new abilities to search print and video data bases to find information teachers needed to prepare their lessons.

Because of our ongoing collaboration, when a need arose at Morningside Eve looked for resources at the College of Charleston. The PageMaker training was one example; another was DIALOG ClassMate. Neither of us, nor anyone at Morningside, knew how to use either PageMaker or DIALOG, but we were able to collaborate to fill the need.

DIALOG ClassMate: Continuing our walk around Room 216, the visitor may find the newspaper "publishers" sitting next to a pair of sixth-grade students using DIALOG ClassMate for on-line research in preparation for a class project. Another of Eve's practicum students, Lisa Marcus, a sociology major with a master's degree in library science, conducted the initial training for DIALOG ClassMate. Lisa was attending the college to become certified to teach social studies and spent a few hours in the school each week to fulfill her pre— student teaching practicum requirement. By second semester, when Lisa was doing her student teaching in another school, the teachers and students at Morningside were able to use the system without outside assistance.

DIALOG, a research system that has been a mainstay of professional research for years, now offers ClassMate to schools. ClassMate allows on-line access to over eighty-five data bases of newspapers, journals, and magazines not found in the school library. Some of the data bases offer full-text articles, which the students may download from the computer and take back to their classrooms. The material includes student workbooks that teach sophisticated data base searching procedures in a format that can be easily understood by middle and high school students. The search procedures are introduced in the classroom; then students come to Room 216 to use a modem to access DIALOG and execute a search they have planned in advance.

The Morning News Show: Continuing to walk around the room, a visitor may encounter a cross-age group of students working on the weekly school television show, which has become a popular event at Morningside. Some of the news team may be using the bank of Macintosh computers to write copy for the show, while another group searches the Video Encyclopedia of the 20th Century for footage to accompany a story.

Once the student researchers find what they need, they record from the laser discs onto videotape to be edited for their final version. Much of the footage contained in the $11,000 video set includes sound — speeches, interviews, and period music. Important decisions must be made by the team when editing. One student group is in charge of using VCR Companion to add graphics and text to the weekly video. Spelling becomes a weekly test in a different sense, here. The students ask several others' opinions and faithfully check dictionaries, as well as word-processing spellcheck options, to make sure no words that will overlay the video footage are misspelled. This is editing in a real-world sense.

Students working on the show must also consider other issues that professionals encounter in the real world. Questions of purpose and audience become more than classroom minilessons; they are daily considerations, which must be understood and acted upon. Important discussion takes place among the students before the final version is produced each week. The news show provides an opportunity for the team to practice many of the skills introduced in the language arts class. Students apply their language skills by interviewing, summarizing, inferring, taking notes, editing, and finally coming up with a segment that is appropriate for the intended audience and purpose. And they must do this on a weekly basis!

About now, having observed and chatted with students working on the newspaper, the morning news show, and other classroom projects, the visitors are usually overwhelmed by what they have seen and are filled with questions about how all of this came about, particularly since these activities may all be taking place at 7:00 A.M., thirty minutes before school opens! The room has become so popular that students come in on their own before school, after school, and whenever they can during the school day, to work on teacher-assigned projects and other projects such as the newspaper and the morning news show.

During the school day, teachers schedule times to accompany their students to the Production Center, particularly when they are working on units such as the one described below.

Sample Unit: Language Arts

A good example of how teachers at Morningside combine classroom activities with the facilities available in Room 216 is Peg Sordelet's presidents unit. Peg, a veteran teacher of over twenty years, was ripe for change and open to trying new ideas. A 1991 CAWP fellow, Peg decided to modify a unit on the presidents, which she had been teaching for several years. Now, in addition to the library research the students have traditionally conducted, Peg's students use their print and nonprint research to produce a HyperCard stack. Each sixth-grade student researches his or her assigned president, using print resources, the Grolier's Encyclopedia on CD-ROM, and the Video Encyclopedia of the 20th Century, where appropriate. Using a Mac Recorder, students add music and speeches from a set Peg had used in the past, scan pictures where needed, and end up with a product far more extensive than the reports on presidents that Peg's former students had produced. With Jeanne's help, Peg linked all the student stacks into one large stack on presidents that has become a resource for other students in the school.

Peg's students, like many others in the school, have become producers of knowledge rather than mere receptors of it. A newcomer to technology, but a teacher with experience enough to see the learning outcome for her students, Peg immediately launched her sixth graders into another project in February 1992 — a PageMaker-published newspaper on famous black Americans. Good teachers are quick to see the power of technology as an invitation for their students to learn and to write.

A Final Look Around: Other activities that students may be working on during a visitor's stay include a National Geographic Kids Network unit on weather for their science class. The unit, "Weather in Action," calls for students to use their writing skills to communicate with other students via modem to compare data they collect with data being collected elsewhere. The students use writing in their science class as a natural extension of what they are learning rather than the "add-on" some content teachers fear when asked to participate in a WAC program.

On the Macintosh computer with a CD-ROM player attached, other students may be using the Grolier's Academic American Electronic Encyclopedia to look up a topic too current to be found in the library's latest set of encyclopedias or other reference guides. Still other students may be creating HyperCard stacks that go along with class-assigned projects such as Peg Sordlet's presidents unit. Some students may be filming each other for a pilot assessment project where each student will have a major project videotaped every nine weeks as part of the Video Portfolio Project. And then there are the other HyperCard stack projects.

South Carolina History Project

Gifted and Talented Program students are producing HyperCard stacks on Charleston and the Low Country region as part of a South Carolina State Department of Education—initiated project going on in three schools in different parts of South Carolina. An addition to the upcoming revision of the South Carolina history curriculum, these stacks will be used all over the state to show third- and eighth-grade students what the three geographic regions of South Carolina are like through the eyes of other students. The stacks will include text, sound, and scanned images, as well as video segments for a computer-controlled interactive video presentation. The Gifted and Talented Program students ask advice on HyperCard from students in lower-level classes who have already produced their own stacks on other topics. This is the type of collaboration that was unplanned, yet is celebrated as an important by-product of what can happen when technology is used as a springboard to writing and collaboration. In the case of the South Carolina History Project, students are constructing knowledge, not only as a classroom exercise but as a real-world project to be used to augment print materials for students throughout the state. Their motivation goes well beyond a desire for a good grade; these students are literally "making history"!

Finally, still other students may be uploading or downloading messages from KIDS-92, a global telecommunications project on Bitnet and Internet for students ages ten to fifteen (Coleman and Sink 1991; *Instructor* 1991), while their fellow students may be working on projects generated by students and teachers and placed on the "Ideas" bulletin board of Free Educational Mail.

Leaving Room 216:   The school climate at Morningside is changing for students more accustomed to failure than to success. The atmosphere at Morningside is becoming one of productive activity and pride. Not one piece of equipment or software in this room containing $100,000 worth of material has been stolen from a neighborhood where crime is endemic.

By this time the visitors are ready for some background information on how teachers at Morningside orchestrate the frenzy of activity they have just seen. Much of that orchestration and planning takes place through their planning for their REACH project.

Project REACH

While most of the equipment in Room 216 was funded through a South Carolina Target 2000 grant, much of the philosophy and spirit of collaboration at Morningside is a direct result of Project REACH. REACH, or Rural Education Alliance for Collaborative Humanities, is funded by the Rockefeller Foundation under an umbrella of programs called CHART. Like other CHART projects, South Carolina's REACH projects focus on the humanities — reading, writing, the study of American culture, and the understanding of other nations of the world — as essential for the improvement of public education in the United States (Adkins and Coleman 1992).

While each REACH site plans its own approach to improving education through the humanities, two common threads link each project. First of all, each REACH project has a university or college partner from a nearby institution who collaborates with the secondary teachers to work toward their common REACH goals and their site-specific objectives.

The second common thread, a statewide computer network, enables the college partners' collaboration with secondary schools to extend beyond the one or two REACH sites of close geographic proximity. It also gives each REACH site Bitnet and Internet access. Bitnet is an "international network of computers that links higher education institutions and other educational and research organizations" (Roberts et al. 1990, 221–231). Internet is "a vast international research and academic networking infrastructure which exchanges information among its thousand of university and research institutions" (Rogers 1991, 2). Bitnet is one of "many computer networks presently connected to the Internet via electronic gateways," according to Rogers (2). Bitnet and Internet access has been integral to broadening Morningside's collaborative efforts outside the school and even outside the country. As REACH partners, we have worked together to use Bitnet and Internet to the advantage of students. One example of the use of the Bitnet and Internet gateways is Morningside's participation in KIDS-91. Morningside students were able to participate in a global telecomputing project (described below) because of their access to Bitnet and Internet.

Project REACH enabled the two of us to expand our personal collaborative efforts into a formal partnership. In spring 1990 we attended a computer training session together and worked with the teachers at Morningside to plan the 1990–91 REACH grant, with the theme

"Against the Odds" (Coleman and Sink 1991). We found that against all odds, 350 Morningside students were able to participate in KIDS-91, an international on-line computer conference started by Od de Presno from Norway. The October 1991 issue of *Instructor* magazine reported the success of Morningside's participation in KIDS-91. The article tells how "three teachers got hooked on classroom technology—and the projects that reeled them in" (32). In the case of new Morningside teacher Cissy Meyers, the hook was KIDS-91. KIDS-91 (and KIDS-92) asks students to write responses to the following four questions: Who am I? What do I want to be when I grow up? How can the world be a better place? What can I do to make it happen? During the first year of Morningside's participation, 350 students not only wrote and posted their own responses to the conference but also read responses from other kids from all around the world. The idea of reaching out to others throughout the world showed such promise that the REACH team members decided to extend the idea. The theme for Morningside's 1991–92 REACH grant became "REACH Out to the World." That is just what Morningside students are continuing to do with the help of technology.

REACH Out to the World: Morningside Middle School's 1991–92 REACH project, REACH Out to the World, focused on the students, teachers, and administrators reaching out to discover more about other continents and cultures and collaborating with others from around the world. Because of the Bitnet and Internet access provided through REACH, all 850 Morningside students were able to participate in KIDS-92, with each student in the school answering the four questions listed above. This is in keeping with the goal of the '92 conference: "to get as many 10–15-year-old children as possible involved in a global dialog continuing until May 19, 1992" (de Presno 1992, 1).

Posting responses to the four questions was also in keeping with one of the goals for the school's commitment to WAC. Students wrote for a real audience with a specific purpose. They were well aware that other students from all over the world would be reading their responses. Likewise, Morningside students read responses written by young people their age from around the world. One result of reading responses from other parts of the world was a dawning recognition by the Morningside students that there really was a purpose for learning a second language. Many of the Morningside students commented on the fact that almost all of the responses they read were written in English, although English was a second language for many of the students participating in the conference. Once students responded to the four questions, they became eligible to go on-line and read and send messages to KID-CAFE, "an international, electronic conference for kids 10–15 . . . to talk about whatever they like, establish relationships with new friends in other countries, discuss the future, school, hobbies, environment, or whatever" (Oldenburg 1991).

Seventh-Grade REACH Team

Collaborating as an interdisciplinary group, the seventh-grade REACH team took the KIDS-92 project even further. Using KIDS-92 as a springboard, the students developed HyperCard stacks on one of the world problems they identified when they wrote responses to the four questions. Writing was at the heart of this project, and students used writing for real purposes and to address real audiences.

Eighth-Grade REACH Team Focuses on Africa

Led by social studies teacher Odessa Wilson, teachers on the eighth-grade REACH team brought the continent of Africa to the students of Morningside Middle School. For the "kickoff" of the unit, the teachers brought in Ron and Natalie Daise, experts in African culture. Great storytellers, these experts told tales from Africa and introduced students to many of the songs that slaves brought to the United States. Students learned how certain songs were sung for dual purposes and were part of a communication system among slaves. Later in the unit the students learned about the communication role that drumming played in Africa. The culminating activities for the unit were individual oral presentations, many of which were multimedia as a result of students' research and production in the Production Center—Room 216.

In preparation for the oral presentations, eighth-grade students went to the Production Center to conduct research and develop their projects. Students researched different countries in Africa using *The Encyclopedia of the Twentieth Century* on laser discs, the Groliers Encyclopedia on CD-ROM, and DIALOG ClassMate. For example, students researching South Africa searched the multivolume laser disc set of *The Encyclopedia of the Twentieth Century* in search of footage for their oral presentations. Students were able to see Desmond Tutu speak, see black prisoners in South African jails, and see cities that were destroyed as a result of violence associated with apartheid. Those researching other countries found information on the great many newsworthy events that happened throughout Africa during the twentieth century. One student combed the electronic encyclopedia searching for clips to show African clothing, ranging from traditional to modern dress. Later, she transferred the clips from videodiscs to videotape, which she edited to use as part of her oral presentation.

As part of this unit, Morningside students used the KIDCAFE component of KIDS-92 to telecommunicate with students in South

Africa. During this period of time, students read a story about South Africa in their language arts class and wrote reactions to the story. Later, they sent letters to South African students via KIDS-92.

After the students had researched and collaborated on their African project for four weeks, Martha Overlock, who lives in Asheville, North Carolina, and is an expert artist in African drumming and the peoples of the west coast of Africa, worked with the students for two weeks as an artist in residence. Students learned that drumming was, and continues to be, an integral part of life in Africa. As part of the unit, students wrote their own "rhythm," as well as Africa fables. At the same time, students were writing mini—research papers, which tied in with the unit, in their science class. The culminating activity was a community presentation on the unit.

Finally, eighth-grade students wrote reflection essays about the African unit. The samples below echo what many of the students had to say. According to Odessa Wilson, many of the students, white and black alike, approached the unit with little interest. But the more they learned, the more they were drawn into the learning process.

Patrick, a white student, wrote:

> My knowledge of Africa has improved greatly. I understand what the colors on flags resemble, what entertains the people. Before the presentations or any research ... I thought that Africa didn't have cities in some countries. After the research, I realized that some cities in Africa are as modern as the ones in our country or any other country. Before the presentations, I thought the drumming was when they were going to invade another tribe. When I realized why and all the reasons the Africans play [drums], I was like—wow!—this is really cool stuff! I must admit though at first I was skeptic. I thought, I have no ties with Africa, let the blacks research their mother land. Don't get me wrong, I am not racist but that is the way I thought. Now my feelings have changed greatly.

In the rest of his reflection, Patrick goes on to theorize about Africa as the cradle of civilization and even speculates that Kenya may have been the site for the biblical Garden of Eden. His final sentences reflect on race relations between blacks and whites. He ends the essay with the statement, "We are all God's children." It is interesting to note that Patrick begins his essay with the impersonal statement, "My knowledge of Africa has improved greatly." From there he goes on to include a few facts he has learned. The more he writes, the more he reflects upon his newfound knowledge, even using prediction and analysis. By the end of his reflection, the unit has become very personal to him.

Another student, Benjamin, points out a personal connection he has made because of the unit as he describes his developing sense of pride in his heritage. Benjamin writes:

On the unit on Africa, I learned that I don't have to be shamed by my heritage; but to be proud of and happy with it. I learned how to play some African beats on African drums. I also learned how to sing some African songs along with their purpose and meanings. I learned African traditions and the Africans dress and styles. Also, the presentations and information presented in Mrs. Wilson's History classes helped me realize how important my heritage is. The unit also got me involved in African studies, which I never knew was as fascinating and interesting. In fact, I wanted to dig and dig until I knew everything there is to know about the continent of Africa. I wanted to get so far in this unit that I knew more about it than the Africans that live on the continent of Africa . . . .

Also, I would like to thank you all and Mrs. Overlock for allowing me to learn so much from the Motherland; after all, some people don't have the opportunity to learn about their homeland and their heritage.

The unit on Africa demonstrated the realization of Morningside's goal to involve students actively in their own learning, something the Morningside team had envisioned during their initial planning for their Target 2000 grant and also their REACH project.

REACHing the Goal

Working toward the goal of involving students in their own learning continues to be satisfying to teachers and students alike and has gained national attention (Coleman and Sink 1991; Dunham 1991; *Instructor* 1991). A section of the narrative for the 1991–92 REACH grant says a great deal about the spirit of collaboration at Morningside and sums up how writing and learning have come to be viewed within the school. According to the REACH grant:

The main goal of our project is to get all students actively involved in their own learning. We want our students to be producers of knowledge rather than receivers of knowledge. All teachers will have high expectations for all students. In a school like Morningside, it is often easy for teachers and students to have low expectations. By working as a team on a common topic, students will have a fresh start. When they go into the Production and Communication Center at Morningside, they all become both student and teacher of the technology. They must be willing to share their knowledge with classmates in order for all students to be the best they can be. We want to take the competition out of the classroom and replace it with team work. By taking away the competition, school will become a more positive experience for the students. This will bring about changes in their attitudes and in their attendance.

The teachers put a lot of thought and work into planning our REACH project. The activities they have planned for (telecommunications, host professors, artists-in-residence, multi-media productions, and visual and performing arts opportunities) are activities which allow all content areas to work together. The students will not be learning content in isolation. Students will be able to see how the content areas work together in real life. School will become real. (Sink 1991)

The Future of Collaboration

As we stated earlier, some collaboration is carefully planned from the beginning, but ours evolved over years and has involved many teachers and administrators who were ready to collaborate with each other, their students, and people from outside the school in order to help students overcome tremendous barriers to their learning. Can this type of collaboration be planned for and replicated? We don't know, but we suspect it can be, judging from other models we know of where schools have become partners with colleges, universities, and businesses. We have learned that when teams of teachers are empowered to plan meaningful learning experiences for students, learning becomes more exciting for students and teachers alike. Yet we know that our collaboration is unique, due to the combination of our personal friendship and common professional interests. As for our professional collaboration, it is continuing down a new avenue.

During the 1991–92 school year, events occurred that have set off continuing evolution of our professional collaboration and that of the programs at Morningside. Jeanne was selected as South Carolina's 1992 Teacher of the Year. In that position, she went on leave from Morningside to travel the state with her technology message as a representative of the South Carolina Center for Teacher Recruitment. One of Eve's former students was hired to temporarily staff the Technology Center. After much consideration, Jeanne accepted a new position to help steer technology for a whole district, which includes a high school with which Eve has a close working relationship. The professional collaboration of Eve and Jeanne will continue in a new direction.

As for Morningside, something positive has happened as a result of the programs initiated during the past two years. One positive factor in that new leadership is emerging in the void left by Jeanne, who wrote the initial grants to fund the programs at Morningside. One of the key new leaders is Odessa Wilson, the teacher who spearheaded the African unit. Odessa participated in the Charleston Area Writing Project (CAWP) in 1991 as a fellow. Since then, she has spoken to state REACH groups and a national CHART group about the successes of the REACH project. She has recently been asked to serve as codirector of CAWP and is quick to tell others about the marriage of technology, writing, and learning at her school. Eve hopes to maintain her ties with Morningside and support the continuing relationship between Morningside and the College of Charleston.

Good programs will always face the problem of teachers who transfer, move, or retire and leave a program to die because it has been the particular province of one teacher. One lesson learned at Morningside is that a core of teachers must "buy in" to new programs in order to assure continuity when staff changes occur. If a program remains the province of only one or two teachers, then the program is likely to die when the key teachers leave the school. Fortunately, in the case of Morningside, a core of teachers, supported by their principal, did buy in. Our best hope for Morningside is that new leadership will continue to emerge and that students will continue to accept the invitation to take an active role in their own learning. For the sake of students, we invite other teachers to use technology as an invitation for writing and collaboration. We have seen students accept the invitation.

Appendix
Further Information About Materials and Services

The Apple User Group Connection
Apple Computer, Inc.
20525 Mariani Ave. M/S 48AA
Cupertino, CA 95014

Computer Eyes
Digital Vision, Inc.
66 Eastern Ave.
Needham, MA 02026
(617)329–5400

DIALOG ClassMate
Dialog
Marketing Dept.
3460 Hillview Ave.
Palo Alto, CA 94304
(800)334–2564

FrEdMail (Free Education Mail)
4021 Allen School Road
Bonita, CA 92002
(619)475–4852

Grolier's Academic American Encyclopedia
Sherman Turnpike
Danbury, CT 06816
(800)356–5590

HyperCard
Apple Computer, Inc.
20525 Mariani Ave. M/S 48AA
Cupertino, CA 95014

INTERNET
c/o the Consortium for School Networking
EDUCOM K−12 Networking Project
1112 16th St. N.W., Suite 600
Washington, DC 20036
(202)872−4200

KIDS−92
Od de Presno
Saltrod, Norway (Europe)
+47 41 27111
Internet: opresno @ ulrik.uio.no

National Geographic Society Kids Network
Dept. 90
Washington, DC 20036
(800)334−2564

VCR Companion
Broderbund®
San Rafel, CA 94903−2101
(800)527−6263

Video Encyclopedia of the 20th Century
CEL Educational Resources
1515 Madison Ave., Suite 700
New York, NY 10022
(800)235−3339

South Carolina Center for Teacher Recruitment
Canterbury House
Winthrop University
Rock Hill, SC 29733

References

Adkins, Polly, and Eve Coleman. 1992. "South Carolina Students REACH New Frontiers." In *Proceedings, Ninth International Conference on Technology and Education*. Paris, France.

Coleman, Eve B., and Jeanne C. Sink. 1991. "Concentric Circles: Morningside Middle School Students REACH Out. *Telecommunications in Education*. 2: 4.

de Presno, Od. February 3, 1992. *The KIDS-92 Newsletter: Global Networking for Youth 10−15*.

Dunham, Marla H. 1991. "Computer Windows in Room 216: Urban Middle School Students Look Out at the World." *Middle Ground* 19 (2): 6.

Fulwiler, Toby, and Art Young. 1990. *Programs That Work: Models and Methods for Writing Across the Curriculum*. Portsmouth, NH: Boynton/ Cook.

Oldenburg, Dan. 1991. *The Washington Post* Style section.

Papert, Seymour. 1992. Keynote Address. Centre Pompidou, 9th International Conference on Technology and Education. Paris, France.

Roberts, Nancy, George Blakeslee, Maureen Brown, and Cecilia Lenk. 1990. *Integrating Telecommunications into Education*. Englewood Cliffs, NJ: Prentice Hall.

Rogers, Al. 1991. The National Research and Education Network (NREN). *FrEdMail^{TM} News* 6 (1).

Sink, Jeanne C., et al. September 1991. REACH grant proposal.

Solomon, Gwen. 1990. "Using Technology to Reach At-Risk Students. *Electronic Learning* 9 (6): 14−15.

People magazine. 1991. "Students don't fear her byte." (Fall Extra): 78−79.

Instructor. 1991. "Turned on to technology." (October): 34−35.

12

Collaboration as Sharing Experiences: A Detroit Public Schools/ University of Michigan Course

Barbra Morris and George Cooper with Constance Childress, Mary Cox, and Patricia Williams

We meet together once a week from 4 to 7 P.M. in the imposing Rackham building across the street from the Art Institute in downtown Detroit.[1] All of us have been teaching throughout the day, and four o'clock hardly seems like the best time to begin anew talking about our days at school. Despite fatigue and the inconvenience of the hour, fifteen teachers from the Detroit Public Schools arrive for our graduate course: Composition 600, Theory, Practice, and Implementation of Writing Across the Curriculum Programs. Teachers fill their cups of coffee, tea, or maybe glasses with water and then take seats around a set of library tables arranged in a square. The class begins slowly and informally, with stories of the past day or week, sometimes recounting joys, sometimes concerns, sometimes academic activities, sometimes social ones.

As with any course we have prepared an overall plan for each session, which we would sketch out briefly to begin the three-hour class. We might have readings to discuss, projects to present, group activities to complete, proposals to evaluate, or occasionally a speaker to receive. As we introduce our proposed schedule informally, we invariably take time to encourage talk among teachers who, throughout the week, have not seen each other. Even teachers from the same school report feeling isolated from their colleagues. Therefore, informal exchanges are an essential ingredient of our course plan: our theory is that teachers will motivate each other when they have an opportunity to talk about teaching and learning. In fact these teachers often remind us that the demands of their full school days ordinarily prevent much regular interaction, even among colleagues in the same discipline, let alone among different disciplines in different buildings.

We begin each class by listening to teachers' stories: A junior high special education teacher talks animatedly about a visitor she had in her class that day, an African-American hockey player; she shares some of the writings and drawings that her students produced as a result of their discussion with him. A language arts teacher, originally from India, talks quietly about introducing her students to Indian culture by bringing in music, drawings, and artifacts. A French teacher reflects on a recent Pride Day held at her school, telling how the excitement of the festivities surrounding it made conventional academic work difficult. A high school science teacher describes working late into the night monitoring activity in one of Detroit's neighborhoods. He is tired but proud that the coalition of parents, teachers, and business people of which he is a part have helped make the week of Halloween safer for the city's inhabitants. After ten to fifteen minutes, this conversation gradually dies down; we turn our attention to the afternoon's agenda.

Introductory Reflections

As college teachers, we are often looked at as depositories of information to whom students can turn for answers. We like that role; however, to play the role too heartily means we spend considerable amounts of time lecturing instead of listening. Students might like this, insofar as it allows them to be passive learners; but educators, especially those in the field of composition, know that learning happens best when students are active participants in the knowledge-making activity. Moreover, because our students are also teachers, their voices and reflections on course information centrally contribute to developing the subject matter for our discussions. We want to explore theory with teachers through examining their actual practice, whenever possible vitalizing theory through their perspectives as educators.

We also know that using writing to learn in the disciplines is a more complex activity than simply requiring students to write (not to suggest that teaching people to write is ever simple). Writing to learn as a new curricular objective requires interdisciplinary coordination that eventually results in students writing in all classes, not just in language arts. Using writing effectively in many kinds and levels of courses depends upon teachers articulating and acting on a common set of assumptions about students' learning through writing. For these reasons we help teachers to articulate their own assumptions about writing and learning upon which they might then design new initiatives. We need to explore with them assumptions about how students learn and about the expectations about language that shape academic discourse. Finally, we want teachers to begin talking with other teachers in their schools to uncover attitudes toward writing held by teachers in disciplines other than their own.

In each class meeting, two or three teachers took responsibility for discussing main issues raised in readings we provided, and for relating issues raised in readings to situations in their own schools. For example, in Detroit a heated discussion about institution of all-male academies had been fueled by a disproportionally high dropout rate of young males; the essay "Countering the Conspiracy to Destroy Black Boys" by Jawanza Kunjufu (1985) took on immediate relevance, as teachers voiced opposing sides in a spontaneous debate over the merits and problems of gender-differentiated schooling. In another session, work by Gardner and Hatch (1989) on multiple intelligences was regarded to be justification for bringing into the classroom a number of different language experiences that would allow students to build upon their own strengths as thinkers and writers. In a third instance, a lively discussion of differing forms of academic argumentation emerged from teacher-led reports on the significance and possible application of Jack Meiland's proposition (1981) that a discernable format for written academic argument can be taught quite directly to students, regardless of the content being taught, and is of considerable assistance to students as they try to understand the complex nature of academic and social problems.

In what appeared to us to be a striking contrast to abstract discussions of theoretical issues, our group consistently interpreted theory with respect to their concrete experience. The results were sometimes unexpected. For example, teachers read an article by Imani Perry (1988) in which she contrasted her experiences as a student in both public and private schools. The result is an indictment of the public school system as a cold, impersonal environment that favors superficial qualities such as good behavior and factual precision over intellectual development. In another article, Else Weinstein (1988) relayed her difficult experience as a high school teacher in an honest and forthright manner. She depicted a public school setting similar to that of Perry, revealing difficulties she experienced assimilating herself within rigid, entrenched practices of a large and sometimes adversarial system. Conversations resulting from both these articles surprised us. We had selected these articles assuming teachers would sympathize with the authors, finding in their critiques of public school a language by which to better critique the daily school environment. Instead, our teachers argued against the attitudes revealed in these two essays and preferred a picture of the public school environment as a place where there was no time for self-pity and where teachers must not find reasons to quit. It might be argued that we had been naive in thinking that our teachers would not challenge problem-centered depictions of their schools. Indeed in listening to these teachers talk about their determination, we were reminded of how little is written about the personal qualities that lead to success in education despite obstacles. For our purposes, the teachers' resistance to negativity in the articles we had selected provided an excellent transition into deeper individual evaluation of good teaching — and the relationship of students' writing and learning to that commitment.

Following our discussion of attitudes toward teaching, we assigned practical activities outside of class to encourage teachers to try more writing in their own classes and then talk with other teachers about using writing to learn. For example, one of our assignments asked each teacher to talk with a colleague who might be hostile to using writing in her or his subject area. In part, the assignment read:

> We have discussed the pitfalls and obstacles which you anticipate to be the hardest to overcome if you were to start a writing to learn initiative in your school. For this week, and you can work collaboratively on planning this (be sure to include all of your names on the report), make some contact with your biggest adversary. Plant the idea of writing to learn in your conversation with this person and see what happens. For next week write a report of what happens including:
>
> - who you talked to
> - exactly why you considered this person an adversary or obstacle
> - how you approached the person or persons
> - how you talked about writing to learn
> - the person's or persons' reactions

The responses to this assignment were varied. In general, teachers received a warm reception to their overtures, a somewhat surprising phenomenon since they contacted people they had thought would resist using writing in their teaching. One teacher, after advocating writing in disciplines to her administration and colleagues, concluded that

> our school does seem ripe for writing to learn. It seems that almost everyone is trying some kind of writing. Even the principal is anxious for this kind of writing to learn across the curriculum and the crossing

of all disciplines. She is encouraging teachers to form cross-discipline teams to share ideas and activities.

Perhaps not all of our teachers are so willing to try learning to write activities, but a great many are. At least most of the people I know are. (Of course I do have a tendency to avoid people who are likely to give me a hard time.)

Another less sanguine, though not so surprising, report from one of our science teachers indicated that the typing teacher "is an obstacle because she feels the educational system is under a strain and over-worked. So she would resist any change that would cause more work." Further conversation revealed that the typing teacher was not familiar with strategies of writing to learn and after hearing more about them became more positive, saying that "she would cooperate with a team of teachers if she did not personally have to generate or design an activity, nor persuade her co-workers in the business department to cooperate also." In each case of reporting back to our entire class, teachers described their efforts to introduce writing to learn in their schools as a process of talking together and gradually understanding each other's teaching situations. In doing so, they developed increased confidence in their own colleagues' willingness to evaluate their school's potential for change and support of classroom innovations.

Teachers as Agents of Change

In addition to the stimulating classroom discussions and initiatives that grew out of assigned readings, we thought of ourselves as preparing teachers to serve as school leaders in writing to learn beyond our course semester. Toward that end, we spent several weeks working on proposal writing for funds available in Michigan for teachers; some of our class members actually received funding for classroom projects in writing to learn during the year. However, we found that not all teachers were comfortable taking on projects that extended beyond their already challenging classroom responsibilities. Nonetheless, we felt that even those teachers who did not submit proposals at the time benefited by writing them for the class and from general presentations and discussions of proposal writing. In other words, everyone practiced analyzing and presenting a proposal in specific categories: needs, objectives, materials, results, and evaluation techniques.

In connection with our proposal writing and presentations, we asked teachers to imagine a possible timeline of activities during a typical school year that might promote writing to learn in all disciplines. For this activity, teachers from the same school or same discipline formed small groups to consider sequential initiatives within their respective situations.

At the end of the semester we assigned a reflective essay, the goal of which was threefold: (1) reconsideration of readings and initiatives and synthesis of them, (2) discussion of actual classroom needs and practices, and (3) formulation of an image of one's self as an agent of change. These goals were incorporated into a handout we provided teachers for writing these essays:

> Here are some things to think about as you reflect on this class and your work as a teacher.
>
> 1. Think ahead to next semester. Are there specific things from this course that you would like to incorporate into your course? into your school?
>
> 2. Are there other goals you have for fund raising? What are they? And what, if any, relationship is there between your fund raising goals and the ideas we have raised this course?
>
> 3. What reading had the greatest impact on your work as a teacher? And why?
>
> 4. As honestly and frankly as you can, describe why you believe writing to learn works. Use examples both from the readings and your students' work.
>
> 5. Consult with members of your faculty about writing to learn across the curriculum and begin mapping out strategies with them whereby more writing, or more coordinated writing, might be assigned among various courses, and report on those plans and conversations.

Three Teachers' Voices

By the end of the semester-long course, then, we hoped to develop a shared history of common knowledge that would be useful to teachers. We observed that our arrival-at-class conversations gradually developed into familiar stories, rather than random details about school days and isolated events. One of us speaks again about a parent who is very ill. We discuss his health, which has not improved, and the difficulty of sustaining all aspects of our lives. Another teacher catches us up on the progress of her son's computer course, while a third teacher, excited by her students' development, has brought more writing to share.

To the final meeting of the class in December, each of us brings a colleague from our schools. We have a table spread with different kinds of food: chicken, salads, desserts, and breads that represent a collective preholiday dinner for everyone. In this last three hours, some teachers present model writing to learn lessons; all of us, guests included, participate in the writing "lessons" and talk about them afterward.

On this night, teachers give us their final reflective papers; we recall that there have been six out-of-class writing assignments prior to this one, and all papers were intended cumulatively to create and refine individual perspectives on using writing to learn and to encourage plans for future schoolwide writing projects. The final reflective essays proved to be distinctively different statements that demonstrated teachers' thinking about writing, personally as well as professionally. The teachers' voices eloquently addressed educational issues that we had raised throughout the semester: the need for school-based faculty development, collaborative classroom and program initiatives, and opportunities to develop direct relationships between one's own students and professional development. Here are excerpts from three teachers' reflective essays.

School-Based Program Development: Mary Cox, Martin Luther King Jr. High School

An assistant principal once told me, "There is nothing new in education. If you stay around long enough, it all resurfaces." This is certainly the way I felt that first evening I walked into the Writing Across the Curriculum class. I was not at all sure it was where I belonged. After all I had been dealing with writing as a process for years. What more could I learn, especially from teachers in other disciplines? Besides, I wasn't sure it was necessary that I know what other disciplines were doing about writing.

I was wrong.

Sharing class time with teachers in other disciplines was stimulating and inspirational. I learned that we all share a basic concern for student learning and achievement. More important, I learned there is a great deal of teaching going on in the Detroit Public Schools in all disciplines. The class turned out to be one of rewarding exchanges.

I should have known that of course. After all, the most interesting literature class I have taken was populated not just by English teachers but by a doctor, a chemist, a social worker—all who brought different interpretations to the readings in the class. Why wouldn't this be true for a class on writing?

Listening to the exchange of ideas between the science teacher and French teacher taught me that English teachers are not alone. All teachers realize that writing is an essential part of learning in any discipline. What is it about writing that makes it essential to all classes? The answer came from a science teacher: "Writing about something tells you how much you don't know about it."

Gradually, listening to this led to a change in my writing assignments. I still assign very structured papers, but I also discovered that having students write short, informal papers ("What I learned from the first four chapters of *To Kill a Mockingbird*") teaches me things about their learning. I learn what important points students have missed and I learn which students are reading and which are not. I learn which students have the greatest understanding.

I learned this from a science teacher.

Although students have been writing in social studies and science classes, language arts or history teachers often do not know it. High schools are very departmentalized and the opportunity to share, to sit and talk about writing rarely occurs. I believe sharing ideas among teachers is important, and the ideal situation would be to create cross-discipline teams.

These cross-discipline teams could create writing to learn activities that offer the students and teachers many advantages. These activities could be used to allow students an opportunity to think through a lesson they had just covered. They could help students organize ideas about a subject or tackle new material. They would force students to make judgments about material that is new to them and, at the same time, give teachers insight into how well students are comprehending a lesson or how students feel about a method or technique used.

The inclusion of social studies and science papers in the ninth-grade students' portfolios is one way various disciplines could encourage writing. Although teachers would help to design the assignments, students would choose the papers representative of their best writing in each subject area. A combination of cross-discipline sharing and writing to learn activities will produce the best examples of a student's work.

The senior Research Writing class I teach especially lends itself to the exchange of ideas between disciplines. We are proposing a series of writing to learn activities designed to lead to a final project of the student's choice. I hope this approach will encourage students to exercise abilities that are in various areas of intelligence and interest.

It is time we turn our attention to individual needs. By allowing our students an opportunity to choose more varied assignments, we are not only encouraging them to learn more but to become better acquainted with the world outside the classroom. Combinations of teachers across disciplines create new strategies to guide students and make clear to them the importance of writing in all areas of study and careers.

This was the original plan, wasn't it?

Writing and Professional Development: Patricia Williams, Marshall Elementary School

Very timidly I approached the Composition 600 course — with little confidence in my ability to write or in the personal value of the course. It didn't improve when I met the other class participants: they were teachers at either the middle or high school level. Somehow I ascribed qualities to them I had not accorded elementary school teachers, especially myself. As an elementary reading lab teacher, with no class of my own, it was definitely a challenge to motivate myself to continue in the course.

In the ensuing weeks I found myself surrounded by the kind of educational atmosphere I had often desired: the faculty provided the kind of positive support both helpful and sometimes *necessary* to keep us interested and motivated. All participants were there to *learn*, to share. Classroom surroundings became a kind of secure, comfortable arena that allowed me to overcome reluctance to write: I began to "blossom," if you will.

My inspiration to write came from all sources: the faculty, guest presenters, and classmates. Even syllabus readings were thought-provoking. Presentations by the participants varied. One science teacher dealt with a scientific experiment. Responses to his ideas in class were written creatively and quite humorously, giving us the experience of integrating our thinking with writing in another discipline.

Another presentation was more somber in mood, but richly rewarding. On a half sheet of paper, we were told to write about one problem in our lives we wished resolved. The "problems" were placed in a hat; each person pulled someone else's and had to write a solution; we read the problem and solution aloud and discussed them. As both the problem and the solution were read, class reactions ran a gamut of feelings depending upon the content. Some caused tension and release; others required nurturing support, warmth, compassion. You could *feel* it!

Depending on the content, participants cried quietly; became overwhelmed; or smiled contemplatively. No one remained untouched. This was a moving, worthy exercise — teaching much about the value of writing and instantly bringing the class closer together. We all know the power of the written word, but very often attribute that ability to move others to professional writers. Here were teachers writing with that same power, evoking strong feelings in listeners. Based on this experience, I began to believe children must learn to write with power; we must guide them.

These exercises (and others) helped me become more aware of my own feelings as I responded in writing. They also provided an avenue of exploration to discover activities I could invent and share with my fellow "classmates" as well as my school colleagues.

With the gentle, lively, warm, thought-provoking discussions, I began to open up to the writing process. It was the kind of support, that gentle nudging that says, "You can do it." It kept me trying. Being part of the class gave me a new perspective, a different appreciation and compassion for what some young children might go through when given a writing assignment: utter anxiety and sheer anguish. And yet the climate created in *that* classroom led me to think how important it is to provide students with an "incubator," so that their "seedling" thoughts can take hold and develop.

I tested this belief in an experiment with Mr. Miller, the science teacher at my school. After agonizing over his willingness to cooperate, I finally asked him if he would ask one of his classes to write a summary or story about a lesson as a means of assessing what they understood and to give them exposure to writing in that discipline. To my surprise, he quickly accepted the idea and wanted to know if I would grade it. (Teachers always feel swamped with paperwork.) I offered to make comments on each student's paper: an acceptable compromise.

Mr. Miller was extremely pleased with the outcome: his students' writings were clear and orderly, and they felt cared about. Both he and I felt rewarded. His pride in his students and his work was evident! He fairly beamed as he pointed out excerpts, and developed plans to use a writing exercise after each unit. (Mr. Miller recognized that some of his students could verbalize about the subject but are not fluent writers — a sign that he cares.)

My success with Mr. Miller has encouraged me to motivate other teachers, to nudge them toward having their students write "across the curriculum." With my influence, writing processes might expand to creative writing assignments in disciplines.

A refreshing, positive comment sometimes transports students a lot farther along the educational spectrum. As educators, we become so accustomed to grading, we often forget all learning does not have to be labelled A through F. We must sometimes allow students to write unencumbered by "fear of a grade." We must provide a "safe haven" from harsh, negative criticism. Composition 600 and my experiences there demonstrate to me that teachers must be nurturers.

Classroom Initiatives: Constance Childress, Beaubien Middle School

As an instructor in the social studies department, I never considered writing to be among the essential skills and objectives to be mastered in my curriculum. Writing, I always believed, belonged to the English department. During this class, I began to change my mind. Then, an article assigned for our discussion titled "Multiple Intelligences Go to School," by Howard Gardner and Thomas Hatch (1989), provided a useful approach to expanding classroom learning: "each human being is capable of seven relatively independent forms of information process-ing, with individuals differing from one another in the specific profile of intelligence that they exhibit."

I found myself making an effort to incorporate writing into my courses. I began by requiring students to imagine living in colonial America during 1775. Students wrote a business letter, convincing a proprietor to purchase farm produce, livestock, or personal wares from them rather than from another farmer. A picture of the product had to be drawn by students to accompany the letter. Students became interested in learning more about slavery, the triangular trade, and even religion.

One of my students (I will call him Frank) was a below-average student and had completed only a few of the assignments before this one. But Frank's business letter was full of energy, excitement, and much detail. I praised Frank, "I didn't know you could write this well." He replied, "Oh, I like writing; I write all the time at home." Somehow, I had helped Frank want to write in school, too. My students were motivated, and I could watch active participation increase with all students completing the assignment.

After having completed several similar, successful writing to learn activities with my students, I was ready to take that "One Giant Step for Mankind." I asked myself the following question: If I had the opportunity to develop a program for my students, what would its goals be? My answers were

1. I want to move students from being passive receivers of information to being active shakers and movers in their community.
2. I want to empower students to motivate and influence the behavior of parents, relatives, and friends to accept their civic responsibility and unite to form a community that supports a healthy democracy.
3. I believe school must provide an opportunity for students to have real purposes, and participate in the real world.

I created the social studies "Street Law" curriculum. This project turned out to be a collaborative effort between students and a special education social studies class taught by Ms. Carolyn Cleveland, who worked with me. I received a $1,500 grant from the Ponting Foundation through the help of Dr. Morris and Mr. Cooper to support this project.

Students start the project by sharing details about their neighbors. Comments are collected on the board for future reference. Then, an index of important vocabulary terms begins to develop on the bulletin board. A street map four feet wide (created by the students) of the Beaubien community also is displayed on a wall with student's individual maps. A color-code system is used to connect a student's individual map to the large wall map.

Each student surveys people living on their street. Students write narrative essays, describing their street map and the people surveyed.

Using the facts from their surveys, students write a narrative letter, describing positive and negative interactions between a survey participant and the law. Students share their final drafts with classmates. Using a computer, students create a data base of survey results. In cooperative learning groups of three, students write a collaborative essay, derived from one of the confrontations, in which they discuss pros and cons of the issues and offer solutions.

The following activities take place throughout the project:

- Students write creative stories, poems, and/or letters using terms from their vocabulary index.
- Various speakers are invited to address the class about the Beaubien community and the law.
- Students view videos about the Detroit community.
- Students select essays to be mailed to various city officials inviting them to class to discuss the topic presented.
- A writing to learn in-service for teachers encourages writing across the curriculum by talking about this project and future possibilities.

A classroom bulletin board titled "Beaubien Family on the Move" is created by the students. The board is divided into two sections, green light and red light. On the green-light side, students display pictures and essays about the positive aspects of their neighborhood, and on the red side, pictures and essays of issues and situations they would like discontinued.

The first edition of the "Beaubien Connection" will be published by team volunteer students from eighth-grade "Street Law" class, and from eighth- and ninth-grade special education students. Each class votes on selections for publication. To understand criminal, civil, and misdemeanor violations in our community, students take a field trip into the business community to survey various business proprietors. A computer game, "Simulation City," will allow students to design and build the utopic city of their dreams.

Current-events articles, pictures, and announcements about the Beaubien Community are posted on a bulletin board maintained by the students. Students visit the Better Business Bureau. A field trip to the Thirty-sixth District Court allows students to view actual civil or criminal court cases. Students conduct in class a mock trial of a criminal case with a lawyer from the community or graduate law student as the judge and with parents representing the jury.

Every student writes a personal commitment statement and obtains additional commitments from family, friends, and community. The commitment statements identify a community problem and solutions that the applicant actively campaigns to institute. Writing to learn activities of this project are assembled by the students in a "Street Law/Urban Politics" portfolio.

Reflections on Reflections

A writing to learn course is more than just writing. The course demonstrated to us how valuable it is to bring teachers together in an environment where they can reconsider their own assumptions about teaching and can learn from and support one another. Moreover, not every teacher comes away with the same experience. In a climate of mutual support, teachers feel empowered to develop their own professional directions. As we see in the three end-of-term reflective papers, for example, each teacher describes a unique perspective on the meaning of teaching and learning. Mary Cox, the first of our writers, reminds us that change requires a leap of faith. Her initial reluctance to enroll in the course is understandable. She is busy and, as an experienced language arts teacher, had participated in the past in workshops to develop writing across the curriculum (WAC). She feared repeating the same subject matter. On the other hand, extended talking with teachers in other disciplines proved to be a unique experience for her, and strengthened her desire to experiment with using writing in her classes.

We were reminded that, as an educational movement, writing in the disciplines has existed in the literature for some time. Many schools, at all levels, developed curricular materials intended to support teacher initiatives; however, a missing ingredient appears to us to be time for teacher dialogues to develop working partnerships across disciplines. If dedicated teachers such as Mary are to be able to follow up on this important innovation with others, development of WAC must facilitate opportunities for teachers to meet regularly and gain an understanding of each other's teaching situations.

Patricia Williams, our second author, speaks about her sense of isolation from other teachers. She is an elementary school teacher who thought, prior to enrolling in the course, that she could not contribute to or participate in discussions about writing with teachers from other grade levels and fields. Gradually, through her own writing and listening to other teachers read aloud during the class, she established her own voice. Her confidence developed.

For example, in response to our assignment she approached Mr. Miller, a science teacher in her school, and discovered an ally where she thought none existed. In the end, they collaborated on designing an assignment and both of them responded to their student writers. The building of a creative teaching partnership is told about warmly, a sign that the school environment does not have to be a cold and unresponsive place. This positive experience tells Patricia that more dialogue can occur in her school when teachers have opportunities to work together openly and creatively across classrooms and disciplines.

Our third teacher is Constance Childress, who came to understand how writing could further the goals of a social studies curriculum. She had always believed that writing was a one-dimensional skill taught by English teachers. After our discussion of implications of the Gardner and Hatch (1989) article, "Multiple Intelligences Go to School," Constance envisioned writing as one of many interrelated learning processes. Beginning with an assignment of a business letter that locates students directly in the life of colonial America and ending with the "Street Law" curriculum, she makes writing integral to her students' multiple ways of learning.

Unlike courses that culminate in a final exam toward which discussion and readings have been directed, our course primarily encouraged teachers to reconsider their own teaching situations in light of controversial readings and discussions, as well as practical writing to learn activities. According to this model, we do not simply emphasize different forms of writing in disciplines, although we recognize such distinctions; instead, we nurture teachers' various plans to include writing to learn in their regular school life. Although we certainly set parameters for the course by choosing readings and by designing particular assignments and activities, as a regular classroom practice we consistently elicited and validated teachers' daily experiences. Outsiders might not understand how important this sustained process of personal validation is. In contrast, teachers often spend an in-service day listening to an expert from outside their school setting present an educational idea and distribute materials related to it. According to this "transmission" model, teachers will assimilate new information quickly and use handouts effectively to make changes in classroom practice, as though transference of information and incorporation of methods could be automatic. According to our "dialogic" model, individual teachers have time to explore and adjust what can work in their classrooms. We believe that teachers asked to implement new writing to learn initiatives need to acquire methods in incremental steps and share efforts and advice with others.

Concluding Thoughts

During the past several years, national reports have referred to a growing population of at-risk students, those young people whose images of their futures are disconnected from their images of themselves as successful in school. Equally disturbing is the troubling phenomenon of at-risk teachers. Isolated from each other and frequently maligned in media characterizations of their performance, teachers have had very few opportunities to analyze, discuss, and shape their challenging work. They face increasing pressure to respond to standardized test scores, which have little connection to motivating already alienated students to learn or to helping students relate schoolwork to their own lived circumstances.

Too often, teachers' professional development is limited to brief encounters with "experts" who know relatively little about the specific teaching situations of those gathered before them. Undoubtedly, some information can be more efficiently delivered in half-day or full-day sessions; on the other hand, regular dialogues about one's own teaching in a course setting that emphasizes cooperative learning offer a distinctly beneficial and self-reflective range of benefits: open discussions of current publications, trends, and theories; multiple, developmental planning sessions; individual teacher-presented reports and group critiques; extended investigations of new classroom strategies; and establishment of an analytic climate that supports continuing self-study. This is an experience Clifford Geertz (1980) describes as people being "free to shape their own work in terms of its necessities rather than received ideas as to what they ought or ought not be doing" (167).

As we discovered in the design and development of our semester-long graduate course, despite few models or resources for sustaining dialogue across school levels and across disciplines, our teachers, who received reasonable, adequate support for advanced, professional course work, steadily developed renewed creative energy that became translated into their own designs for interdisciplinary projects, funded proposals, and constructive, fresh approaches to difficult and persistent classroom problems. Similarly, in *Enquiring Teachers, Enquiring Learners*, the positive impact of cooperative teacher dialogues is described as a preparation for problem-solving classroom interactions because "teachers who have been taught to question and construct creative possible solutions will be empowered as professionals and will be able to facilitate such empowerment of children" (Fosnot 1989, 13). Indeed, in the proposal to institute our course, we had needed to find creative solutions to financial and logistical problems in order to make the course a reality: The Detroit Public Schools paid tuition of their teachers, while the University of Michigan provided a comfortable, convenient meeting room, current course materials, funds for several speakers, refreshments weekly, and supplied a university car for our round trips between Ann Arbor and Detroit during the semester.

In other words, our institutions overcame financial and bureaucratic obstacles; we all received official sanction and incentives to meet and work together. Despite differing schedules and commitments, the group's collective energy grew. Week after week, we learned how to learn from each other. Our interest was nourished by shared interests in our students and a developing knowledge base, greater than any one of us alone could have provided. Certainly, we each arrived with private beliefs about writing and learning, and we had individual expectations about student learning in our classes. Week by week, we talked together about obstacles our students faced in our school settings and how we could help them succeed. We learned how and why differing teaching strategies met the needs of our students or failed to do so. In these exchanges, we always established teachers as central to evaluation of their own students' progress. In *Plain Talk about Learning and Writing Across the Curriculum*, Mary Ann Norcerino (1987) notes the centrality of teachers' classroom evaluations, planning, and flexibility to an eventual success rate with students. We, too, noted that each teacher's regular reflections on lesson outcomes became the key to an incentive to try something again:

> Evaluation is an ongoing process associated with activities and methods used by educators to know when and what students are learning and to reflect on that knowledge in order to make decisions about what to do on Monday morning. (160)

Evaluation and innovation, therefore, are not processes that can or should belong to people outside of our classrooms. They need to be an integral part of our teaching days, year in and year out. Therefore, our own evaluation of our teaching requires each of us to consider and discuss our own daily practices. Courses, such as the precollege/college collaborative course we have described here, dignify, inform, and sustain the energy of good teaching through an environment of creative collegiality. Moreover, our central pedagogical tool, writing to learn in disciplines, turned our collective attention to an effective common method of teaching and to students being recognized as writers who learn course concepts as they engage with them. In this regard, writing to learn speaks to time-honored classroom practices of learning by doing, during which learners regularly and individually engage with complex and challenging subject matter, regardless of discipline.

Finally, perhaps one of the strongest arguments for instituting cross-school collaboration through jointly sponsored courses is the opportunity it offers for teachers to experience education as a working continuum, not as a fragmented system in which their individual voices cannot be heard. We renewed our commitment to our students at all levels of their schooling. Indeed, we enriched our teaching selves through the establishment of an extended teacher-colleague community, confirming our shared professional goals.[2]

Notes

1. All teachers from Detroit who enrolled in the 1992 class we describe in this essay, and the schools represented, were Constance Childress, Carolyn Cleveland, Beaubien Middle School; Agnes Kimbrough, Lena Teagarden,

Mackenzie High School; Patricia Williams, Marshall Elementary; Lola Black, Cheryl Green, Dora Myers, Northwestern High School; Hattie Cason, Mary Cox, M. L. King High School; Janet Bobby, Redford High School, LanDonia Richardson, Knudsen Middle School; Edgar Griffey, Harlan Hosey, Rupinder Syal, Southwestern High School. The Composition 600 course has been taught once before, in winter term 1990, by Barbra Morris and Ele McKenna, both faculty from the University of Michigan English Composition Board. The first course resulted in production of a manual written by the Detroit teachers in the course for their colleagues in the Detroit Public School system: *Writing to Learn in Disciplines: Detroit Teachers Combine Research and Practice in Their Classrooms.* This manual was distributed to administrators and teachers who attended the April 20, 1991, Collaborative Conference held in Ann Arbor. The manual can be found in the ERIC system or can be requested from the English Composition Board (313 764−0429).

2. In January 1992, immediately after the completion of the course described in this essay, the Herbert and Elsa Ponting Foundation supported faculty enrolled in the course who developed and proposed grants for the 1992 winter or fall semesters. Morris and Cooper administered awards of nine grants to seven schools.

References

Fosnot, Catherine. 1989. *Enquiring Teachers, Enquiring Learners.* New York: Teachers College Press.

Gardner, Howard, and Thomas Hatch. 1989. "Multiple Intelligences Go to School: Educational Implications of the Theory of Multiple Intelligences." *Educational Researcher* 18: 4−10.

Geertz, Clifford. 1980. "Blurred Genres." American Scholar 49: 165−79.

Kunjufu, Jawanza. 1985. *Countering the Conspiracy to Destroy Black Boys.* 3 vols. Chicago: African American Images.

Meiland, Jack. 1981. *College Thinking: How to Get the Best Out of College.* New York: Signet.

Norcerino, Mary Ann. 1987. "How Do We Know?" In *Plain Talk About Learning and Writing Across the Curriculum.* Richmond: Virginia Department of Education.

Perry, Imani. 1988. "A Black Student's Reflection on Public and Private Schools." *Harvard Educational Review* 58: 332−36.

Weinstein, Else. 1988. "High School Teacher." *New York Times Educational Supplement*, November 6.

Ways of Implementing Programs

Collaborations among teachers frequently lead to the sustained relationships that underlie Writing Across the Curriculum programs. The move from individual classroom WAC activities to a school or district WAC program involves a complex array of support systems, teacher initiative, and administrative advocacy. While much of this development operates by local rules, there is still a great deal to be learned from the ways groups of teachers have worked together to develop WAC programs that extend across schools or districts. The chapters in this section describe how particular programs took shape and in so doing suggest how others might do likewise.

In the opening chapter Betty Beck delineates the role of the school writing center in fostering WAC in many classrooms. Gloria Caldwell, Melissa Delosche, Lyn Zalusky Mueller, and Edwin Epps consider the roles played by many individuals in developing a school WAC program. In chapter 15 Pamela Farrell-Childers, Peter LaRochelle, Cissy May, Catherine Neuhardt-Minor, Lance Nickel, and David B. Perkinson outline a three-year plan for developing a school WAC program and describe strategies being used in art, chemistry, mathematics, and biology. The development of another school WAC program is detailed by Elizabeth Clifford, Dean Ellerton, Heather Prescott, Anna Romano, and Hilary Russell. Judy Buchanan and Andrew Gelber underline the importance of partnerships as they explain the development of a district-wide WAC program initiated in 1984. In chapter 18 Nana Hilsenbeck explains how a district-wide WAC program began, developed, survived, and changed during the last decade. Finally, James Upton's letter to colleagues offers definitions, questions, and imperatives for individuals beginning a WAC program.

13

One Vision at a Time

Betty Beck

The class came idling in, looking for familiar faces as they chose seats away from the front of the room. Eight o'clock approached, and the noise level grew. The teacher spent a few minutes welcoming everyone back to school on that hot end-of-summer day. Then, she began.

"For the next three minutes, write how you feel about your writing. Do you like to write? What are all the kinds of writing that you use in your daily routine? Are you concerned about your spelling and grammar? What kinds of writing do you most enjoy?"

After a moment of hesitation, the class settled down and wrote quietly. The only sounds were the movement of pens across paper and the uneven hum of the portable fan. Relaxing, the teacher looked around the newly opened J. P. McCaskey Writing Center and observed the diverse group of teachers who had volunteered for the August Writers' Workshop. The center's first students — teachers from science, industrial arts, English as a second language, home economics, social studies, English, reading, special education, and business departments — filled the room.

From these teachers had come the idea for a writing center. Before bringing their classes into the center in the fall, they would experience their own struggles and discoveries with writing as they composed, revised, edited, and published their contributions to the first workshop anthology, *Page One*.

That was eight years ago. Much has changed since then. Pens and paper have been replaced with two twenty-computer networks and a desktop publishing center, but the enthusiasm for writing has not abated. Prospering in a Lancaster, Pennsylvania urban high school of 1,700 students (45 percent white and 55 percent minority), the McCaskey Writing Center has published hundreds of books chronicling the experiences of thousands of students.

From today's vantage point, the Writing Center's success seems predestined; a closer look confirms that the eight-year evolution of acceptance within the school has been an uneven process. The proposal for the Writing Center written by Morris Krape, English program coordinator, and Joyce Syphard, assistant principal at McCaskey, gave the center its uniqueness: it would not be an English department program; its emphasis would be writing in all disciplines. The center's staying power has always been its ability to change to meet the demands of students and teachers who use writing process and who are comfortable with the place of word processing in that process, regardless of subject areas.

Every time a teacher is willing to take risks, to change, and to grow, the vision of the Writing Center changes; each teacher's vision impels change within the Center. Collectively, these visions guide the growth of the writing and learning across the curriculum program at McCaskey.

Before the Center Opened

When the Writing Center opened in the fall of 1984, it had a three-year history. Principal John Syphard became intrigued with the idea of changing the ways that students learn and teachers teach. He called upon the expertise of SUNY Writing Center director Lil Brannon to present a series of writing strategy workshops for teachers, and the process of change had begun.

One would think that Brannon's workshop would have been met with enthusiasm; however, it turned into a forum for some teachers to vent frustrations at a system unresponsive to the "real" issues: a high dropout rate, problems with tardiness and absenteeism, drugs, alcohol, child abuse, a rising rate of pregnancy. The group had started with forty teachers, but one-third left after the first workshop, citing a number of reasons for not wanting to use writing as a process: too much work, too difficult to grade, cannot cover enough content, cannot be done in my subject, don't want to eliminate the teaching of grammar. Fortunately, others saw it as a springboard into a more open class setting where they could stress process rather than lecture and large-group work.

Tom Wentzel, remedial reading teacher, remembers, "One day, probably in 1981, a Franklin & Marshall student doing a field experience with my classes asked me if I had ever tried expository writing in my classes. I fended off her questions with the standard rationalization— my kids can't read, how could they write? But the seed was planted. When Lil's workshops came along, I signed up."

Wentzel, along with a core of other teachers, stayed with the workshops. Some surprising results emerged when these teachers applied theories in their classrooms. Even reluctant writers responded with clarity and honesty when confronted with nonpunitive writing assignments. Now, constructive dialogue during student-teacher conferences affirmed the student's ideas and encouraged elaboration. The "errors" traditionally stressed — spelling, mechanics, grammar — took a backseat to making meaning. When thought-provoking questions replaced red editing marks, students responded with enthusiasm. Teachers, buoyed by their successes, wanted a visible commitment to writing process in the school; and the vision for the Writing Center was born.

The Early Years: Finding Our Way

In the summer of 1984, I was hired by the school district of Lancaster as the center director; concurrently, I was a fellow in the National Writing Center Project at Penn State Harrisburg.

My first task was to arrange one-third of the cavernous old library into five working areas: a classroom area, a conferencing and writing area, a word processing area, a reading area, and a production area. The teachers could generate ideas and read in large groups in the classroom area. Teachers and students could write, read, and listen to individual stories at the tables and chairs in the conferencing area. In a corner of the room, students could relax and read other students' writings in the Writing Center's library of publications. In the production area, students and staff could assemble books at the oversized table with a paper cutter, a GBC binding machine, and a supply of binders. The ten Apple IIe word processors, which did not arrive until second semester, would be lined against a wall. We discovered it was a room arrangement that worked.

My next task was to work with the group of teachers who formed the support group for the first year. Assisting me were seven teachers, one each period, assigned to the Writing Center as a duty period. These teachers came from the science, history, English, reading, home economics, and business departments. Together, we planned the opening of the center relying upon students trained as peer writing tutors. One hundred twenty-six tutors were trained in writing process during the month of September. In October, the doors opened, and we knew almost immediately that we had used the wrong model.

The peer tutors could not effectively work with students who knew nothing about writing process. Students who came for help wanted a quick fix: grammar and mechanics. There was confusion about the writing assignments. What had the classroom teachers actually assigned? As in the game of "whispering down the lane," the versions of the assignments we heard from the students were dramatically different from the actual assignments given by the teachers. Tracking down assignment information was time-consuming and, too often, did not give us enough information to help improve the student's writing.

A new vision was needed. If students could not tell us what the assignments were and if seeing each teacher to discuss the assignment and grading process was too time-consuming, what would work? And then the computers arrived. With the computers came the curious: first, the students; then, the teachers. We suspected we had something special, but how to use it was still a mystery. The students were fascinated with the computers; I was not because I wanted to emphasize writing. The connection eluded me.

Watching the tutors work with the Apples gave me an idea. If the teachers needed experience with writing process, which I understood, and if we needed students, then, why not bring entire classes to the center? I would teach the writing process while the teacher controlled the content. The student tutors would teach the students to use the word processors. We could all listen and react to student writings. The computers could print out clean copies that would be easily published. Everyone contributed, and everyone benefited.

The most significant benefit turned out to be using the computers for the publication of class anthologies. When teachers began to see their students' pride in the publication of their writings, they realized that tangible publications were more effective than grades in motivating students to revise and edit.

We developed a process for publishing a class anthology. After we collected a piece of writing from each class member, the class would brainstorm titles until one was found that summarized the contents of the anthology. The class artist would incorporate this title into the cover design. The manuscript was sent to our print shop where one copy for each student was printed. When the books came back, we put plastic binders on and gave a copy to each student in the class. On the day of distribution, we held "Great Authors' Parties" to celebrate each publication, inviting friends and family for public readings of the stories. *The Eclectic Anthology*, *Eyeballs in the Water*, *McCaskey Fables*, *Nursery News*, *My Wedding Book*, and *Blacks Who Built America* became some of our best sellers; everyone wanted a copy. Teachers became enthusiastic about teaching units that included writing because their students were eager to publish.

From this enthusiasm came the second summer workshops. The first Writers' Workshop anthology, *Page One*, contained only personal experience stories. In this workshop, I wanted the teachers to publish a second anthology, *Page Two*, that would be a blueprint and a resource for teachers who wanted to construct their own writing units. Teachers grouped themselves according to subject areas so they could share ideas about content while styling individual writing to learn experiences. Teachers practiced all the techniques that they would later implement in their own classrooms: learning logs, multiple drafts, conferences, revising and editing, and response groups. Each teacher acted as scribe, shared a personal experience story, and constructed a plan for using writing as a process during the next year. Then, they scheduled time in the Writing Center to implement that plan.

Page Two consisted of three parts: a learning log detailing concepts covered in each workshop session; personal experience stories; and units of writing that required the teachers' classes to come to the Writing Center the following year to write, revise, and publish a classroom anthology. What did these McCaskey teachers design for their students? In biology, Cyndy Dinsmore had her students imagine that they were a McDonald's hamburger so they could describe the journey through the digestive system. June Schwar, who supervises the Child Development Center, had her child care students publish a parents' newsletter four times a year. The family relationships instructor, Mary Shawkey, had her students produce two reference books: *Families in Crisis: Where to Turn in Times of Need* and *My Wedding Book: A Guide to Planning a Wedding*. In Jo Stokes's math class, students kept learning logs, analyzing their progress as math students. George Resh's local history class compiled interviews with World War II veterans. In a class with high absenteeism, Fran Keller used scribes to record and read aloud the concepts and assignments from the previous day. Tom Wentzel had his remedial reading students publish high school "survival guides" that were sent to the junior highs.

As teachers began to use what they had learned at the Writers' Workshops, more class time was spent talking about, editing, and revising one piece of writing instead of just producing larger numbers of papers. In slowing down the number of papers and by concentrating on the development of one paper, teachers showed students how writing could be improved. The computers became an integral part of that process. Word processing facilitated revision and allowed nearly painless publication of student writings. With ten Apple IIe's, groups of students composing at the terminals formed spontaneous collaborative learning groups.

Because of the increasing demands during the second year, ten more Apple IIe's were added. Now, individuals could work on their writings but with less collaboration than occurred at shared terminals. Student writers still wanted feedback, and conferencing with writing became the norm—not just at the terminals but in every corner of the center.

By the mid 1980s, we had become simply another part of the school. Students took the Writing Center for granted and were surprised to find out that not all schools had one. Student publications appeared everywhere: in the in-school suspension room, the library, the principal's office, and the community. We believed that we had created a state-of-the-art center, but we could not have foreseen the changes the future would bring.

The Middle Years: The Years of Acceptance

Based upon the success at McCaskey, writing centers moved into the libraries of the four junior high schools. When the writing centers opened in the junior highs, students became familiar with word processors. This, in turn, brought a trend toward students' composing directly at the terminals and away from paper and pencil composing. Some students felt composing with paper and pencil slowed their thinking processes. Having writing centers in the junior high shifted McCaskey's emphasis from teaching beginning word processing to spending more time on development and revision. About this time, two writing activities appeared that would refine the way we worked with student writers.

I remember that it was a hot day. The Writing Center has no air conditioning, and in the September heat the west windows baked the room and all of us. Sitting at my desk, I turned to see Fran Keller, a friend and colleague, walking toward me. "I'm teaching paperbacks," she announced. She was not happy. "How do you *teach* paperbacks?"

Without too much thought, I said, "Have them write a paperback." We looked at each other and realized the potential of using the Writing Center for a full semester's work rather than the usual five-day visit. That simple exchange has resulted in a six-year, twelve-semester discussion about the most effective way of having students become writers.

So, what happened when we asked a group of non-college-bound urban teenagers to write a paperback? Like publishers or editors, we dealt with many real issues of writing: appropriate language choices, PG-13 ratings, character development, setting, plot, symbolism, and dialogue. We learned that there had to be some limits. If we set no limits, some students would mirror in their writings only the violent, sexual behavior seen in the media.

Although early in each semester some students resisted, we have never had a student who refused to write a paperback. A bigger dilemma was that many of Fran's students could not stop writing in time to publish. It was not unusual for students to write fifty-page stories; it was not unusual for them to spend all their spare time in the Writing Center living in their writings; it was not unusual for them to continue writing long after the class was over and the final grades had been given. As teachers, Fran and I needed only to get out of their way, to give up control, which was harder than it sounds.

When students believed that they had ownership of their writing, there was a writing explosion. It happened every semester even with some of our most reluctant writers as they lost their writers' blocks. They also loved to read each other's stories. Sometimes, it sounded as if they were talking about families.

"How is Kayla? Did she make up with Jake?"
"No. He left her for Marly."
"Good. I didn't like Kayla. She lied too much."

Part of the difference in this writing activity was that the students worked for a whole semester on one piece of writing that evolved over an eighteen-week period. So that there would be no requirement to force closure, we decided not to publish their writings in a class anthology, but to call them works in progress. This was a critical decision, a departure from the Writing Center's philosophy. Taking away the publication requirement has lessened the responsibility of assisting students in extensive editing. To work with a student to standardize mechanics and spelling for publication was a massive job and required too much of the student's time away from writing, although some students requested help. We stressed proper paragraphing for direct quotations, and we had students use the spell checker. Creating a paperback enabled students to feel a connection with professional writers by experiencing firsthand the decisions and struggles a professional writer encounters. In addition, this activity turns writers into more discerning and analytic readers.

Not publishing the students' paperbacks gave me some insight: all students' writings were works in progress; and publication, while an important element, was not the only goal in the Writing Center. Fran asked one of her students, "Did you ever expect that you would be able to write this much?"

"Certainly," she replied, "I was just waiting for the opportunity."

Another English teacher, Andrea King, used writing in all her courses. When she first brought her classes to the Writing Center, I was impressed with the independence of her students, particularly since her class size was over thirty. I noticed she used a class plan that communicated her expectations and showed them the concrete steps in writing process.

We have adapted her class plan for other classes. The following is a sample:

1. Read your draft to the class.
2. Type and revise your draft at the computer.

3. Print your draft. Mark it **Draft 1**.
4. Read your draft to another student. Listen to his/her draft.
5. Write your comments about his/her draft on the conference sheet and return the conference sheet to the writer.
6. Revise your draft. Mark it **Draft 2**. (There should be some significant changes. If not, see a teacher.)
7. On Draft 2, underline the changes you have made.
8. Have a conference with a teacher for final editing. Have the teacher initial draft 2.
9. Use the computer's dictionary.
10. Print out two copies:
    Print one draft quality, double-spaced (for Mrs. King to grade)
    Print one letter quality, single-spaced (to be published in a class anthology)
11. By Friday, paperclip these together and give to Mrs. King:
    Your handwritten draft (on top)
    Your conference sheet filled out by another student
    Your drafts 1 and 2 (underlined and initialed)
    Your final drafts: one single-spaced and one double-spaced

The weekly plan generally follows the sequence above; however, the conference sheets are specific to the writing assignments. These weekly plans make the students independent learners who no longer ask, "What do I do now?"

Expanding Andrea's idea to research papers, particularly in Ann Pinsker's sophomore American Cultures classes and Carroll Staub's Global Studies classes, we concentrated on thesis statements. On the conference sheet, the student reader must identify the writer's thesis statement and find at least three supporting concepts. Students discover the construction of thesis statements by listening to others.

Although we do not use these plans and conference sheets with all classes, I think the classes that use this process accomplish more because the teacher's expectations are clear from the beginning of the class, and the structure is sequenced logically and understandably for every student.

Believing that written expectations facilitate the transition from the classroom to the Writing Center, I developed a checklist for teachers to explain what to do with their classes before coming to the Writing Center and to explain what to expect when they get there.

What to Do Before Bringing Your Classes to the Writing Center

For the Writing Center:

- If you are planning to come to the Writing Center this year, schedule as early in the 1991–92 school year as possible. As of June 1991, there are only four weeks unscheduled for the next school year.
- Discuss the assignment with Mrs. Beck, including any special needs you may anticipate such as a minilesson on documentation, special computing requirements, and so on.
- Give a written copy of your assignment. This should include the due date and the criteria for grading (if you are grading this piece).
- Indicate if you want your class to produce a publication such as a class anthology, letters, contest entries, college essays, and so on.

With your classes:

- Conference with students to make sure they have the necessary information before they come to the center.
- Discuss your deadlines for your students' writings.
- Explain about the Writing Center's hours before and after school. No pass is needed for these hours. If students want to come from a study, they must get a pass from the Writing Center before or after school.
- Check to see that every student has a piece of writing, a first draft. You may want to collect those drafts on the Friday preceding your visit to the center.

What to Expect in the Writing Center

Here is a basic plan of action. If you have special requirements, we can plan your days to suit your writing unit. Just let us know how we may best help you and your students.

- Part of the first day will be spent in a large group planning session. Each student will read a portion of writing (one- to two-minute limit) and tell where the writing is going.
- The remainder of the week will be spent word processing, sharing writing with small groups, revising, and individual conferences for editing.
- Students who have not finished may schedule time in the center during a study or before/after school by obtaining a pass from Mrs. Beck before school from 7:15 until 7:50 or after school until 4:00

Another idea that works is what I call "conference progression." It started in an English as a Second Language class where some students who are new to our country lacked confidence when using English. I have the student read to me, listening carefully so I can think about the content. Then, I read the writing back to the writer, choosing one or two details to discuss with the student, who will then make a few additions, elaborating just a bit more. After printing out a revised draft, the student sees another teacher who repeats the process. Although it sounds painstakingly slow, our goal was to help the student gain confidence and independence by taking small steps with different teachers; it was not our goal to "correct" everything.

Although this conference progression seems obvious to us now, we teachers did not understand the importance of collaboration in the beginning. This team approach to helping students was the most significant result of working together in the Writing Center during the middle years. We learned how interdependent we teachers had become. We needed to share ideas about writing and about students. The students benefited from seeing us working together as a team.

Vision for the Future

Just when we thought twenty computers were enough, the center experienced a surge of activity. More teachers wanted more class time for their students. Students, on the other hand, having experienced the ease of writing with word processors, wanted more individual time using the computers. They were now coming to the high school with better keyboarding skills and more knowledge about software.

Enter the networks. What were ten Apples became twenty Apples. What were twenty Apples became forty IBM PS/2s on two local area networks each run by an IBM Model 80, which manages the Novell system and the I-Class software. Separate from the two networks is a desktop publishing center, loaded with Pagemaker software and complete with a scanner and laser printer, which produces the school newspaper in camera-ready layouts. The newspaper staff makes use of our "technology to go," three Radio Shack laptop computers. These laptops move the Writing Center throughout the school.

With the arrival of the networks, we outgrew our original one-third of the old library and moved to the other two-thirds. We also outgrew our old schedule. From an 8:00 A.M. to 3:00 P.M. day, we changed our opening to 7:15 in the morning and our closing to 4:00 in the afternoon.

The expanded hours allowed us to accommodate a new tutoring program that runs both semesters and complements the school's initiative to use principles of the Johnson and Johnson Cooperative Learning Center of the University of Minnesota. During nine weeks of each semester, approximately sixty Millersville University education majors come to the Writing Center to tutor individuals and small groups. Volunteers also come from the community, from Harrisburg Area Community College, from Franklin & Marshall College, and from McCaskey to tutor our students.

We continue to schedule classes for writing activities. Fran Keller's paperback class has just finished the semester's work with five students still writing their paperbacks into the second semester—after the class ended. Joan Kochel's tenth-grade general English classes have published individual family books with unique covers and pages for photographs. One student dedicated her book to her newborn son. Alison Carzola's Spanish classes published magazines and newspapers in Spanish. In his Advanced Placement composition class, Frank Gray formed collaborative groups that researched, wrote, and presented material on topics such as "restructuring schools" and "gender differences." Each student in the collaborative group was responsible for a specific part of the final project. Business teacher Donna Freeseman had her students researching their individually chosen business professions to discover if they want to pursue a specific career. Sociology teacher John Valori had his students write a present and future obituary for his death and dying unit. Health teacher Frank Albrecht had his students publish books entitled "Where I Find Meaning in My Life." He pasted a photograph of the class on each cover.

A new writing assignment involves students' writing their college admission essays for Kathy Novosel's Collegiate Power Reading class. College-bound juniors and seniors write their college essays in Kathy's class and come to the Writing Center for additional feedback. Kathy explains, "Writing the college essay is unlike any other writing assignment our students face. Their personalities, their outlooks, and their perspectives will be judged by total strangers. These strangers can grant or withhold a very important prize—admission to the college of their choice. While this is a wonderful opportunity to show themselves as unique individuals, so much more than the sum of their cumulative GPA and SAT scores, it is also a daunting task for student writers. The Writing Center defuses the anxiety. Supportive adult 'strangers' and peers react in a constructive way to these critical writings. The opportunity to gauge the reactions of others before mailing these essays is an invaluable benefit. The Writing Center is an indispensable part of this very practical writing assignment."

Besides scheduling writing classes, teachers are making more extensive use of the center's network capabilities. Because of the network, Tom Wentzel could bring in his remedial reading class to experience a text and graphics computer adventure game called "King's Quest IV." As part of a unit on folktales, his students played, "King's Quest IV: Perils of Rosella" by Sierra. Having been taught the elements of the folktales, the students came to the Writing Center to experience these elements in this interactive game. In five days' time, students who were reluctant readers or who were using English as a second language became independent readers in their quest to "save King Graham." After playing the game, which takes more than five class periods, students will write a folktale of their own, demonstrating their understanding of the traditional elements.

At the same time that Wentzel's students were in the back room kissing frogs or stealing the witch's eye, students from Charlotte Spinella's psychology class were using "Psychology on a Disk" to do a shaping experiment: training a computer rat to exert more pressure on a lever by rewarding with or withholding a food reinforcement. Her students must write about their learning process when using this software.

Having seen the success of collaboration in the Writing Center, teachers and administrators continue to seek other ways to use these principles. This year McCaskey has become part of the Coalition of Essential Schools (CES) coordinated by Brown University. In CES, writing will become a strong component because evaluation is based on performance and portfolios.

The Writing Center continues to be a laboratory where students can use technology to write, but the human element remains most important. It must continue to be a place where students receive encouragement and support. It must remain a place where students can discover their strengths and their talents. Our student writers, anticipating a larger audience for their writings, collaborate with teachers, peer tutors, and each other to polish their works; our current generation of writers expects this process. Their vision will guide the future.

Acknowledgments

Response group: Donna Freeseman, Debbie Gardner, Frank Gray, Fran Keller, Andrea King, Kathy Novosel, Ann Pinsker, Mary Ann Rudy, Gloria Spangler, Carroll Staub, Tom Wentzel.

14

Tiger Talking Time: Writing Across the Curriculum at Saluda High School

Gloria Caldwell, Melissa Deloach, Lyn Zalusky Mueller, and Edwin C. Epps

The Idea (Gloria Caldwell)

This year, as in the past two years, Writing Across the Curriculum (WAC) has been the focus at Saluda High School in South Carolina. Each morning at exactly 11:05 after the Pledge of Allegiance and the announcements for the day, a silence descends on the classrooms. Students and teachers open their neon-bright journals for "Tiger Talking Time," a fifteen-minute time slot named after the school mascot built into every day for recording ideas and concerns in personal journals.

This free-writing time is one of the components of Saluda's emphasis on WAC. On August 19 when school began, each student in the fourth-period class received a bound book containing one hundred blank pages and one page of simple directions. Students were told in these directions that they are free to write whatever they like in their journal since no one will read the writing unless the student chooses to share it. The teachers keep the booklets in file boxes bought for each classroom.

Every week one fourth-period class chooses a topic for the entire student body to use as a writing prompt for the following Wednesday. These prompts are timely and thought-provoking, reflecting the concerns and problems that teenagers face today. On the other four days students simply write about anything they choose. Should a student fill up the journal, he or she may request that more pages be added, and many students have had supplemental pages added to their books. As a means of sharing and publishing the writing generated in these journals, each week on a rotating basis fourth-period classes have an opportunity to share pieces of writing from their journals with the entire school.

Generally, student response to Tiger Talking Time has been positive. Many view their writing time as a way to focus what is in their heads and, as one student said, "to get rid of frustrations and go through the day easier." Another said that he thought it would be good to "later on in life . . . look back at the record I kept."

A second component of WAC is the use of writing as an aid for student learning in every curriculum area. All of the forty-five teachers at Saluda High School use writing as an instructional tool in their classrooms; during the year according to a schedule, each department publishes student writings in the magazine *Tiger Talk*.

The Context: Test Scores and Faculty Development

Saluda High School is a comprehensive public high school with a student body of approximately 560 students in a small town in a rural, primarily agricultural South Carolina county with a total population of 16,357, two-thirds of whom are white. In 1987 the percentage of students at Saluda High School meeting the state standard on the writing sample of the state exit exam was 77.8 percent; in 1988 the percentage dropped to 77.5, and in 1989 it dropped to 74.8. In the fall of 1989, after examining this decline in student writing scores, Saluda High School decided to begin a WAC project to try to raise student and teacher awareness of the importance of writing and thus eventually raise student achievement in all areas. As a result of this schoolwide effort, the 1990—91 tenth-grade class passed the writing portion of the exit exam with 91.3 percent at or above standards. This means that of the 115 sophomores taking the exit exam for the first time, 105 students met or exceeded the standard and only 10 failed to meet the standard. It also means that in only two years' time, the percentage of students at Saluda High School who met the minimum writing standard *increased from just under 75 percent to over 90 percent.*

In September 1989, Lyn Zalusky Mueller, director of the Writing Improvement Network (a teacher assistance project), spent two days in two of the classrooms at the high school conducting classroom demonstrations and discussing problems teachers were encountering, particularly with their reluctant writers. In November, Saluda High School conducted a survey of its students, teachers, and parents to solicit community input into its WAC project. This survey revealed among other findings that 43 percent of social studies students, 65 percent of science students, 76 percent of math students, 70 percent of vocational students, and 79 percent of physical education students *never* "write a composition for the purpose of learning information about the content." In December, partially as a result of this survey, Lyn was invited to conduct a WAC workshop for the entire faculty.

The Consultant's Perspective (Lyn Zalusky Mueller)

It started off like every other staff development day.

Teachers were milling around, not very anxious to get started. Most of the teachers at least recognized me — I had been hanging around the school a bit. I had even taught two days in the school, although no one really seemed to notice (except of course the teachers whose classes I had taught). The school was applying for a grant for a writing lab to help their students. It was an impressive grant — they were all very hopeful. At least the English teachers were.

Most of the English teachers sat at the front tables in the library that day. After all, *this* was something they were interested in!

I knew the principal was more than interested. In a previous conversation he had told me about a piece that his son had written about him several years earlier and published in their award-winning high school literary magazine. "My Father, My Principal" it was called. "There's just something about publishing," he tried to convince me. "It just does something to kids to see their work in print. And, you know what? That article did something to me, too."

Since a great many of the pieces in the literary magazine were written about the local community, the principal seemed (perhaps without knowing it) to already have a good, down-to-earth, real-life understanding that writing and improving writing don't come from additional skill sheets. He was also facing the recent results from the statewide basic skills tests that showed that many of his students were not going to receive diplomas unless they could adequately demonstrate their abilities on the writing portion of the state exit examination.

"The whole school has to be involved," he told me. "There's just no other way." So we decided to start with staff development for the whole faculty. After all, the WIN (Writing Improvement Network) project had been funded to assist teachers and schools with their writing programs. However, it seemed like we were proposing to water a garden for just five minutes a day and expecting a healthy crop to flourish.

By the afternoon of the in-service, teachers were reading and writing together in small groups — but sparks weren't flying. It wasn't until I asked the groups to respond to a provocative quote found at the National Aquarium in Baltimore — "Without firing a shot, we may kill one-fifth of all species on this planet in the next twenty years" — that things got interesting. As the teachers in each group read their reactions aloud, heads nodded and mutual concern appeared in their eyes. Then one of the science teachers read his. To say he didn't agree with the others would be an understatement. People began to fidget in their seats. Then they started making huffing noises, like horses impatient to get out of their stalls. Finally, the "oh no's" and "ah come on's" started to erupt from the group. Before I knew it there was a knock-down, drag-out verbal fight going on. I let it go. At last, I sighed to myself, something meaningful.

In January I met with the teachers in small groups to address specific concerns in their respective content areas. In the next session the English teachers barked—"It's *we* against *they*" (meaning the teachers in the content areas weren't doing much for the cause of helping their remedial writers). In the second session the problems seemed overwhelming. Teacher comments were typical but genuine: "What can we do?" "I wish we could get those kids to write." "But how?" "Publishing would help them so much. They need so much help."

We all knew that the purpose of these WAC in-services was to involve the whole school in helping those kids write, write better, and care about their writing. During the final session an industrial arts teacher pointed his index finger at me and said, "I hate to burst your bubble, lady, but my kids can't even write a complete sentence!" Quietly, one special education teacher responded, "You know, my students publish a class newsletter about what they're doing in school for their parents. If my kids can do it, can't those kids?"

That one comment started a smoldering revolution. From my perspective, it was at that point that the teachers took ownership. Now I could switch from in-service person to scribe of their ideas. I knew that somewhere in that comment was a solution to the "those kids" problems and to the we/they dilemma that many schools face. As I met with each group and proposed the previous group's thoughts, the publication idea began to form and snowball. By the end of the day, we had an across-the-subject-areas committee, an idea for a publication, and a commitment from the principal to cover the typing and publishing expenses of whatever form this publication was going to take.

I was excited that day when I left the school. But as I drove the ninety miles back to my house, the industrial arts teacher's comment haunted me. I couldn't figure out how they were going to come together, how I was going to help them—or even if I should.

The Teachers' Perspective (Missy Deloach and Gloria Caldwell)

From Lyn Mueller all teachers learned that English teachers could teach the writing process but could not give students enough writing opportunities to perfect the process. As a result of the workshop, a committee of teachers was organized to create a schoolwide project emphasizing WAC, and a pilot issue of *Tiger Talk* was published in May 1990. This magazine contained a sampling of the various types of writing produced by students as they used writing to learn content in all courses.

During the school year 1990−1991 Saluda High continued its emphasis on WAC. First, consultants were brought in to work with teachers individually in building writing to learn activities into their lessons. As a result, five issues of *Tiger Talk* were published with each department responsible for one month's magazine: English and French in November; science in January; social studies in February; vocational and physical education in April; and fine arts, special education, and math in May.

All teachers chose for publication three samples of writing from each class they taught. Each department was also responsible for the magazine cover, which was created by a student. In addition, some students also submitted related artwork to be used in the magazines. The magazines were each typed, edited, and designed by several teachers. Although the covers were printed professionally, the magazines were simply copied on the Xerox machine at school. Then they were assembled by students and teachers.

Unfortunately, this process was not without its pitfalls. Several teachers had to be reminded by the principal, a firm supporter of the project, to submit writing samples. Also, assembling the magazine took away from instructional time. Of course, the copying of the magazines took a toll on the school machine as well. Since only a few teachers were involved in the actual typing, editing, and layout of the five magazines, the task became overwhelming, with publication deadlines having to be extended. As a matter of fact, the last magazine was not completed until June.

However, the magazines received much recognition from the community, parents, and students. The publications had a vast audience because they were mailed to each student's home and to businesses in Saluda County. Every teacher received the magazines to display in the classroom.

Because of this recognition and improved exit exam writing scores, the faculty and administration agreed to proceed with the WAC project in 1991−92. This year the project also received special funding through REACH, the Rural Education Alliance for Collaborative Humanities. With a grant of $3,000, "A Tiger Talks: Writing Across the Curriculum" became the schoolwide REACH project.

In 1991−92, the project had three components. The first component was *Tiger Talk*, the magazine itself. According to a set schedule, each department again published student writings in a magazine of fifty-two pages. Each teacher now selects two pieces from each class for publication, and summarizes the activity that generated the writing.

Subject-area writing activities were thoughtful and varied, and student writing showed a high degree of originality. Math teacher Louise Sanders gave her students the assignment to "use the unit vocabulary in a creative manner." Student Brandy Miller took up the challenge:

> Tiffany has a 1985 Mustang G.T. 5.0 she wants to sell. She placed an ad in the Saluda paper and it read as follows:
> I have a 1985 Mustang GT 5.0 for sale. The car's fuel economy, or miles per gallon, is 28 miles. The depreciation would be $9,600. The variable costs, such as gas, oil, tires, on the average are about $1,106 per year. The fixed costs, such as insurance, license, etc., on the average are about $4,258 per year. As for maintenance, it comes to around $1,000 per year. The car is in excellent condition.

Angie Shealy applied her talents as a poet to Joshlyn E. von Szalatnay's computer programming class to produce the following verse about popular software for the IBM PS/2:

Wonderful Link Way

"Click"
1023 KB OK
"Press enter to continue"
"Enter your user ID:"
Shealy A
"Enter your password"
#@
"Computer Programming One"
Let's see. What to do today?
"Link Way Version 2.01 for the PS/2"
"Loading Program"
Where's the mouse?
"Link Way Program"
"Start Link Way with default start options"
Which one? "Getting Started, Link Way Tutorial,
Link Way Tools, Useful Buttons, or Exit Link Way"?
I know ... Link Way Tools
"Link Way Paint Program"
Waiting, waiting
"Picture, Open"
No, that's not it.
"Pictures, New"
"New Picture Name"
**$*#
"Click"
Now ... Let's draw!

Subject-area teachers often used writing to help students master essential processes by generalizing from observed examples or explaining key operations. Physical science teacher Deborah Minick involved her class in this activity: "After reading and solving density word problems, students described the step-by-step process of how to determine the density of an object." Student Jamie Minick responded this way:

> You want to find the density of a block of wood or even a round object. This is how you find density.
>
> Using a ruler, measure the length, width, and height of the block. Next take the measurements and multiply them. Now you have your volume. Weigh the block. Now divide the mass by the volume and get your density.
>
> To find the density of a small, round object, take a graduated cylinder and put 25 ml of water in it. Next drop the object in the water. Write down that measurement. Then subtract 25 ml from that measurement. That is your volume. Then weigh the object. Next divide the mass by the volume. This equals your density. This tells you how to find the density of a block and a round object.

Another way teachers in areas other than English at Saluda High School used writing as a learning tool was to relate subject-area content to students' own lives — to make it relevant, in other words. For instance, personal health teacher Patsy Rhodes's students were studying life spans of America's aging population and how our older adults were treated and cared for. A discussion came up about how some older adults act youthful and that every young person has an older adult that they admire. Students were given ten minutes of class time to write about their favorite or most youthful older person. Students shared their writings with the class.

This is what Kendrick Stevens shared about his grandmother Mama Minnie:

> The most youthful, older person I knew was my grandmother. She died a couple of years back, leaving behind her a family of twelve. She inspired us all and found time during her working hours to be with her family.
>
> My grandmother was 72 when she died, but just because she's dead doesn't mean she's gone. Her influence is still with us. Along with her hard work and dedication, she was wise. She always told me, "If you are going to do something, do it right the first time and you won't have to do it again." I'll always remember those words.
>
> Mama Minnie, I won't forget the time you spent with me and just for me. For you I will try to do things right the first time.

Other examples could be given, but the point is simply this: Once they committed themselves to utilizing writing as a strategy to promote learning, the faculty at Saluda High School had little difficulty in deriving specific writing activities for their individual subjects.

This year a journalism student volunteered to be the editor of each *Tiger Talk* under the direction of teachers Bela Herlong, Gloria Caldwell, and Melissa Deloach. This student types the writing samples and lays out the pages. Art students design a cover for each magazine and are in the process of creating a clip-art book to be used for design of the magazines throughout the year. With the $3,000 REACH grant, the publications will be printed professionally instead of on the school copier.

The second component of the WAC project is the free-writing period, which began in August when students entered school. Each student during the Tiger Talking Time chooses from his or her journal a selection of writing to share with an audience. The student copies the selection on a prepared page. Then students read their selections aloud to the class, and the class votes on which selection should be spotlighted on the bulletin board. There was much initial opposition to this component of the WAC project because a number of teachers mistakenly felt that it would require extra time and effort on their part. Therefore, the media specialist provided each fourth-period teacher with colorful pages and banners for the display boards.

Display-board writing was often personal and informal, but it was also heartfelt and reflective, the kind of writing that reveals the writer making meaning of experience. Melissa, for example, wrote "Forever in My Heart," a poem and prose piece about her grandmother:

> I sit at my desk, thinking of the past.
> Eight years ago, yesterday, they came to get me with the bad news.
> "She's dead!" My Grandma! My heart!
> How can I fend without her? The teardrops roll, but they cannot wash away my pain.
> No longer can I hug her, or feel the wrinkles and cracks of skin tarnished with age and the task of time.
> No more walks along the creek, holding her gentle hand in mine, as my long, blond hair, as it was then, blew in the cool summer breeze.
> No more games of her youth. No more soft kisses on my forehead.
> No more of her praise for my sweetness and good accomplishments.
> No more Grandma!
> How have I lived my life without her this long? She dwells in my memory.
> She hugs me in my thoughts. I can feel her warm skin, her simple kisses, her joy, her love.
> It's all there, deep inside my mind, and forever in my heart.
> I'll always love you Grandma!

One measure of the support given the "Tiger Talking Time" project by the entire school staff is the principal's key participation as an audience for the display boards. Each piece of student work displayed received Bill Whitfield's personal mark of approbation: his rubber-stamped message, "I saw your work today!! Mr. Whit," always accompanied by the handwritten addition of the date he read each piece.

The third component of the project is to have consultants once again work with teachers in all subject areas in using writing to learn content. That aspect of the project has not yet been realized this year because of a very busy school calendar.

Since 1989, Saluda High School has made every effort to permeate its atmosphere with the importance of skillful, effective writing as a part of every student's academic achievement; the results have been encouraging. Of the 111 eligible seniors this year (1991) taking the exit exam, only four did not pass the writing portion; and as explained above (see "The Context"), tenth-grade writing scores improved by fifteen percentage points. Those scoring below standard will have several additional opportunities to pass the exam before they graduate.

In commenting on the impact of the school's emphasis on WAC, Gay Mullinax, school guidance counselor, stated, "In my position as a counselor, I am quite involved with testing, both with administration and interpretation. I have seen a remarkable difference in the students' attitudes and abilities with regard to the writing portion of the exit exam. The phenomenal success of this year's juniors and seniors on the writing subtest, in my opinion, is directly related to the positive impact being made by our writing across the curriculum program. The value of this teaching concept should ultimately be reflected in grades and other tests as well."

In November the South Carolina Department of Education informed the school that it had been selected as one of four high schools in the state to be reviewed for recognition by the Writing Improvement Coordinating Council as having an exemplary writing program for 1992. In April 1992 the council officially designated Saluda High School as the site of an exemplary writing program.

Why it Worked (Ed Epps)

To many the need for WAC seems obvious. We have students write about what they are learning because in so doing they learn more, not only about the content they are studying but about their own learning process and, ultimately, themselves as well. Progressive educators since at least the time of John Dewey and, more recently, many English and language arts teachers in all parts of the country have internalized this belief to such an extent that it is a given in their classroom praxis.

To others, however, especially teachers of such traditionally skills- and content-centered disciplines as mathematics, science, and even physical education, this truth is not self-evident. Non-English teachers often worry that "adding" writing to their own lessons will necessitate eliminating some essential knowledge in their already overcrowded curriculum. Some also worry that their administration or their colleagues are trying to turn them into — heaven forbid — English teachers. Both concerns are natural enough, and at Saluda High School both concerns resulted in some initial resistance to the WAC project. Over time, though, most resistance abated and some of those who had been initially skeptical eventually became enthusiastic supporters of the project.

What things made the difference? For one, teachers were involved early on in the planning and implementation of all project activities. For another, Bill Whitfield, the principal, was involved as instructional leader from the outset; his commitment of local funds and his gentle prodding of a few reluctant staff members made a significant difference in the ultimate success of the project. Too, the consultants from the Writing Improvement Network were perceived as *colleagues* with valuable insights based upon actual classroom practice rather than as outsiders isolated in an ivory-towered office somewhere in the abstract realms of academe.

A final factor contributing to the success of the Saluda High School WAC project was teachers' personal realization that writing in their subject areas was making a difference in their students' learning. Writing is one way to achieve both student involvement and integration of content. In responding to an informal request for comments about the program, teachers in all subject areas at Saluda High School expressed numerous benefits of the WAC initiative. Comments included the following:

> As a teacher of learning disabled students, I have discovered that the daily writing time has been an outlet for my students' emotions. They are able to express their feelings about school problems on paper thus avoiding some verbal or even physical conflicts with their peers or teachers. (Joyce S. Berry)

> As a United States History teacher, I have found writing to be an invaluable tool in my classes. Through writing, my students can actually become historical characters. They can live their lives and dream their dreams. History comes alive. The students learn and actually enjoy learning! (Patricia D. Cockrell)

> Child care students have had to keep journals as a part of their graded effort while working in their classroom centers. I have noticed an improvement in these journals as they described details of what their children did, how they felt, etc. I attribute this to our writing emphasis this year. (Linda L. Padgett)

Teacher comments were not universally positive, of course. A special education teacher observed that "an every-day writing task became boring and nonmotivational [to these students] as the year progressed" and that "I'm not sure their skills improved to a great extent" since they didn't receive "corrections and reinforcement instantly." Another teacher noted, "Students get bored with [the] idea of writing—need variety of ideas to write from Science, Phys. ed., English, history, etc." Even this teacher, however, admitted, "It needs some refinement but we have a great start"; and only these two teachers expressed reservations of any kind about the project.

Most teachers shared the opinion of Scarlett E. Hardin that "[t]he writing across the curriculum [project] at Saluda High has been a tremendous enabler for teachers, allowing us to encourage expression and creativity while giving the students an arena in which they define the boundaries and, as a result, feel comfortable in exploring the territory of their own abilities." Linda Bodie agreed: "Our writing program has been a wonderful addition to our school. . . . The warm glow generated by [students'] success in writing in various content areas pervaded our halls and classes as we saw a new desire kindled within the students—a desire to share their ideas."

At Saluda High School the principal and faculty committed themselves to the belief that students would learn more, better, faster through writing and then proceeded to develop a set of procedures and activities to integrate writing into all areas of the curriculum. The result has been greater student involvement in learning, increased mastery of content, widespread community enthusiasm for a series of anthologies of student writing, and expanded participation by the community in the life of the school.

15

Writing Across the Curriculum at the McCallie School

Pamela B. Farrell-Childers with Peter LaRochelle, Cissy May, Catherine Neuhardt-Minor, Lance Nickel, and David B. Perkinson

A Plan for Change at McCallie (Pamela B. Farrell-Childers)

An endowed chair of composition dedicated to writing across the curriculum (WAC) at an independent boys' school in Tennessee? It sounds highly unlikely, yet innovative, even logical. A family by the name of Caldwell believed that such a position needed the commitment of money to make it a reality. As Hacker Caldwell said, "I had learned [at the University of Virginia Business School] that the primary value of improved writing was clearer thinking with a secondary value that it improved my critical ability to read." So in 1991 the Caldwell Chair of Composition became a reality at the McCallie School, an independent day/boarding school of over seven hundred boys in Chattanooga, Tennessee.

The first job of the new chair was to design a three-year strategic WAC plan for McCallie. The two most important concepts of the plan were the creation of a writing center and the implementation of a WAC retreat for faculty. In the fall of 1991 the Writing Center officially opened for students and staff. Designed as a place where there is a reverence for writing, the Writing Center has become a hub for the composing of language and a writing resource for students and staff. With fifteen Macintosh Classic computers and three DeskWriter printers available for student use, the double room offers a writing workshop

Figure 15−1
Caldwell Writing Center Floor plan

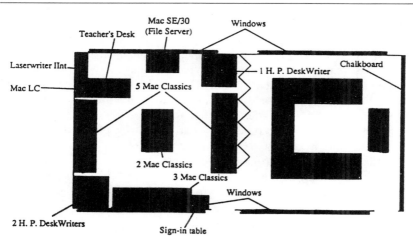

environment plus a computer area for writing with the word processor (Figure 15−1). Students and staff across the disciplines use the facility for work with specific writing concerns, writing to learn activities, peer editing, collaborative writing projects, class writing workshops, and individual or personal writing projects (college application essays, grant proposals, etc.).

The first WAC weekend retreat with Art Young as facilitator, held at Cohutta Lodge in the mountains of Georgia, included fifteen members of the faculty from all subject areas. With a focus on writing to learn, Art encouraged participants to develop writing activities to use in their classes. (See essay by Cissy May.) This retreat became the beginning of ongoing WAC faculty workshops and collaborative writing projects throughout the school year. Individual training sessions continue, and retreats are planned for future years until all faculty have attended at least one. Through the faculty newsletter, teachers have an opportunity to share WAC activities from classes in all disciplines, and regular articles keep them informed of guest artists and other opportunities to participate in WAC. For example, each December the faculty presents a poetry reading in the school art gallery. Teachers in all subject areas have participated.

As teachers begin to share the writing activities that work for them, the Writing Center will create files of lessons as resources for other teachers. Teachers and students are changing their focus to reflect writing to think, learn, and know; therefore, the curriculum has begun to reflect those changes. For the future, we plan to involve the entire faculty in writing, create a McCallie Press to publish professional materials and student works, increase the amount of technical equipment, continue emphasizing the role of guest artists across the disciplines, and improve student and faculty writing, thinking, and learning.

What makes the program at McCallie unique, however, is the faculty. They are willing to take risks, learn from each other, and grow as professionals. On any given day, a student may walk into the Writing Center and see teachers in all disciplines working on pieces of writing at the computer, reading and responding to each other's writing, or planning writing activities for their classes. This modeling of the importance of writing is something that cannot be planned; it cannot be staged, and it cannot exist without teachers who believe in the importance of writing across all disciplines. The selections that follow reflect the first-year activities of the program by such faculty members and demonstrate the possibilities for writing in all subject areas.

Writing and Learning Chemistry (Cissy May)

After attending the WAC retreat, I was eager to try some ideas in my classroom. One of the concepts I learned was letting students write about problems they were having in class, then having other students write back with a solution to the problem. Since we had just completed the factor label system of problem solving that always seems to be a difficult concept for most students, I chose this method for several reasons. First, students were more receptive to help from their peers than from their teacher early in the school year. Second, if students could identify and key in on their problem, they had a much easier time solving the problem. Third, students thought they were alone; but through this activity, all realized that everyone was having some difficulty with the concept. I found that most students took the exercise seriously even though it was not graded. Also, it was a wonderful confidence builder. As I read each of the answers, I added other comments that I thought might help the student (Figure 15—2).

At the end of the semester, I tried another writing assignment in which I asked students to evaluate different aspects of the course. I received some very frank and helpful replies about problem areas as well as information about what students liked about the class, demonstrations, lab work, and help sessions. After compiling the information, I gave the students the results so that they could get an overview of what others felt. This activity made the students feel that they had some ownership in the class and increased their awareness of how other students felt on the classroom issues. Accelerated students don't always realize that some of their classmates spend twice as much time on homework as they do. Students who don't like labs need to understand

Figure 15-2
Writing to Learn Chemistry

Factor   Labeling   (Phil Hudson)

Getting the conversion factors mixed up + when I'm deciding what to find in the problem how do I tell if it is A factor: for example $\frac{11 miles}{1 gallon}$?

$$? \longrightarrow \times \quad \frac{km}{10^9 nm}$$

Do not know what goes here + how do i tell if it is a fraction or not.

Look for words like contains, per, in any word that relates 2 items.

CMay

Phil,

Well, it is very simple on how you can stop getting your conversions mixed up. You must memorize them. However, once that is completed and the memorization is over with there are several other key factors and steps you must take into consideration before calculating the problem. Don't forget to have what it is that you need to find as the product of the problem ready so that your labels will cancel out neatly when you begin the problem. Also, this makes it so that you will be less prone to confuse your factor labels. A factor is something that is set equal to each other. In other words km = 10^9 nm. That is how you decipher what is and is not a conversion factor is by whether or not it is equal to each other.

(Chris Loker)

that it is the high point of the class for others. Where it was appropriate, I wrote comments back to the student explaining why some techniques that I use are important. A few examples of questions and answers follow:

What part of class do you enjoy most?

"I find the demonstrations are enjoyable, but what it is that I really enjoy is when we do challenging problems in class that involve several different aspects of chemistry. I find that those types of problems are more of a jigsaw puzzle that take time to figure out and challenge the student." Chris Lokey

What changes would you make in the daily routine?

"Overall the classroom routine runs smoothly because we cover most of what is needed and the time passes quickly. Perhaps a few more demonstrations to break the routine could add the spice we need." Ben Boardman

"I like the way we spend a lot of time just working problems. We do them one by one. You give us a problem, let us try it, then explain, then repeat. This is very effective for me." William Lavin

I really like the idea of students writing freely in settings that are not threatening to them. Chemistry is not an English class. I don't expect anything more than an honest answer on exercises like this, and I don't get upset when students don't meet my expectations for grammar and punctuation. The situations above allow students to unburden themselves, to feel that they have a right to their opinions, and to have the fulfillment of helping someone else.

Writing and Pre-Calculus (Lance Nickel)

When students walk into my pre-calculus class fresh from a year of advanced algebra, one of the first questions I ask them is, "Why do you write up problems?" Their silence makes it quite obvious that they have never considered the question. Invariably, their answer boils down to "so you can grade it." Algebra fosters the belief that the only goal is the correct answer and that any intermediate step to "show work" is merely an attempt at partial credit in the event that the boxed-in solution is incorrect. It takes the better part of the first semester to convince students that writing up the solution to a problem is an attempt at communication.

In writing a sustained problem such as the long-answer portion of the Calculus Advanced Placement (AP) exam, I constantly stress three points (besides correct mathematics):

1. Use good prose including full sentences, connectors, capitalization, punctuation, etc.
2. Use a well-written solution that can stand by itself; i.e., a knowledgeable reader should be able to reconstruct the question from the write-up.
3. Use precise mathematical vocabulary.

The purpose of the following exercise is to stress the third point. My goal is to convince students that it is nearly impossible to engage in technical writing without the necessary vocabulary.

The Exercise

The class is divided into two groups designated Group A and Group B (Figure 15−3). Each student in a group is given one of two complicated graphs with the following directions:

> In the space provided below, write a well-developed paragraph describing the graph above to your reader. You must use descriptive English and may not simply list ordered pairs.

The following day, each student receives a description from the other group and must attempt to reproduce the described graph (Figure 15−4).

The message to the students about communicating without the necessary vocabulary comes through loud and clear. Out of eighteen Honors pre-calculus students, only one was able to reconstruct the graph described by his peer, and he admitted to a great deal of lucky guesswork. The point was made — in technical writing, each word needs to convey one and only one meaning, and that meaning must be the same for the writer and the reader. Use of metaphors describing a graph as "a series of sand dunes" or "like the arches of McDonald's" left too much ambiguity to describe the reality of the graph.

After more than eight months of studying elementary functions, graphs, and vocabulary, students are again challenged with the same task. By the end of the year, the writing of the description (Figure 15−5) and the reproduction of the graph are deemed trivial by the students. The first year I did this exercise, the students were 100 percent successful (except for minor errors) in their efforts. They had learned to write to communicate to a particular audience for a specific purpose.

Figure 15–3
Mathematical Vocabulary Exercise

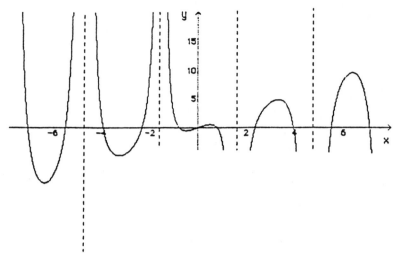

A

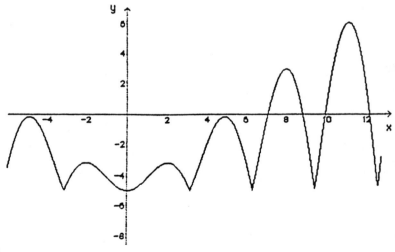

B

Figure 15−4
Reproduced Graph

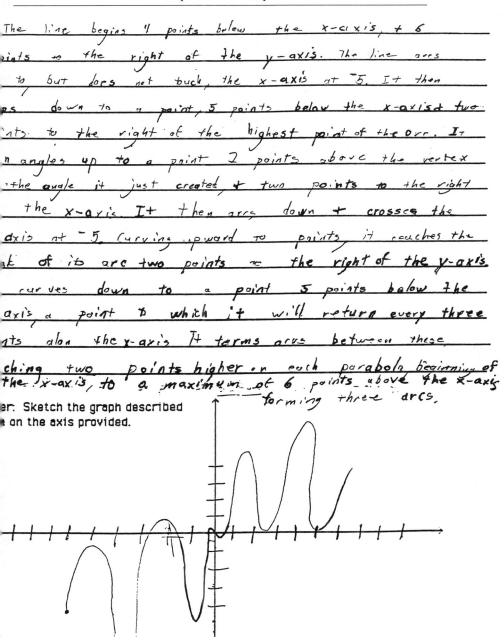

The line begins 4 points below the x-axis, + 6 points to the right of the y-axis. The line arcs to but does not buck, the x-axis at ⁻5. It then ps down to a point, 5 points below the x-axis + two 'nts to the right of the highest point of the arc. It n angles up to a point 2 points above the vertex +the angle it just created, + two points to the right the x-axis. It then arcs down + crosses the axis at ⁻5 curving upward to points, it reaches the k of its arc two points ~ the right of the y-axis. curves down to a point 5 points below the axis, a point to which it will return every three 'ts along the x-axis It terms arcs between these. ching two points higher on each parabola beginning of the x-axis, to a maximum of 6 points above the x-axis forming three arcs.

er. Sketch the graph described
on the axis provided.

Figure 15–5
Mathematical Exercise Revisited

The graph has **vertical** asymptote at x = 8 and x = -3.
Its horizontal asymptote is y = 3, for both positive and negative
value for x. X - intercepts are at x = 1, and x = -1.
Y-intercept is at y = 0.2. There is a cusp pt at
(5, -0.3). Relative maximum is located at (-0.2, 0.
Parity changes at x = 8, x = 1, x = -1, and x = -3.
Relative minimum is located at (4, -1). Other than
the cusp pt, the graph is nice and smooth curve

Yoshi Hishinuma

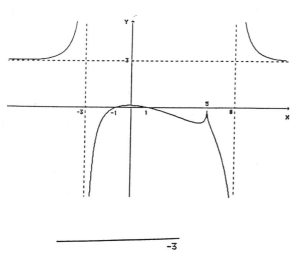

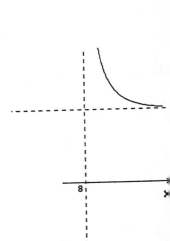

Honors Biology Writing Projects (Peter LaRochelle and Pamela B. Farrell-Childers)

Based on Pete's experiences in the lowland tropical rain forests of Ecuador in the spring and summer of 1991, he suggested that his students learn biology by creating alternatives to basic textbook learning. He felt that the intensive study of an ecosystem would provide an interesting context for the study of many biological concepts. Pete approached Pam with the idea of combining a more traditional approach to high school biology teaching with an intensive study of tropical biology as part of a year-long project using *Tropical Nature*, a collection of essays written by Adrian Forsyth and Kenneth Miyata (1984). This holistic approach would involve the development of a need for knowledge through discussing, questioning, and writing, followed by more intensive study of biological processes. In a sense we were testing a hypothesis that students would be more motivated to learn in this context and, therefore, would learn more. We agreed to offer the students possible writing projects to meet the objectives but also give them the option of creating their own learning project. The class met every Wednesday morning in the Writing Center to discuss the topics presented in each chapter and to see how the students' projects were progressing. All students were required to keep a journal documenting their writing activities.

Pam was primarily responsible for implementing the writing aspects of the course and for promoting discussion. Pete was responsible for guiding the discussion and touching on the critical points of each essay. Pam and Pete presented options to the students for their writing projects. The students selected their projects and wrote a description that included their direction, goals, and procedures. We gave them passwords and created computer file folders for each project within a master folder (LaRochelle) on the fileserver. The following projects were selected:

1. Articles to inform — Students would write articles for the school newspaper and for publication elsewhere to inform others of specific aspects of tropical biology.

2. Action letters to key individuals — Students would locate and write to key international organizations and individuals regarding specific political issues and environmental concerns.

3. Creative Writing — Students would write short stories set in similar environments to the rain forests described in the text and/or write poetry inspired by chapter content.

4. Theme writing — Students would write a booklet based on a year-long study of a particular aspect of tropical biology (one team chose opportunism; another, coevolution).

Branen and John described their goal "to become well-informed, maybe even experts, on the wide use of opportunism and the many contributions it has to the diversity of the rain forest and the survival of its inhabitants."

Pete and Pam questioned each other and offered several "What if" questions to include in this new collaborative project. Also, we questioned students periodically to evaluate how they were doing and how we were doing as resources. As a year-long project, we gave students a two-part questionnaire at the end of semester one. Part One evaluated this program along several lines:

1. Did they perceive this approach as interesting and effective?
2. Did they have enough time to complete the reading, written assignments, and projects within the regular schedule?
3. How often should their progress be evaluated?

All students felt that although this approach was interesting and thought-provoking, there was too little time to complete their work with no scheduled time to work during the school day. In other words, this project could not be done *in addition to* the customary content goals of the course. We, therefore, gave them open time every two weeks when they were required to be in the Writing Center working on their projects. Finally, with the students' approval we chose to evaluate their progress at the end of each grading period (each month) to keep them accountable. This part of the questionnaire also led to a detailed schedule (syllabus) for the second semester.

Part Two of the questionnaire aimed at our performance and their intellectual growth. When asked to share what they had learned "about biology, yourself, other new information," one student wrote, "I have learned a lot about rain forests that I never knew. ... The one thing I've learned about myself is that I can do a project like this without someone hovering over my shoulder." Other students said that what they learned was "how little I'm aware of"; "I have to read to know what in the world is going on ... I better start studying and reading more"; and "I want to preserve the rain forest and make others aware of the rain forest so they will want to preserve it, also."

What have we as teachers of biology and writing learned? We have found support for our hypothesis (students would be more motivated to learn in this context and, therefore, would learn more). We also reached the following conclusions:

1. The development of a "need" to learn through reading and questioning sets an effective stage on which to learn biological science and models the more observational and investigative approach that students will experience in graduate research and professional work.

2. The selection of reading material is critical to helping the students learn many important biological concepts in a relevant and interesting context.

3. The thought processes lead to the research to discern design in nature and to the communication skills for students to express their own ideas and those of others.

4. The boundaries between disciplines are contrived and not real.

5. The study of biology can be more than microscopes, muscle types, and memory—it is the perception of design and function in nature that is not static but the result of many dynamic and integrated processes.

6. The study of biology necessarily involves verbal, quantitative, and historical aspects among others.

Writing to learn and writing to inform can effectively help students learn about the subject matter, the world around them, a self-directed project, and their own learning styles. We have learned from each other's knowledge and expertise. Pete shared his experiences through slides of the rain forests of Ecuador and his presentation of the subject matter in each chapter. Pam offered suggestions for writing and presentation of materials and parallel readings. For instance, when we covered the chapter on plants emitting toxic defenses against herbivores ("Bugs and Drugs"), Pam suggested that we all read "Rappacini's Daughter" by Nathaniel Hawthorne (1993) to see how accurate the author was in describing the poisonous plants. We both also learned that students were discovering how to write in new ways. Jeff, Rajeev, and Daniel had to learn how to write business letters using the school letterhead. Some used *Writer's Market* (1993) for the first time, and others had to make business phone calls to the Library of Congress and Tennessee Aquarium. Through WAC we have discovered worlds that each of us would not have traveled without the other.

Writing in Math or Math in Writing? (David B. Perkinson)

How can writing reports on math articles or research papers on the history of math help my students become better math students? How can I cover the material I need to cover if I devote several days to writing reports and papers? Why should I change what I am doing in my classes to incorporate writing in my classes? As I began to investigate the idea of WAC, I discovered that these questions did not need to be answered. I thought of writing as a means to an end—simply the way students in the humanities communicated their ideas to their teachers. Fortunately, I came to understand writing is a much more dynamic process than that. Writing is thinking. The process of writing develops ideas more clearly by slowing down the thought process. Writing requires a more thoughtful understanding and a better organization of ideas. Understanding writing as a way to think is the first step to understanding the benefits of WAC.

With this understanding of two levels of writing — writing to inform and writing to learn — came further questions. How can I use writing in my classes? Should I change my math classes to incorporate writing? Since it was easier to develop some writing exercises to use in my class than to change what I was doing, I started with a simple writing to learn exercise. While reviewing the homework problems in class, each student described his or her mistakes. Initially, students were not adept at correctly describing their mistakes, but I could still see the benefits of this exercise. If students could not describe the mistakes they made, they did not understand their mistakes.

As I read that first set of homework papers, I was convinced students needed time to learn how to write in this way. The writing required them to analyze their work in a way most of them had never done before. I also discovered that I needed to develop a more structured system for doing the homework so that they could find their mistakes the next day in class. I developed the idea of a double-entry journal to give them room to make corrections and describe mistakes next to every problem. I gave the students the following homework guidelines:

1. All problems should be done either in a column down one side of the page leaving space next to each problem or across the page leaving space below each problem.

2. As we reviewed the problems in class, the correct solution to any incorrect problem should be worked in the available space.

3. Students should attempt to find and circle the precise point at which they missed the problem.

4. For each mistake, students should describe as accurately as possible why they missed the problem.

In order for students to be able to find their mistakes, they must have well-organized, completed solutions to the problems (Figure 15-6). I used to plead with students to show their work. Some would do so reluctantly without any understanding of why they needed to do so. With this focus on homework, the students understand the difficulty of finding their mistakes if they do not show their work. Furthermore, the students see the benefits of doing homework, and they are more motivated to do it. The entire process is more meaningful to them simply because I asked them to write.

Recently, I began to require students to write questions about

Figure 15–6
Double Entry Math Journal

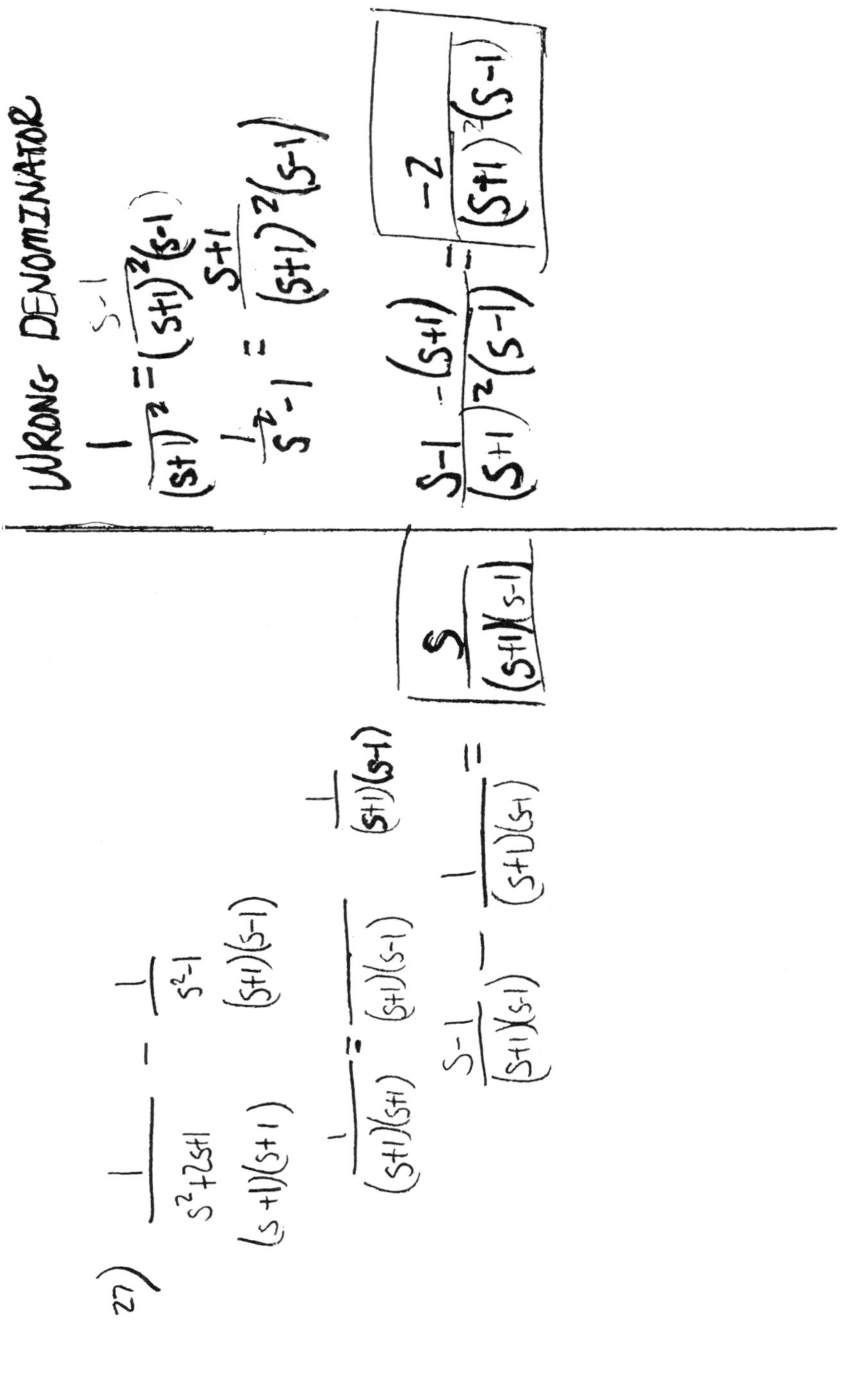

WRONG DENOMINATOR

$$\frac{1}{(s+1)^2} = \frac{s-1}{(s+1)^2(s-1)}$$

$$\frac{1}{s^2-1} = \frac{s+1}{(s+1)^2(s-1)}$$

$$\frac{s-1-(s+1)}{(s+1)^2(s-1)} = \boxed{\frac{-2}{(s+1)^2(s-1)}}$$

27)

$$\frac{1}{s^2+2s+1} - \frac{1}{s^2-1}$$

$$\frac{1}{(s+1)(s+1)} - \frac{1}{(s+1)(s-1)}$$

$$\frac{1}{(s+1)(s+1)} \quad \frac{1}{(s+1)(s-1)}$$

$$\frac{s-1}{(s+1)(s-1)} - \frac{1}{(s+1)(s-1)} = \boxed{\frac{s}{(s+1)(s-1)}}$$

their homework problems. If students cannot do a problem, they must write a specific question about the problem or state what they understand about the problem and at what point they are stuck. Instead of getting some homework papers with a few completed problems and an "I don't understand" from students, I get evidence that they struggled with the problem. After writing their questions, the students have specific questions to ask the next day in class. Through the process of writing, the students are forced to analyze the problem as well as their own thought process.

As I began to see the benefits of these two writing exercises, I also began to see the importance of writing in other parts of my courses. These exercises not only involve using writing to enhance the students' understanding of mathematical concepts but also provide me with valuable feedback. The writings give concrete examples of the level of understanding of each student. This honest feedback from the students is the best way to analyze my teaching performance. I can also use the writing exercises to establish a dialogue with the student. Thus, writing to learn exercises in mathematics enhance the learning process for both teacher and student.

Other exercises that can be used in math classes include the following:

- Write a cooperative problem-solving report.
- Submit a math column to the school newspaper.
- Have each student write his or her math history.
- Have students write letters to each other explaining a concept.
- Allow students to bring summaries of each unit into the test. The summaries could be written at the end of each unit in class.
- Have students keep journals on their progress in math: attempts, failures, difficulties, feelings.
- Have students write short stories about mathematical concepts.
- Ask qualitative questions such as: Which method is better? When is it better?
- Have students write their own descriptions of mathematical concepts.
- Write word problems.
- Have students write reports on articles pertaining to math from news magazines.
- Research the history of math.
- Draw a figure, have one class describe it, and another class draw it from the descriptions.

Words and Images (Catherine Neuhardt-Minor)

Students in Art I have no trouble telling you whether they like or dislike a work of art, but they rarely can tell you why. What they are responding to is the total impression of the work. Writing, in conjunction with making art, focuses students' attention on specific details. Verbalizing these details places newly found information into familiar vocabulary. Students are able to talk about directional forces, light sources, and relative values because they have ordered their thoughts enough to write about them. "There is a hat placed to the right of the door with a shadow that tells of a light source shining on the door and its objects," Dan Chandler explained in his critique of the illustration in Figure 15—7. Having to write about a piece of work also forces the students to observe details they might skip over in a casual conversation.

Figure 15—7
Illustration Critiqued by Chandler

Figure 15–8
Picture Critiqued by Buckner

This is a picture of a door. There are two objects hanging from the door. One is a jacket, the other is a cow skull. These objects are hanging from top left (jacket) and top right (skull). There are three objects at the foot of the door. There is a log, a wooden broomstick, and a large sack. The stick is propped at an angle toward the sack. The log is on the left side of the door. The door is old. It has no door knob; it is cracked and looks as if it is fragile. There is shadowing to the bottom left side of all the objects except the jacket. The jacket is not complete. (David Buckner, critique of Figure 15–8)

This kind of objective reporting sharpens the students' observation skills and leads to more detailed and thoughtful renderings. This not only makes them better artists but also helps them to appreciate and evaluate the work they have just created.

Critiques of still lifes, as well as other artworks, are especially useful when a whole class is working on the same exercise. For instance, critiques were written by two students about different drawings of the same still life (see Figures 15−7 and 15−8). What is especially gratifying is the way their direct observation leads to the use of imagination and self-revelation:

> This is half finished, but still it is beautiful. The artist took his time and paid close attention to detail. If we pay close attention to the things we consider small and unimportant, even if we don't finish our main goal in life, we still have produced a beautiful picture. A picture that is probably more beautiful than that of a rushed sprint to the big goal. (David Buckner, critique of Figure 15−8)

Words not only describe but also may be used to stimulate the creation of images and indeed entire compositions. To introduce this idea, I give each student a large piece of paper and several oil pastels of various colors. I then ask them to "draw" the noises I make, using an appropriate color. At first no one believes that they can draw a sound, but after experimenting they are quite pleased with the results. This new skill of translating noises to marks on a page is then extended to sounds and words. A discussion of Poe's "tintinnabulation" and Kadinsky's synesthesia further integrates the students' understanding of words, sounds, and images. Using writing to learn activities gives both student and teacher visual and literal insight into themselves, their world, and the world of art.

Conclusion

The McCallie teachers have learned a great deal about themselves and their students through the use of writing to learn activities in their classes. Cissy discovered how her exercises "allow students to unburden themselves, to feel that they have a right to their opinions, and to have the fulfillment of helping someone else." Lance's students have "learned to write to communicate to a particular audience for a specific purpose." Through their collaborative work, Pete and Pam "have discovered worlds that each ... would not have traveled without the other." David realized that his "exercises in mathematics enhance the learning process for both teacher and student." And, finally, Catherine has expanded the horizons of creativity of her art students through writing. Every new writing to learn activity will bring new discoveries for both students and teachers. The possibilities are infinite.

References

Forsyth, Adrian, and Kenneth Miyata. 1984. *Tropical Nature*. New York, NY: Charles Scribner's Sons.

Hawthorne, Nathaniel. 1993. "Rappacini's Daughters." In *Elements of Literature*. Fifth Course. Chicago, IL: Holt, Rinehart & Winston, Inc.

Kissling, Mark, ed. 1993. *Writer's Market*. Cincinnati, OH: Writer's Digest Books.

16

Development of Writing Across the Curriculum at Berkshire School

Elizabeth L. Clifford, with Dean Ellerton, Heather Prescott, Anna Romano, and Hilary Russell

Inception to Practice (Elizabeth Clifford)

At Berkshire, a private, coed boarding school for 410 college-prep students, located in Sheffield, Massachusetts, our writing across the curriculum (WAC) program has influenced the faculty and students' ways of thinking, learning, and writing since 1983. This chapter will describe the WAC program that has evolved at our school since that time, highlighting a variety of branches of the program that are evident in the philosophy and practical teaching/learning strategies we use at Berkshire. All of us who contributed to this article have developed and modified our teaching styles in different ways that we can trace to our roots in the WAC program.

During the first three years, Berkshire's WAC committee was formed of volunteer faculty from every discipline that cared to participate. We published *The Writer's Handbook*, a guide to teach students and faculty in all disciplines to use a process approach in their writing; we hoped to encourage intelligent thinking and writing, thoughtfully directed towards the author's audience. We also created a common key for corrections, which became known as "The Berkshire Hit List." During those first years, we attended conferences and held mini-workshops for our faculty, *encouraging the use of active student learning, writing as a vehicle for discovery, and "coaching" rather than lecturing as an effective teaching method.*

In 1986 we added the "T" to our committee's name. We became

the Thinking and Writing Across the Curriculum Committee (TWAC) in an attempt to broaden the scope of faculty involvement, particularly to include the mathematics and science disciplines. Since then, our committee has met weekly to discuss ways to implement cross-curricular thinking, writing projects, and teaching strategies within our curriculum, as individual teachers and as an entire school. We have spent much time encouraging the development of a grassroots network of teachers concerned with TWAC, successfully extending our philosophy beyond the bounds of our ten-person committee to an everincreasing number of the faculty at large. We have learned how much more effective it is for faculty to choose to experiment with their curriculum and teaching strategies, rather than to be forced to make changes. We greatly appreciated administrative support for TWAC when we introduced alternative methods of teaching and learning, in which students and faculty must see themselves as equally responsible for successful learning. Faculty and students now engage in more collaborative group work, use journals as a means of communication, and view learning as a process that includes thinking, writing, and revising in ways appropriate to the discipline. The process leads to better products, and both are valued. For both faculty and students, the premise that all share equally in the educational process can be very unnerving: faculty members often find it difficult to share the authority, and students balk at accepting the necessary responsibility for learning.

Since 1986, regular TWAC meetings have been a welcome source of professional enrichment and support. All of us on the committee have found that our teaching styles have developed in ways that we trace back to three ideals: *encouraging active learning, using writing as a vehicle for discovery, and "coaching" as the most appropriate teaching model.* The projects we have taken on and the changes in our teaching styles reflect the needs of our students at Berkshire and our own special interests.

The weekly meetings of TWAC provide us with a regular source of reinforcement to practice rather than to preach. We have learned by experience, still the best of teachers, that creating a list of "thou shalts" for the faculty at large is counterproductive; too forceful "encouragement" makes colleagues shudder and avoid contact with overly zealous proselytizers! Instead, the TWAC committee experiments with new teaching strategies and creates projects that serve as models; interested faculty will investigate what we're doing and adopt methods that are appropriate to their own classes or individual students. Thus, the grassroots network grows.

During the fall semester of 1991, the TWAC committee considered the concept of interdisciplinary independent study projects for seniors — in our opinion, the perfect culminating academic exercise of a student's four years in high school. The prospect delighted us because independent study involves all three aspects of our philosophy. Certainly, a student would practice *active learning* in the process of formulating and researching a topic of choice. Writing the final paper challenges any student to synthesize all the work he or she has done, not merely to record it in a grocery list of footnotes and facts; thus, the student enjoys the potential of *writing as a vehicle of discovery*. Finally, we stipulated that the student must choose *a faculty sponsor* from each discipline, whose role is *to coach* the student in the process of narrowing the research topic, selecting appropriate research material, and then meeting necessary deadlines on the way to completion of the project. Naturally, the sponsors take part in the final evaluation of the project. At the completion of the project, students then publish their work and share it with peers by keeping it on permanent file in the library. That way current seniors would gain from each other's learning experiences, and future seniors would also have the opportunity to learn from the experiences of those who had completed interdisciplinary writing projects.

With all of the guidelines in print, the TWAC stepped back from the description of the project to discuss how to promote it. Ten years of committee experience saved us from the potential disaster of believing that all of the faculty and all of the seniors would be equally eager to undertake the projects! After presenting the project to the seniors and to the faculty, we invited them to take part. We acted upon our belief that choice is critical to the long-term success of the program. The course was offered as a second-semester elective in English. The project has started with a group of eight seniors, under my supervision as project coordinator. Students meet weekly with me and monthly with their faculty sponsors in the Writing Center, where they draft, revise, and edit their final projects on the computer. The grassroots network of TWAC is working. Interested faculty have agreed to sponsor students in subject areas of mutual interest. The TWAC committee has devised several ways to provide incentives for more seniors to take part in future years: a book prize for the best project to be given at graduation, honorable mention in the graduation program, earlier promotion of the project to juniors through interaction with seniors who participated and as a transitional experience between high school and college. I have traced this description of a project from inception to the first stages of practice to point out a few practical strategies TWAC employs and some pitfalls we were able to avoid.

Anna Romano, director of the English as a Second Language (ESL) Program, and Heather Prescott, French teacher, use journals in several ways that have grown out of their experience on the TWAC committee and graduate training.

A Community of Teachers and Learners: TWAC
Philosophy Shapes the Curriculum (Anna Romano)

Writing is a thinking process. This is the basic premise that our TWAC committee is built upon. More important, however, it is the lesson that I learned once again as a teacher-researcher when I conducted a year-long study of my intermediate level ESL reading and writing class. In this class, my students read historical fiction and responded to the novels in a dialogue journal. This journal consisted of letters that the students wrote to me. I instructed them not to simply retell the story, but to respond to it. I asked them to write what they thought about the story, the characters, and the situations in which the characters found themselves. I then responded to those letters, adding my observations and asking questions. I discovered that by writing about their reading my students had become active readers and critical writers.

My students were able to think about the situations that the characters of the story found themselves in and make some inferences and judgments about those situations. In writing about the book *The Tamarack Tree* by Patricia Clapp, Shinichiro Satoh wonders,

> If Rosemary and [her] brother Derek could go to the Northern America, Rosemary wouldn't be in complicated situation. She could talk to her friends normally about whatever she wanted to talk [about]. ... Unfortunately, she have come to the Southern America where her thoughts don't belong. People in the Southern America thought the Negroes should not be free. If I was in Rosemary's situation, I would move to the Northern America, and I would fight with the people who live in the Northern America against the South. All people should have [the] right to have freedom.

In this single entry, Shinichiro has demonstrated three critical thinking skills. Shinichiro imagines how Rosemary's dilemma would have been resolved if she had gone to live in the North rather than in the South. Then he puts himself in her shoes and decides what he would have done had he been in her situation. Finally, he makes a value judgment — people should be free — and then applies it to all people, not only to the black slaves in his book.

In another entry about the same book, Yurie Aizawa writes,

> After I read *The Tamarack Tree*, I knew that even in the South, during the Civil War, there were people who were against the slavery and helped slaves escape to Canada.

This kind of information is important for Yurie to learn for two reasons. One, she has more accurate information about the Civil War, and two, she learns that not all Southerners fit into the stereotypes created about them.

In a different entry about the same book Yurie writes,

> As I read this book, I feel that any kind of war makes people uncomfortable and I think war shouldn't be existed. I know that when war happens, there are some reasons and arguments, but still I think to kill people isn't a way to solve [problems].

In this entry, she is able to look at the consequences of the Civil War and determine that war in general is not the best way to resolve differences or solve problems. Comprehension is the skill that all my students demonstrated every time they had to write a journal entry, for all their entries required that they practice paraphrasing and summarizing.

While reading the letters my students wrote to me, I realized that these historical novels permitted them to become involved in the situations and problems of the people living in different historical periods in a way that their textbook did not allow. Furthermore, because they were able to identify with the characters in the stories they were reading, they came to a better understanding of what had occurred historically. Finally, by writing about the lives and problems of the people they were reading about, my students were able to read and write critically. It was only after having studied their letters that I realized that those letters in my students' journals were a form of literary analysis in disguise.

Journals in French Class (Heather Prescott)

I encourage my French students to use their journals to think about writing, to become more able to write about thinking, and to explore ways in which they best learn. Although some balk at first, for many the self-reflection has been useful and revealing.

My ideas for applying journal work to the beginning French curriculum were inspired by William Zinsser's book, *Writing to Learn*, which our TWAC committee read as a group. We then invited Zinsser to visit Berkshire and address our faculty on using WAC.

From the ideas generated by Zinsser's book and his visit to Berkshire, I designed a journal program for French Levels One through Three. The system has increased my ability to identify my students' needs and respond to them. It has also enhanced my respect for the process of discovery my students go through as they learn from their mistakes. A negative (spotting mistakes) then becomes a positive learning experience.

My primary goals for Level One are for the students to look critically at their work, ask themselves whether or not their writing makes sense, and learn to proofread more thoroughly. They also have to hone their communication skills by writing their responses clearly enough for me or others to understand. All of the students' work is returned to them with no numerical or letter grade on the sheet. Thus, it is up to them to peruse their tests, discover their mistakes, write about any patterns they see in their work, devise methods to improve their performance, and evaluate their own work. That is, they are using a writing to learn activity. Students in Level One write almost all journal entries in English.

In response to his own test corrections, John Jaxheimer writes:

> I was a little disappointed in myself with the results of the test (especially after feeling confident about the conjugation of all the verbs). I was surprised how much I struggled on the vocabulary. I was puzzled on part #9! I know I can do better, and I'll prove it on the next test.

John's perceptions of his performance are integral to his developing ability to see patterns in his work. He draws fairly sophisticated conclusions about the effects of his preparation and review of material. Thus, his test responses become more accurate, and his long-term retention of the concepts is more sound.

At Level Two, the students' tasks are similar to those required at Level One, with the added expectation that they write summaries of stories and dialogues we are reading. The students in French Two are also required to produce more thorough and detailed explanations of grammatical concepts. Level Two students write in both French and English — their plot summaries are in French; their grammatical essays and test evaluations in English.

In course evaluations of June 1991, French One and Two students completed the sentence, "The purpose of the journals in this class was to . . .". Their responses reveal diverse perceptions about the value of journal writing. The following excerpt proved significant because the student was able to draw a connection between the act of thinking and the act of writing, skills I try to help students hone through the journal exercises:

> The purpose [of the journals] was to give us a chance to write and therefore think about any errors that we had made on tests and other exercises. The journals gave us a chance to realize and correct our errors. (Benjamin Rood)

Many responses from Level One indicated that the journals helped because the students had to write out and think about correct responses and how to learn them. They recognized patterns in their own work.

In the advanced section of French Three, the purpose of the journals is more complex. In addition to the requirements of Level One and Two students, Level Three students frequently write assignments describing the process they go through to solve linguistic or organizational problems. Writing in journals becomes writing to problem solve. For instance, a student incorporates perceptions of different concepts in the example that follows:

> While I was taking the test I thought part one was easy, but I . . . missed obvious answers: *à* + *le* = *au*. I was surprised at how well part two went, because *ces, cet, cette* and determining gender is usually difficult for me. The verbs were O.K. *Dites* and *veulent* are [forms] that I often confuse with the common mistakes 'disez' and 'voulent.' I was confident about my essay and it turned out well. The map was not difficult, but spelling, as usual, hurt my grade. I think I earned a grade in the low 80s. (JoAnn Barett)

JoAnn evinces the ability to synthesize information and to examine problems that hindered successful performance. The detail she applies to her analysis is made more readily available to her through the act of writing.

Other examples of process writing include entries from culture projects during the first semester. Students keep a record of the process they go through to do the research, glean the material, produce the outline, and write all the drafts. This way I am able to see where they need guidance and how well they are coming up with ideas on their own. Throughout the entire process, students interact and respond to each other's thinking and writing. Most of this is done in English.

June 1991 Level Three course evaluations revealed that students saw value in the journal exercises, and for different reasons. One student commented on the merit of the examination of tests. The following example reveals the specific importance of student statements to improve the quality of their work through writing to think and writing to learn:

> We could write our goals and expectations down and they would be right there always staring us in the face, reminding us of what we had committed ourselves to. (Brandi Hopper)

Using writing to learn through journals in the French classroom has been an exciting way to see students grow. Journals help students learn material because they are accountable in writing for the concepts taught to them. The journals give students the tools to learn through writing. From clear thinking, clearer writing becomes possible. My students and I feel that journal writing creates a more solid foundation for learning.

Berkshire School's Writing Center: The WAC Committee Puts Philosophy in Practice (Elizabeth Clifford)

One recent and very physical accomplishment of the TWAC committee's planning is the Writing Center, a pair of adjoining classrooms that house twenty-one Macintosh computers of various types, as well as five printers, a scanner, a Mac Recorder, overhead projection equipment and software that allows students to share screens and files. The planning, researching, purchasing, and running of the Writing Center has been accomplished by members of TWAC. Dean Ellerton and I currently share the task of running the Writing Center. Members of TWAC frequently use the facility to teach classes. Because of the grassroots network developed by TWAC during the last ten years, many faculty members from various disciplines make use of the Writing Center: for instance, chemistry, political science, ESL, English (including several senior electives taught exclusively in the Writing Center), music theory, Spanish, French, and ethics. Berkshire students and faculty write a great deal and quite well. They enjoy the natural integration of the writing process with the word processor and the facility of Microsoft Word 5.1. The integration of computers with writing, collaboration, and student interaction in the Writing Center have helped our TWAC program. During our first year and a half, the Writing Center has been an overwhelming success and a productive gathering place for faculty interested in innovative teaching methods. As we move into the next year of operation, we look forward to expanding our capacity to produce desktop-published documents, to examining the feasibility of training a staff of peer tutors to work with individual students and teachers who assign special projects, and to implementing the two-week, team-taught modules in the Writing Center for sophomores.

Hilary Russell, chair of the English department, and Dean Ellerton, computer specialist in the Writing Center and chemistry teacher, will comment on ways they have incorporated writing into their courses, and assignments that they ask students to accomplish in the Writing Center.

Computers and Writing (Hilary Russell)

The big change in my teaching came during the 1990−91 school year in the TWAC-sponsored Writing Center. Formerly I had eschewed computer rooms, primarily because the students looked not at me but at screens and keyboards and because the rooms tend to be impersonal and too public to encourage the private activity of writing (I still cannot imagine writing anything of personal value in a public place.) I also felt awkward looking over students' shoulders at what they were writing. (Wearing bifocals, I had to stick my nose very close to the screen to see.) Furthermore, if something broke, no one was there to help fix it. Perhaps my greatest reservation was that I felt, and still feel, that computers can distance students from teachers, the machine becoming the focus instead of the person. My ideas about the use of computers as a tool for writing were limited by the facilities that had existed before the creation of our Writing Center.

Since all of the members of the TWAC committee wanted a warm, user-friendly Writing Center, we brainstormed about how to achieve this goal. With the assistance of faculty members and students who offered suggestions for student interaction, collaborative writing, and ways of using the computers for writing in all disciplines, we managed to create the warm atmosphere. In order for students to feel comfortable when they worked in isolation on a piece of writing, we put dividers between computers, effectively creating carrels, each having its own shelf above the computer for extra books and a slide-out surface for the keyboard, thus leaving space in front of and next to the computer for texts, drafts, reference books, or other material that students may need as they word process. The result is that students work in relative privacy, undistracted by their neighbor's books, elbows, and nosy stares. If students want to interact with their teacher or classmates, the rolling chairs enable them to move quickly from private to public space with relative ease. (See Figure 16–1.)

Thinking and writing across the curriculum solved the problem of teachers looking over students' shoulders by placing a large table in the center of the room, lining the computers around three of the walls, and leaving one wall blank for a screen on which to project images from a central computer. Sitting at this central table with one's back to the blank wall, a teacher can easily confer with a student while keeping an eye on the class. Since the printers are also located on this large, rectangular table, students who want to discuss their work can simply get up, retrieve the hard copy they have sent to the printer, and move to this area to share their work with each other or the teacher. Carpeting and office chairs on rollers make all of this movement quiet and simple while aiding communication among students and between student and teacher. This mobility allows me to do something that we teachers rarely have time to do, even in schools where the student-teacher ratio is favorable—I sit down with each of my students two or three times a week and confer on a piece of writing that the student usually cares a good deal about. I am now using the computers in the Writing Center as well as in my own classroom when the Writing Center is not available for student interaction or collaborative writing. Rather than

Figure 16-1
Berkshire Writing Center Floorplan

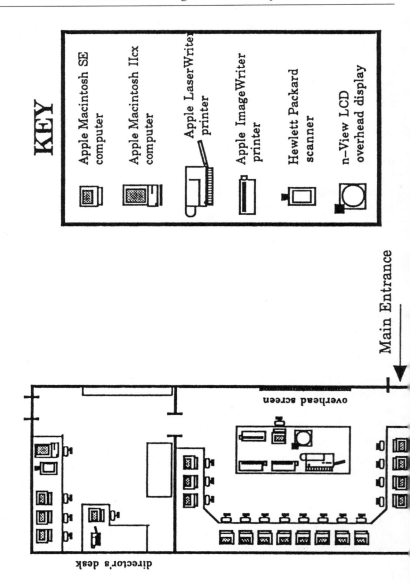

standing between me and the students, our computers (thanks largely to the furnishing, layout, and personnel of the Writing Center) have served to bring us together.

Writing in Chemistry (Dean Ellerton)

As a chemistry teacher at Berkshire, I have been using the school's Macintosh computers to aid in the teaching of laboratory report writing for the past three semesters; consequently I have noted a dramatic improvement both in the quality of the students' word-processed reports and in their general understanding of the material presented in the laboratory. Chemistry students at Berkshire are currently required to write a portion of a weekly laboratory report on a word processor. This report is then graded not only for its scientific content, but also for its clarity and style. Although grammar and syntax are not graded specifically, students are reminded that these elements have a significant impact on the general impression of the paper and that they may be asked to revise a section of the report if these errors are excessive or the scientific content of the report needs to be rethought.

The laboratory element of the general chemistry course at Berkshire School, a weekly event, is generally a three-step process. First, on the night before the lab, students are required to write a "pre-lab." This assignment, consisting of a prepared series of recipe-like steps, is designed to prepare the students for the actual procedure of the lab. The student handwrites a pre-lab in a laboratory notebook and gives a copy to the teacher immediately before the lab session. Next, the students collect data on the day of the lab and enter this information in the laboratory notebook as well. Finally, the students are asked to answer some questions about the data collected in the lab and to write a report featuring two sections entitled "Discussion" and "Conclusion." The discussion section of the "write-up" is the student's chance to elaborate on events that took place during the lab and to comment on various anomalies or relevant observations. In this section students can think out loud and ponder the significance and accuracy of certain measurements taken the previous day. The conclusion section serves as a means for the student to synthesize the collected data and to summarize any trends, completion of objectives, error management, and so on. The discussion and conclusion sections of the final report must be word processed and submitted to me approximately three days after the actual laboratory.

Unfortunately, high school laboratory report writing has evolved into more of a spontaneous reaction than an exercise in process writing. Typical conclusions have included sentences like:

I really liked this lab. It showed me how oxygen and magnesium
react. Wow, I could hardly look at it because the light was so bright.
I'm not sure why they did it, but it was really neat. I hope we can do
stuff like that again.

I have recently tried to stress the concept of using writing to
develop ideas — to get students to view their reports as vehicles to aid
in the understanding of chemical principles, rather than as documents
produced purely for a grade. The use of word processing seems to have
helped with these objectives in several ways. First, it makes the idea of
revising a section of the report a lot less painful for the student than in
the past. Second, the physical act of going to our Writing Center seems
to focus students' attention on the task at hand. Thus the writing is
much more thoughtful and all-inclusive than in the past. Students now
seem to view their work as a piece of *scientific writing*, rather than just
a response to an assignment. Finally, students have a great deal more
pride in the appearance of their work than they ever have had before.
This concern for cosmetics, although apparently superficial, is vital
when a student must prepare an accurate, clear laboratory report in
college. Many high school science students are at a great disadvantage
when they enter university science courses never having completed
such an extensive report during their secondary education.

Although evidence of drastic improvement in the overall quality of
laboratory reports is hard to quantify and the means of measurement
are purely subjective, it is obvious from just a quick inspection of
recent reports that passages such as the following are no longer the
exception but the rule:

In this lab, I learned to tell the difference between physical and
chemical properties from my observations. I now realize that chemical
properties are those that involve reactions with other species, and
that physical properties can simply be observed with the five senses. It
is also possible to measure physical properties without changing a
substance. For example, when I observed that magnesium reacted
with oxygen to form a new substance (magnesium oxide), I had to
"destroy" the magnesium; however, to measure the density of magnesium, a physical property, I merely had to drop it in a graduated
cylinder of water and measure the volume change. (Amanda Wonson)

In the preceding case, the student has had time to process the
relevant data, analyze her observations, think about the ramifications
of this information, and synthesize all this into a lucid conclusion about
an experience. In other words, she is writing to learn and to communicate what she has learned. In previous years, I, as well as others,
placed far too much emphasis on calculations and impromptu observation for this type of advanced scientific thought to occur. Now,
however, the students are encouraged to use writing as the tool to

improve their analytical skills and to improve the actual process of thinking through a complex concept.

In conclusion, I highly recommend the use of process writing and word processing in the preparation of laboratory reports. The improvement in the quality of the final product greatly outweighs the time and energy expended to learn the new system for both teacher and student. In short, the results of this experiment in writing in science class far exceeded my hopes for slightly improving the thought and effort that went into producing a readable chemistry laboratory report.

TWAC Past, Present, and Future: The Effectiveness of Grassroots Committee Work (Elizabeth Clifford)

The success of each of the projects and teaching techniques described in this article can be attributed directly to the effective work of the TWAC committee. Writing across the curriculum programs thrive in schools that utilize a grassroots network to spread the word and to put philosophy into practice on a daily basis. The Writing Center, for instance, would not have been the overnight success that it is if TWAC had not provided the faculty with the groundwork of philosophy and practical teaching strategies before its inception. Because any teaching facility has to meet the needs of the faculty and students who will use it, effective preliminary study of the school's needs and training in practical use of the equipment are critical. The interaction between students and faculty is essential to such a program. Through the work of the committee and the grassroots network that has grown from it, the school's programs reflect the needs of the students and the interests of the faculty.

References

Clapp, Patricia. 1986. *The Tamarack Tree*. New York, NY: Viking. Penguin, Inc.

The Writer's Handbook. 1990. Sheffield, MA: Berkshire School.

Zinsser, William. 1988. *Writing to Learn*. New York, NY: Harper & Row.

17

Projects and Partnerships: Writing, Teaching, and Learning in the School District of Philadelphia

Judy Buchanan and Andrew Gelber

What institutional structures support teachers as writers, researchers, and reformers within their schools and school districts? What does it mean for organizations to collaborate in providing that support? Discussion of these questions is at the heart of the partnership among the School District of Philadelphia, PATHS/PRISM: The Philadelphia Partnership for Education, and the Philadelphia Writing Project (PhilWP).

By describing the history of the partnership and detailing the development of specific structures for supporting teachers and schools, we hope to illuminate some important issues for others engaged in collaborative work of this kind. Through looking closely at two programs, the Cross-Visitation Program and the Writing Assessment Program, we will demonstrate the power of partnerships in creating supportive structures for school and curricular reform in the teaching of writing, as well as some of the struggles and problems that arise in attempting to keep such a partnership responsive to the changing needs of teachers, administrators, and schools.

Beginnings of the Partnership

Since 1984 the School District of Philadelphia has been engaged in a systemwide effort to help teachers change their understandings and uses of writing in their classrooms. From the beginning Philadelphia's

228

writing across the curriculum (WAC) efforts have included a strong focus both on writing for teaching and learning across the disciplines and on professional development opportunities for the teachers who ultimately realize the systemwide goals through their classroom practices. This vision was articulated by Dr. Constance Clayton early in her superintendency of the School District of Philadelphia. At the outset, Dr. Clayton's vision gave priority to the role of writing for students' engagement in learning in school and to the formation of partnerships that would enable her goals for the school district to be realized.

Nationally a number of foundations and business and university consortia had already joined together to support reform efforts in K−12 public schools. In Philadelphia in the early 1980s Dr. Clayton's reform agenda attracted the interest and support of area corporations, universities, foundations, and cultural institutions and led to the formation of the Committee to Support the Philadelphia Public Schools (CSPPS). The membership of CSPPS made the innovative decision to found an organization that would work directly with Philadelphia teachers and schools. This strategy resulted in the creation in 1984 of PATHS/PRISM: The Philadelphia Partnership for Education.

Dr. Claytons vision for change in classrooms included the development of teacher leadership, a broad view of writing, and opportunities for educators at all levels of the school system to engage in rethinking the purposes and practices connected with the teaching of writing in schools. PATHS/PRISM launched the pilot WAC effort in the 1984−85 school year, involving 28 of Philadelphia's more than 250 schools. In each of Philadelphia's subregions, teams of teachers, administrators, and faculty from area universities came together in professional development workshops that explored a wide range of issues and practices concerning the field of writing.

Participants in the regional workshops then returned to their schools to share, discuss, and implement some of these new ideas and classroom practices. During the pilot year, goals included both the introduction and dissemination of new approaches to using writing to learn and the building of collegial structures that supported change in classrooms, within schools, and within regions. Each region benefited from university consultants who provided both leadership for the professional development workshops and advice on program structures.

Positive evaluations of the pilot year led to expansion of the program and to discussions of ways to support and deepen the work that had begun in the schools. Of particular importance were the connections between the university consultants and the school teams, as well as the opportunities for teachers to work closely with other teachers. A problem teachers identified early in the program was the need for more time to talk about the new ideas in the writing field and more opportunities to try new practices in collaboration with their colleagues. Teachers rightly observed that many of the innovative ideas in the teaching of writing would require significant change in their overall classroom practices and that these changes could not be accomplished quickly or easily.

During the fall and winter of 1985 conversations and discussions that were focused on meeting these emerging needs led to the conclusion that Philadelphia's efforts to enhance writing in the classroom would benefit substantially from the founding of a National Writing Project site, specifically dedicated to School District of Philadelphia educators and students. The National Writing Project (NWP), currently comprised of more than 150 sites, is an organization established to create school-university partnerships to improve the teaching of writing in schools. The NWP makes clear its basic principles to accomplish this task: teachers themselves are the best teachers of other teachers; teachers of writing must write themselves; as researchers in classrooms, teachers can inform both theory and practice; and real change in classroom practice happens over time.

University of Pennsylvania faculty at the Graduate School of Education, working in collaboration with PATHS/PRISM and the School District of Philadelphia, designed a proposal to create a site of the NWP, the Philadelphia Writing Project (PhilWP), which then began offering summer institutes and a range of ongoing professional development opportunities for teachers in 1986.

The partnership among the school district, PATHS/PRISM, and PhilWP teachers works in many ways to support teachers, with each partner providing different kinds of resources for the various activities and programs. For example, each summer, intensive invitational institutes are offered by PhilWP, and teacher fellowships to these institutes are provided by the school district. Cross-visitation during the school day by PhilWP teacher-consultants, enabling teachers to learn from and with their colleagues, occurs through the school district's funding of writing support teachers for each subregion. Regional miniconferences, conducted as part of the ongoing WAC effort are supported by the partnership and provide leadership opportunities for teacher-consultants. The partnership works at many levels to foster the teaching of writing in schools and to support teachers working with other teachers.

The Partnership in Action: Structures for Teacher Collaboration

The Cross-Visitation Program

Upon completion of the 1986 Summer Institute a group of thirty-two teachers, K−12, became the first PhilWP teacher-consultants, eligible to participate in cross-visitation with one another and with colleagues citywide. During the school day, teacher-consultants may visit other teachers' classrooms or may receive visitors in their own classrooms to work together on broad questions and practices involving the teaching of writing. These cross-visitations may take place within school buildings or may bring together teachers whose schools are miles apart. Drawing upon ongoing WAC efforts in schools across the city, PATHS/PRISM and PhilWP assist in building the network of cross-visitation by linking teacher-consultants with interested colleagues. Currently there are 250 teacher-consultants in PhilWP; this year about 110 of them are involved in cross-visitation with more than 1,000 fellow teachers.

Gail Sklar, a high school special education teacher-consultant for the Philadelphia Writing Project, wrote a reflective journal on her cross-visitation with colleagues at her school:

> [After an initial invitation to meet together] what I found were teachers anxious to talk about the writing they were having their students do in the classroom. They were also eager for suggestions on how to expand writing activities. . . . I met with teachers of woodshop, auto mechanics, science, and physical education. . . . One of the first teachers I collaborated with was the woodshop teacher. We met and discussed the kinds of writing he already had his students do. Next, I went into his room to get a better sense of what occurred in his classroom. We met again, and decided to collaborate on a final project — an exhibition. . . . Now, when I meet some of these teachers in the hall, our dialogue continues. We discuss what worked and what was not as successful. We've gotten to know each other a bit better. Perhaps this experience has chipped away at a little of the isolation we, as high school teachers, face.

Cross-visitation creates opportunities for collegial learning during the school day and begins to break down some of the barriers that isolate teachers within classrooms, schools, or subject areas. This program is made possible in each region by the writing support teachers provided by the School District of Philadelphia. These teachers, most of whom have participated in PhilWP summer institutes, are specially designated substitute teachers who work only with teacher-consultants and participating fellow teachers.

Among the aims of the Cross-Visitation Program is the encouragement of teacher inquiry and writing about students, classrooms, educational issues, and the program itself. Through PhilWP publications such as *The Voice* and *Work in Progress*, as well as a range of professional journals, participants in the program share their knowledge, practices, and perspectives with one another and with a wider national audience.

Cross-visitation has helped to create a network of teachers who can share ideas and ask questions of their colleagues about the teaching of writing. It provides the opportunity for "teachers to make sense of and improve their everyday practice, not by imitating routines and strategies but rather by questioning, observing, documenting and discussing their own work in relation to the work of others" (Lytle and Fecho 1991).

It also provides much-needed time for teachers to create and implement specific plans for curricular change with colleagues within their school. An elementary teacher-consultant, Jean Farlino, writes:

> This is the fourth year that Mrs. J. and I are collaborating on the teaching of writing with her third-grade class. . . . We have begun to use portfolios for assessing writing. As a start we have been reading through current literature on the topic and looking closely at the logistics of keeping portfolios. Secondly, we have decided to start small by choosing four students. . . . Lastly, we agreed to review the portfolios monthly.

The Cross-Visitation Program exemplifies the ways in which the resources of the partners work together to enable teachers to share knowledge, inquire about practices, and broaden perspectives through classroom-based collaboration. The network of teachers involved in cross-visitation has also helped to disseminate ideas and innovations across schools and throughout the school district. Sharing information within and across communities of teachers has also been an important way for teachers to develop ideas and locate resources to support their work.

The Writing Assessment Program

Another Philadelphia Writing Project teacher-consultant, Carol Merrill, wrote about her colleagues' learning in her final report on a seventh-grade citywide workshop on writing assessment:

> Through the series of workshops the teachers in this group widened the lens through which they saw student writing and the students as individuals. . . . Teachers learned through real experiences . . . that there is value in looking for the positive aspects in a student's writing. . . . Teachers started to see what their students were able to learn from the assignments and that merely evaluating what *is not* present tends to blind a teacher to what *is* present in a student's writing. . . . Participants said that they would look at student writing differently now; they would try to see things more from the student's vantage point.

The Writing Assessment Program was initiated by the School District of Philadelphia in 1986, coordinated by PATHS/PRISM, and led by teacher-consultants of the Philadelphia Writing Project. The program was initially devised to provide teachers with approaches to writing assessment that matched the perspectives on teaching writing that were part of the overall WAC effort. As a result, the school district invited PATHS/PRISM and PhilWP to provide programmatic coordination, university consultants, and teacher-consultant leadership. Over the next several years (1986–1991), the program evolved through a range of structures and formats. For example, groups of teachers of particular grades (three, five, seven, eleven) and subjects (English, social studies, mathematics, science) gathered in citywide workshops to compare and discuss the kinds of student writing taking place in their classrooms and the criteria they used to assess student progress. All of these workshop groups were led by teams of teacher-consultants who not only facilitated the sessions but also designed a workshop syllabus, including resource materials and group activities. More than five hundred and forty teacher-consultants took part in this citywide format for the program.

When the Writing Assessment Program adopted a school-based format, PhilWP teacher-consultants on the faculty of each participating school provided program leadership. The school-based Writing Assessment Program was a response to the growing awareness, both locally and nationally, that the possibilities for real change in teaching and learning were substantially limited unless whole schools, as well as individual classrooms, became engaged in purposeful innovation. Many individual teachers were already trying to make changes in their own classrooms, but were frustrated by not having enough opportunities to discuss these changes with their colleagues or to pursue innovative changes as part of a collaborative whole-school effort.

Within each school the participating teachers reflected a range of grades and subjects. The school-based format encouraged sharing and discussion of teachers' differing expectations and assumptions regarding student writing. These school-based conversations across the grades and disciplines proved extremely meaningful to the participating teachers.

A powerful lesson, as teacher-consultant Carol Merrill stated above, was the need for teachers to look closely at individual students when evaluating their work. This vital link between students' work and teachers' assessment practices came alive when teachers looked at student writing as texts to be learned from, rather than simply as papers to be evaluated.

When teachers within the same school community looked at student writing together, they began to see new possibilities for reshaping both curriculum and assessment in ways that would better support student learning. These school-based teacher efforts received significant school district support through the creation in 1991 of a Citywide Task Force on Portfolio and Performance-Based Assessment. PhilWP and PATHS/PRISM, as members of the task force, were among the organizations providing professional development opportunities to teachers carrying out pilot projects in portfolio and performance-based assessment in elementary and middle schools.

During the spring of 1992, school-based teams of teachers explored and began to develop a range of tools and approaches for assessing student learning, including parent and student surveys, developmental checklists, and interdisciplinary projects. Teams worked to define what kinds of portfolios made sense for their students and their schools. Pilot project efforts drew heavily on teachers' earlier experiences in the Writing Assessment Program and on teacher-consultant involvement on many school teams. Support for the pilot project teams included a seminar, "Assessment and Teacher Inquiry," jointly sponsored by PATHS/PRISM and PhilWP, which provided opportunities for sharing ideas and projects across schools and for learning from current research.

The seminar was designed to support teachers' inquiry into large questions, as well as specific practices, in the area of assessment. A middle school social studies teacher, Dennis Barnebey, reflected on his own learning as he worked to develop an alternative assessment project with other teachers in his school:

> Collaboration is expected, if not required, if we are going to find new ways of helping students to learn. Teachers must collaborate with students, students with students, and teachers with teachers. It seems we will be putting "new wine in old skins" if we don't build in all three levels of collaboration in any project we undertake to change what happens in our schools. ... Without a doubt, there has been no greater boost to my teaching career than having had the opportunity to collaborate with other like-minded colleagues. ... We must be able to look at children, understand what they are able to do, challenge them to learn as much as they can, and assess their growth fairly in a way which does not make us all crazy or exhausted. Key to all of this is establishing the atmosphere in a room, or school, that encourages positive collaboration.

These pilot assessment projects are currently in their second year. While it is too soon to say what effects the projects will ultimately have on changing assessment practices throughout the school district, participating teachers have benefited from opportunities to examine their own practices, develop new approaches to assessment, and reflect on their learning.

Changes and Challenges for the Partnership

The School District of Philadelphia's emphasis on writing as integral to all student learning had encouraged teachers to investigate their own classroom practices in the teaching of writing and to develop some new approaches to the teaching of writing in their classrooms. During the past nine years substantial numbers of teachers have drawn upon the professional development opportunities represented by PATHS/PRISM and PhilWP programs and have used these opportunities to build new connections with colleagues, within and across schools. Through programs offered by these two organizations and with the support of the School District of Philadelphia, a climate for innovation has been created within many schools in the district. Thematic and interdisciplinary approaches, literature-based reading programs, writing in math and science, and learning from colleagues are among the noticeable changes in curriculum, instruction, and professional relationships.

While these changes are both noticeable and positive, many challenges remain. Partnerships require time and energy to flourish; collaboration over time takes time. Writing across the curriculum began with twenty-eight schools in 1984, and PhilWP began with thirty-two teacher-consultants in 1986. As WAC grew to include all of Philadelphia's schools, and PhilWP expanded to 250 teacher-consultants, both organizations have experienced the challenges of program growth. The energy and responsiveness of teachers challenge our organizations to provide growing levels of resources and support structures.

At the same time, responding to the needs and interests of teachers and schools becomes more complex as teachers and schools ask a broader range of educational questions. The investigation of classroom and school practices around writing has widened to include broad issues of restructuring teaching, learning, and schooling. As a result, our organizations are challenged to provide support, technical assistance, resources, and expertise around an increasingly diverse and sophisticated educational reform agenda.

A final pair of challenges concerns responsiveness to divergent but equally important needs. One of these is the significance of maintaining citywide and K−12 dialogue on students, curriculum, and standards, even as individual schools are encouraged to pursue site-based innovations. Both of our organizations are committed to assisting school-based reform while also continuing to support teachers' efforts to overcome the classroom-bound or school-bound isolation that previously characterized so much of their experience.

Perhaps the most complicated challenge of all is that of responding to the diverse professional growth needs of both new and experienced teachers. Keeping programs dynamic rather than static is not easy, but it is essential if we are to meet the needs of an ever-changing population of teachers. At any one time and over time, a range of programs and professional opportunities needs to be available if teachers with varying interests, at different stages of professional growth, are to find the resources and networks they desire.

   If the complicated challenges described above are to be addressed with any measure of success, especially in a large urban school district, partnerships such as those we have detailed are essential. The maintenance of the partnership among the School District of Philadelphia, PATHS/PRISM, and PhilWP has not been without its growing pains. At the same time, this partnership, which has evolved and flourished over more than seven years, is the source of some of the most substantive professional development opportunities available to Philadelphia teachers. While many challenges remain, we are heartened by the continuing efforts of the partners to sustain productive collaboration in support of teachers and students.

Reference

Lytle, Susan L., and Robert Fechol. 1991. "Meeting Strangers in Familiar Places: Teacher Collaboration by Cross-Visitation." *English Education.* (February): 8.

18

From Top Down to Grass Roots: Writing Across the Curriculum Districtwide

Nana E. Hilsenbeck

The Beginning

The young black student entered a classroom for the emotionally handicapped (EH) and announced, "I don't want to work today; can I write?" This student had found the joy of discovery through writing. This young man became hooked on writing when he realized that he had something to write using his own words. When his paper was completed, his peers and adults read and appreciated his writing. The teacher started with a wild animal unit because this eighth grader did not believe he could write anything; he had not been taught from kindergarten that he had something worthwhile to say. The students were to write about a wild animal that they had personally seen. For this young man the only one that came to mind was an opossum. The teacher said the opossum was perfect! The student researched the facts about the animal and wrote a facts list. The requirement for these EH students in this classroom was to have at least ten facts before they started writing.

The program to promote the use of the writing process in all content areas was called Writing Across the Disciplines (WAD) in Volusia County Schools in Florida. This program, which was supported by Dr. Evelyn Lynn, the assistant superintendent of Volusia County Schools in 1981, used writing as a viable learning strategy. This same young man attended a school board meeting in 1982 and told the members of the board that his paper, entitled "Mr. O. Possum," was the first he had ever written. Until he had a trained writing teacher, he had only copied from an encyclopedia.

Top Down to Grass Roots

The WAD has supported writing instruction for all students in all content areas. Writing makes a difference in the way students learn and process what they've learned. With a vision for writing in all classrooms, Dr. Lynn put the plan into motion through two actions: first, she hired Dr. Nancy McGee, a consultant from the University of Central Florida, for one full year to teach teachers how to write and how to coach writing in their classrooms. Payment for the consultant was arranged with the staff development department in the district. Dr. McGee would supply workshop leadership, facilitate monthly sessions of the planning group's work, assist in writing the end-of-year report, and consult in program development.

Second, Dr. Lynn requested that the secondary administrators choose one or two faculty members who were respected by their peers to serve on a writing task force. She wanted to use the "teacher teaching teachers" model. This group of teachers was asked to attend a summer writing in-service and to participate in monthly meetings for updating research-based knowledge about writing and sharing successful strategies in their classrooms.

Sharing the Wealth of Writing

The first week of in-service started with personal writing—writing about what we knew. Dr. McGee had each of us write about ourselves, our dreams, and our fears. She introduced us to the writings of Donald Murray and Donald Graves. Books by Lucy Calkins, Nancie Atwell, and Regie Routman would come later. Many of us were afraid of writing, especially in front of our peers! We learned we could overcome that fear, and we experienced how our students felt when we assigned writing instead of taught writing. As the two-week in-service progressed, we began to gain confidence in ourselves. We acted as coaches assisting each other and sharing what we had written. Sharing was an important process. It gave us insight into the importance of publishing.

The last two days of the summer in-service, our assignment was to devise a plan for promoting and coaching writing at our individual schools. Everyone had a different plan, but we shared and borrowed from each other. The vision from "top down" was beginning to receive "grass-roots" enthusiasm.

After one short month in our schools, every person on the task force came back to the meeting with tales of success. We shared our writing and writing samples from students. One school had started a publishing incentive program. When students wrote something that was published at the school level or outside the school, they received a student-designed T-shirt. The most popular T-shirt had a picture of a dog with the caption: GET ON THE WRITE TRACK. After that sharing session, everyone believed this program was now "our" program.

A newsletter was one of the first suggestions for broadening our base of operation. *Writing Tips* became the first newsletter, and it is still the writing newsletter that our teachers receive each month. Other ways of broadening our base for information were

- module development for major content areas
- development of writing idea booklets(s)
- development of demonstration lessons

At the same time that WAD was developing, the Department of Education in Florida passed the Jack Gordon Writing Act, which decreased the size of English classes and mandated a major writing piece per week for students in the Writing Enhancement classes. The WAD in-service gave many of our teachers the confidence they needed to provide the required instruction to high school students in the Writing Enhancement classes.

Teachers who tried writing as an alternative to workbooks or multiple choice questions saw its value as a learning strategy and as a motivator of students. Math teachers would ask students to write the steps they took in solving a problem to discover where they were having difficulties, as well as to model problem-solving strategies for students who needed help. (See Appendix, Exhibit A.)

An English teacher had her students write about their reactions to what they were learning in social studies (Appendix E, Exhibit B), and music teachers had fun with concrete poetry using the musical instrument as the object of the poetry (Appendix, Exhibit C). Many classes began with content journal writing, in which students respond in their own words to the meaning of a key word or concept for that day's lesson. This technique of responding before learning allowed the teacher to have quick pretests without the students' fearing their responses would be graded or not acceptable. After the lesson, many teachers would again request a reaction to the concept to determine if the concept was clear or if more teaching was needed. (See Appendix, Exhibit D.)

Students who loved science found that writing about aerodynamics in English was acceptable; acrostic poems using science terminology or diamantes transcribed onto kites gave students pride in their accomplishments. After students were exposed to different writing strategies, acrostic and concrete poetry appeared in all classrooms, and writing organizers using drawings or boxes assisted students in understanding problems or the task at hand. (See Appendix, Exhibit D.)

Like our EH teen, students came to class wanting to write because the teacher had provided strategies that allowed them to find success in their writing. Realizing that publishing provides real audiences for writing, many of the schools started their own publishing houses using parent volunteers. The district's two major publications, *Imprints* and *Impressions*, reflected the writing talents of students in all grades.

How it Survived

The program had top-down and grass-roots support; but in a large district of over 45,000 students, the program had to provide ongoing in-service. The in-service each month provided the task force members researched-based information. Individual teachers experiencing success using writing provided school-based workshops, wrote newsletter articles, and encouraged new teachers to integrate writing into content. From October 1981 through August 1982 the task force continued to promote and encourage writing as a viable classroom strategy. With the end of the year and our consultant's contract, many teachers felt that the program needed its own consultant. Therefore, with help from the assistant superintendent for curriculum, a teacher on assignment (TOA) was hired to assist with the management of writing in the district. This person became the catalyst who coordinated the task force meetings, provided in-service for new teachers in writing strategies, and promoted writing in all content areas.

Cynthia Pino, the first TOA, provided in-service to new teachers, gave demonstration lessons, and served as a writing coach in classrooms. She edited *Writing Activities Recommended by Classroom Teachers*, published for and by teachers, plus many other, smaller booklets to assist in teaching writing.

Taking the High Road: How it Changed

From 1982 through 1986, the program expanded to the elementary level, making it a K−12 program. The district continued to support the program with a TOA coordinator. Although there were several TOAs over the years, the original vision has not changed. Writing across the disciplines in Volusia County Schools is a program that believes writing is an essential skill for all students. Humans need to communicate their experiences — ideas, knowledge, and creativity.

In 1986 our new superintendent, Dr. James Surratt, identified as a goal that our teachers and students become technologically literate. His plan included purchasing over 5,000 computers for the classrooms. In his wisdom, he realized that the quickest way to teach computer literacy was through writing. All our kindergarten students began using a computer program called "Writing to Read." Using computers for writing after kindergarten was a natural sequence. Thus, in 1986 all elementary teachers and all English teachers were allowed to take a computer home to learn how to use it as a writing tool. The program was entitled "Process Writing," defined as using the steps of the writing process with the computer as the writing tool.

In addition to the newsletter, *Writing Tips*, *Behind the Screens* provided helpful computer writing hints. The teachers wrote *Computer Writing Activities* to assist in using the computer as a writing tool. Now that all elementary teachers and all English teachers were required to teach writing and use the computer as a writing tool, as well as our high school level writing in the content areas, an additional TOA was hired to ensure support through in-service. This continued support made it possible for our district to grow as a writing district receiving state and national recognition.

A Decade of Writing

October 1991 marked the tenth anniversary of WAD in our district. Veteran and new teachers still are attending in-services and promoting writing in their classrooms and school sites. Writing folders are expected for every student, grades K−12. Each spring, representative folders are read from every teacher's classroom to provide feedback, as well as to plan for the type of in-service needed. Monitoring the folders gives an opportunity to celebrate and praise the students and teachers for a job well done.

Today the program has these components:

- school-based and districtwide writing in-service
- computer writing in-service for all new teachers and others who need additional computer assistance
- *Writing Tips* and *Computer Tips* newsletters for all teachers
- districtwide writing contests culminating in district-published books for elementary and secondary students
- Youth Authors' Conferences for elementary and secondary students
- area meetings for writing task force open to all interested teachers
- classroom demonstration lessons upon request
- technical assistance and coaching in writing
- K−5 integrated curriculum that does not use workbooks — reading, writing, and speaking are emphasized
- teacher publication, *Images*, with public praise for teachers who write
- senior portfolio writing contest in English

- writing folder for all students K−12
- writing audit grades 1−12 from February to April.

Teachers are suggesting that a portfolio follow the students instead of just a writing folder. In the future this will be an alternative form of assessment that directly affects curriculum development and student progress. In this process teachers and students will be the key. No program survives and thrives unless it has the elements of support at all levels, responsive in-service, and a productive monitoring plan that teachers view as positive, not punitive.

The Future?

Writing by its very nature crosses content and cultural boundaries. If we listened to the experts, students need to write about what they know. Everyone has different knowledge; that makes writing interesting. With portfolio assessment as an authentic method of evaluating writing and changing curriculum to meet students' needs, a bright future exists for us. Our EH student, who wanted to write instead of work, graduated from high school knowing the importance of the writing process as a learning and discovery tool. This dynamic instructional strategy— Writing Across the Disciplines—is a vital way of meeting students' individual needs.

Appendix
Exhibits and Examples

Exhibit A

Math Problem

The area of the border in the figure is 225 square meters. How wide is this border if the outside length is 25 meters and the outside width is 15 meters?

Student's Strategy: First, I multiplied 25m × 15m to get the area of the entire rectangle. Then I subtracted 225m (area of the border) from 375 (area of the entire rectangle) and got 150m as the area of the center section. The inside length equals $25-2x$ because you have to take away the two sidewalk widths and the inside width if $15-2x$ (same reason). Next I set 150 equal to the inside width times the inside length. I multiplied this FOIL and subtracted 150 from both sides to set it equal to zero. I tried to factor it but it didn't work so I put it into the quadratic formula. The two answers I got for the width of the border were 16.614 meters and 3.3956 meters. The width of the sidewalk couldn't be wider than the entire width (15m) so 16.614m wouldn't work. I was left with 3.3956 meters for my answer.

Denise Goforth, Algebra II
Grade 10

Exhibit B

English/Social Studies
Student was asked if he felt Phillip Nolan's punishment fair.
Student's response: Was it fair? Did Phillip Nolan really commit treason? Phillip Nolan, lieutenant in the Army of the United States, was tried for treason in the year 1807. At Fort Adams, it was proven that Nolan disliked the Army. He was associated with Aaron Burr and was part of the militia for Burr's new country.

I think Nolan is guilty of being naive. He saw Burr as a god and would undo anything for him. Nolan is a traitor with a childlike belief in Burr.

In the way of a trial, Nolan had an extremely fair one. He got his chance to speak his mind and he did so. I think that his sentence was fair because the judge knew that his "wish" would teach him a lesson.

If the same event were to happen in 1992 the result would be very different. Today, people burn flags and get away with it. Also, we have a freedom of speech which allows us to say what we wish without being penalized. In conclusion, I think that Phillip Nolan was treated fairly according to the justice system available at that time. He was quick to speak and surely regretted his words.

Jennifer Blom
Middle School Integrated Unit
Grade 8

Exhibit C

Music

Notes

Notes
are
beautiful.
They
have a
good
sound.
Notes
will
make
people
fall in
love.
Music is made up of
hundreds of notes.
Melodies are made up
of many of them. So
the next time you think
music, think of notes.

Naquisha Nelson
Grade 8, Music

Exhibit D

Science/English
Assignment: Tell how you made your kite.

We had been studying aerodynamics in science for sometime when we made kites. This project was part of our science class and also part of our English class.

In English we had to write diamante poems. We picked one to place on the kite which we flew.

The other half of the task was building the actual kite. The first step was taping two long sticks together in the shape of a large, lowercase "t."

Mike Rubino
M/S Integrated Unit
Grade 8

Multicultural:
Student's response is to a literature story about fears.

About the war that's nothing to laugh about. It's real hard not to be scared by the bombs, the rifles, grenades and the guns. My country is not free like the United States of America. When I see the news I repeat to myself it's not free. My country is very poor. People live in the streets. When I saw poor people in the streets, I gave them "un colon." That's my country's money name. In my country the guerrillas have killed almost everybody that got in their way. When I was little I was afraid of the helicopters and planes. Now I'm a little scared I guess. I guess my country is still the same as when I left. I'm glad I left El Salvador, Central America.

Rhina Charlaix
Grade 4

Student's Poetic Example:

(more) Finances (grandfather)

I take a message in my grandfather's office.
(a job I earned for being related)
He is a shrewd businessman — fascinated
by capital gain.
If you are a client (with green in your
        hand),
you are welcomed and loved.
If you are a relative (with care in your
        heart),
you are despised and blamed.
But he has taught me one thing-
his affection cannot be won,
it must be bought (and I just
don't have enough money).

Kelle McArdle
English, Grade 12

19

An Open Letter: Why Should Teachers Become Involved with Writing Across the Curriculum?

James K. Upton

Dear Colleague,

As the unofficial spokesperson for those who work in "the Write Place," the Burlington Community High School writing/learning center, I am more than happy to share our perceptions and ideas about writing to learn theory and pedagogy. Whether we were truly farsighted or blindly lucky in establishing the center, our exploration of writing to learn activities has been expanding for over a decade, and our views are based on our continuing research, our work in our own classes, our work in and through our writing/learning center, and our work as consultants for other districts. Many of us who developed the plan for our Communication Resource Center in the early eighties had participated in the Iowa Writing Project and had adopted a process approach to writing and learning. One of our primary objectives for the center continues to be that it "become the center for staff exploration, development, implementation, and sharing of writing-to-learn activities" (School Mission Statement). As in many high school centers, we spend most of our time working with students and staff on traditional writing activities, and we believe that these efforts are important. However, we are gaining converts to writing as a powerful learning tool, and more content-area instructors are beginning to use writing to learn strategies. The staff in the center is very proactive; we seek out, encourage, and assist all teachers in the use of both traditional and writing to learn activities.

Those of us who work with writing to learn activities see our efforts as ongoing processes. For example, we have begun investigation into authentic and portfolio assessment, and we believe that these hold great promise as important components in writing to learn activities. We have also become involved in sharing our efforts with other school districts and often make presentations at professional meetings. I do want to make clear that our perceptions and ideas are more practice-based than research-based. While we continue to explore writing to learn theory and pedagogy, we always emphasize to students and staff to do what works, and what works is our most important criterion for evaluating our efforts.

Our work in the area of writing to learn activities has been an "inside-out" effort. Neither our district nor our building has made the large-scale commitment to exploration and implementation of writing to learn activities. Most of our work in this area has been based in our writing/learning center. We have deliberately sought out sympathetic or semi-interested teachers and have worked with them in incorporating more traditional writing activities into their classrooms. Then, we have further encouraged and assisted them in the exploration, development, and implementation of writing to learn activities. This inside-out approach has been most effective in creating truly committed converts; however, such an approach is limited in its immediate large-scale impact. I do work as a consultant for districts that have made the large-scale commitment to writing to learn, so my reflections are based on my classroom, center, and consultant experiences. However, as with all learning activities, I would emphasize that teachers, departments, buildings, or districts must work with what is available and must be committed to what works most efficiently in their specific situation.

I want to make clear, at least from my perspective, what writing to learn is and is not. Just as "cooperative" and "collaborative" learning are often used interchangeably but may mean entirely different concepts, so too "writing to learn" and "writing across the curriculum" (WAC) are often used interchangeably but may mean entirely different concepts. In the broadest sense, WAC includes any type of writing we ask our students to complete, including writing to learn activities. For the sake of clarification, our approach with students and staff is that WAC is most often "writing to show learning." Such writings are usually summative activities and are formally evaluated to measure what has been learned. In theory, the learning has already occurred and is shown in the written essay exams, research papers, or abstracts. This use of writing may indeed be valuable and justified; however, such assignments often place much emphasis on surface features of the writing (the correctness, external structure, etc.) and do little to engage the student with the language as a means of learning the content or improving skills.

On the other hand, writing to learn activities are usually formative and are designed to engage students with written language to help them improve content learning and thinking skills. Such writings are the means to involving students in their own discoveries and understanding of the content materials and of their own learning. Writing to learn activities are usually nontraditional and creative, are usually not formally evaluated or graded, are always student-centered rather than content-centered, and are often key components in improving the subsequent writing to show learning. Writing across the curriculum may involve both writing to learn and writing to show learning; what is essential is that a clear distinction among these terms be reached to avoid needless confusion and frustration.

The use of writing to learn activities often triggers a debate over the importance of the quality of written expression, and this issue is important to resolve. The ability to "process" oral and written language clearly and correctly is one of the fundamental goals of education, and all teachers need to provide students with positive experiences to achieve this goal. In both writing to show learning and writing to learn activities, all instructors should encourage and positively respond to clear and effective use of language; however, the primary focus in writing to learn activities must always be on the quality of content learning and thinking skills.

Some Reflections

Absolutely essential in the exploration, implementation, and support of writing to learn theory and pedagogy is the commitment of time and resources. Such endeavors are often massive undertakings, and the commitment to provide adequate resources and time both for initial exploration and development and for ongoing implementation, assessment, sharing, and support must be secured. Our experiences have been that it is most often the lack of time for exploration and especially for follow-up sharing and support that is most crucial in the failure of writing to learn activities at the staff level. The exploration and development of writing to learn activities will inevitably raise other educational issues — for example, authentic and/or portfolio assessment — that also involve much time to explore, develop, implement, assess, and share. We have come to realize that we must give students adequate school time to complete both writing to learn and writing to show learning activities to emphasize our belief in the importance of these, and instructors too must have school time to make writing to learn ventures successful.

The actual exploration of writing to learn theory and pedagogy should involve as many staff, administrators, board members, students, and citizens as possible and practical. Some negative reaction to any exploration of new educational strategies is inevitable, and no matter how unfounded, unfair, or unrealistic, such criticisms must be dealt with effectively. Prevention is a major key. All members of the educational and social community must become "stakeholders" and have ownership of the exploration, development, implementation, assessment, and sharing of writing to learn activities. Although the value of these activities has been proved repeatedly, just as students in our classes must discover truths for themselves, so too must staff and the community discover the truths about writing to learn for themselves.

Giving all staff members time to explore writing to learn theory and pedagogy will, unfortunately, not make all of them enthusiastic supporters. There will be some who see any discussion or exploration of new methods as a not-so-subtle criticism of their teaching. People will hear: "I've been teaching for twenty years and my students have gone to college and become successful. Why should I change what has been working for twenty years?" The most effective solution to such difficulties lies in the selection of those who are responsible for the exploration, implementation, and follow-up support. The most effective leaders or facilitators of writing to learn activities are those current staff members who become knowledgeable and truly committed to the value of this approach. While zealots are often counterproductive, there must be a core of staff members who will assume leadership roles to provide training to others and assume the responsibility for the ongoing implementation, assessment, and support needed. Such leaders need not be language arts instructors (indeed a concerted effort to involve a wide range of teachers as leaders should be made), but they should be highly knowledgeable about writing to learn theory and pedagogy and/or be willing to become colearners with all other staff and students in this area. The leaders should be brave, patient, and skilled at cooperative/collaborative learning; they will literally become the models for both staff and students.

Just as no teacher can read books or attend a workshop on whole language and become an expert on whole language, so it is with writing to learn strategies. I must admit that I constantly amaze myself at how much I discover I do not know about learning, writing, and students. Our experiences have been that the most effective staff in-services are inductive experiences in which the staff become learners and later are provided with substantial amounts of follow-up time throughout the year for ongoing development, assessment, sharing, and support. The model of the National Writing Project is one of the most effective, but buildings and districts must develop the most effective initial and follow-up structures to meet their own needs.

Depending on the situation, outside consultants can be effective in exploring writing to learn strategies. If outside consultants are used, they should work with local staff members who will serve as leaders prior to and after the initial training. Involving all staff members in a writing to learn workshop prior to implementation is most effective, and arrangements for the consultants to return for follow-up work should be made in advance. As in teaching, the ultimate goal is to make the staff independent; however, quality consultants can provide effective initial introduction and vital ongoing ideas and support for both the local leaders and the staff.

Convincing staff members to examine writing to learn theory and pedagogy is often frustrating, and the worst approach is for administration to mandate such endeavors. The values of writing to learn activities will be discovered by almost all who become involved; however, some initial "selling" of the approach is often necessary and effective. One important positive approach to induce teachers to consider writing to learn strategies is to emphasize these are to be used *in lieu of* some current teaching activities. All of those involved in the exploration and eventual implementation must understand that such uses of writing are not additions to what they are already attempting to do in their classes. Indeed, attempting to add writing to learn activities guarantees only frustration and failure for staff and students. Substitution is essential.

Some teachers believe that every activity they have students complete is wonderful, but even the use of writing to learn strategies as a matter of variety has some merit. Almost all of us are constantly bombarded with new federal, state, or local mandates; we are expected to do more for increasing numbers of students with fewer resources and less time. The substitution of creative writing to learn activities is literally a welcome relief for many teachers.

Another issue that can be a selling point is that content teachers are not going to be involved in the direct teaching of writing; they will be involved in the use of writing. Writing to learn means determining the student content or thinking outcomes and then developing writing or language activities to help students achieve these. Reading and responding with concern for the learner and the learning are the major instructor characteristics for effective use of writing to learn activities. While we encourage teachers to make positive comments about effective uses of written language in writing to learn activities, the primary emphasis must always be on the quality of learning and thinking shown.

The use of writing to learn activities will demand a new and challenging role for the teachers. Teachers will become literal colearners with their students and will have an opportunity to assume a myriad of challenging roles in cooperative and collaborative activities. Beyond the new excitement in the classroom, the written outcomes of writing to learn activities will be much more interesting and exciting to read than are most traditional written products.

Communication is a major consideration within and throughout writing to learn endeavors. Many process language arts teachers can recount horror stories of early uses of a process approach to writing instruction when children took papers home that did not have all surface errors marked. Many parents became upset and believed that teachers were not doing their jobs because the errors were not noted. We all learned a valuable lesson; we must keep the public informed of new or innovative educational techniques. This is especially true when students become involved in creative writing to learn assignments and becomes even more necessary if authentic/portfolio assessment is incorporated into writing to learn activities. Most parents want the best for their children and will be supportive if they have adequate information *before* the new technique is implemented.

Those who agree to become local leaders and/or the consultants can develop a list of written resources about learning, writing, and writing to learn for use by staff and community, and the quantity and quality of available resources continues to increase. Those interested should also join the "National Network of Writing Across the Curriculum Programs." This is an NCTE Special Interest Group, like the National Writing Centers Association, and the group has meetings at NCTE and CCCC. There is a directory of schools that have such programs, and the contact person is Christopher Thaiss, George Mason University, Fairfax, Virginia 22030—4444.

It is also most worthwhile to visit other schools that have some experience in writing to learn strategies. There is great value in seeing and sharing the practical kinds of activities that others have developed. Although we repeatedly emphasize that schools must develop ownership of their own unique materials, forms, and processes for writing to learn activities, the interschool sharing of ideas, materials, and personnel is an excellent investment. We have developed our own list of resources and materials for writing to learn activities, and we are happy to share these with all those interested.

I again want to emphasize the necessity of an effective follow-up sharing and support system. This can be the vital element in the eventual success of writing to learn activities. Although I am biased, at the high school level the multifunctional writing/learning center seems to be the most effective method to provide for this essential follow-up sharing and support system. As a complement to traditional writing activities, a writing/learning center more than justifies its existence; however, such a center is also a most logical and effective center for writing to learn activities. The center can be the clearinghouse for resource materials, can be the center for storing and sharing of developed materials and approaches, can be the place for formal and informal sharing and support sessions, and is the logical place for students to seek help with their writing to learn assignments. Just as a multifunctional writing/learning center makes coordination of cross-curricular writing to show learning assignments more efficient (having students in history and language arts complete a research project for both classes), using the writing/learning center to coordinate writing to learn activities is also more efficient. The demands of staff and student tutors in such a multifunctional center are much greater, but the benefits for students and staff are enormous. I have been a consultant in districts that have developed coordinating committees, support networks, and other methods to provide the follow-up sharing and support; however, a writing/learning center can readily become a most effective center for such activities.

Enough of the plug for writing centers. The scariest part of writing to learn for most teachers begins after the research and training are completed; they must begin to use these activities with their students. No matter how committed teachers are to writing to learn, this is a combination of Kierkegaard's "leap of faith" and the proverbial patience of Job. For most students, the use of writing to learn activities will be a new and strange phenomenon, and the role of the teacher and the structure of the class must change significantly if the use of these is to be successful.

Most important, the new role for the teacher and new structure for the classroom means a new use of time to model and implement writing to learn activities. Modeling and completing such activities will demand much time early in a course, and it is equally important to provide subsequent, adequate amounts of class time for student work on writing to learn activities. Yes, these activities are to be used in lieu of other learning strategies; however, adequate class time must be provided for introduction, modeling, and ongoing work and for the possible use of authentic and/or portfolio assessments. Just as teachers must develop ownership of the writing to learn theory and pedagogy, students must develop ownership of the activities they are asked to complete. In both cases, the use of school time to underscore the value of these activities is crucial.

In the introduction and initial use, teachers must be honest and admit that these are new activities for them also, and they must immediately begin to establish the trust that is necessary for the writing to learn activities to be successful. The teachers must literally become colearners with students and must be involved in completing many of the writing to learn activities such as large- or small-group work, cooperative/collaborative efforts, or modeling several examples for students. It is also often beneficial to share completed samples of previous students' work as these become available and to share the completed works of students throughout the course as a means of further modeling and encouragement.

Creating the climate of mutual respect and trust is essential. Students are distrustful of the educational system in general and teachers in particular, and it will take honesty and time to convince them that they are not being set up for some hidden agenda and that writing to learn activities can be enjoyable as well as educational. The attitudes and actions of classroom teachers are crucial in achieving this. The efforts of writing teachers who espouse a process approach but evaluate traditionally are more damaging than those who espouse traditional writing methods and evaluate traditionally. The same principle applies to those who involve students in writing to learn activities and then evaluate the work as product. The responses to work must be learning and thinking based, and teachers must practice what this methodology implies. Misusing writing to learn strategies is worse than not using them at all.

One of the keys to successful completion of writing to learn assignments (and of all assignments) is to make sure that students clearly understand the assessment or evaluation criteria. Many materials we have developed stress this essential understanding, and sharing previously completed samples of successful activities that demonstrate the evaluation criteria is also effective.

We believe that the classroom should also become an extensive resource room. Whether the course is math or science or industrial technology, students seem most engaged and have wider exploration possibilities when instructors make a conscientious effort to provide as many sources of information as possible. These sources need not be limited to print. Instructors can provide in-class access to films and audiotapes as well as lists of local, regional, and national "human resources" who may be able to provide additional information. Computer hookups with the ERIC system or on-line search systems at college or university libraries are also relatively easy and inexpensive to arrange.

We have also discovered that writing to learn activities seem to be most effective if they are coordinated with or complement other learning activities rather than being done in isolation. For example, a study of the issue of slavery as a cause of the Civil War might be tied into some independent or group research about the history of slavery, the abolitionists' movement, John Brown, and other related issues; a role-playing debate between Northern and Southern politicians; and then a writing to learn activity creating a newspaper of the time that includes newspaper stories, editorials, cartoons, want ads, and personal ads. The more students can have experiences with all forms of communications and the more they can be led to think critically and creatively, the more effective meaning makers they will become and the more successfully they will complete writing to show learning tests.

The more creative the writing to learn activities themselves, the more engaging and effective they become. We have seen students write brilliant biopoems about endangered species; create biographies of composers set to the music they wrote; create insightful "unsent letters" that reveal the personality and conflicts facing historical and fictional characters; create mock debates among historical or literary figures based on the old TV show "Face to Face" (an argument between Malcolm X and Martin Luther King, Jr., about the effects of each on the civil rights movement); create riveting personal "diaries" of historical or literary characters (the diary entry of Harry Truman after making the decision to drop the atom bomb is heartbreaking); create a heaven or hell so the characters can share their feelings about events they caused but did not live to see used or abused ("Albert Einstein, would you have explored nuclear energy if you knew the dangers it now poses?"); explain a scientific concept for a nonscientific audience ("Explain covalent bonding so that an English teacher could understand it" or "Write a handbook for new players that gives tips on winning at tennis"). The possibilities are limited only by the instructors' or students' imaginations. It is also valuable to have students create writing to learn activities for their own work or as a group or class activity for possible completion by others.

I also want to emphasize the value of computers in writing to learn activities. In addition to extending sources of information beyond the classroom, networked computers can facilitate group completion of writing to learn activities and can allow for most effective cooperative and collaborative writing/learning experiences. Beyond this, many computers can create blank forms to add realism to writing to learn activities. Computers can generate blank newspaper formats for completion of newspapers about historical or fictional time periods; letterhead stationery and memos ("Write the memo that President Truman may have written in firing General MacArthur"); or blank "cartoon balloons" so that students can create their own messages for pictures of historical persons or events. Computer technology is no replacement for the active involvement of students with the language, but the technology can add significantly to the quality of the learning experience.

Publishing and sharing writing to learn activities as well as traditional writing tasks is also important. It is not necessary to literally publish books, but having students share orally, displaying completed projects, and having those outside the class view these are all important parts of the positive experiences students should have with all language experiences.

I must admit that I probably lied a little when I implied earlier that writing to learn activities will not mean more work for teachers. The implementation, especially early in a course, will be a "leap of faith" and will require patience until students buy into the use of writing for learning (although students will be far less reluctant than staff). The work, however, will be of a different kind, and the eventual rewards will be most satisfactory for both students and staff. Because a different kind of work will be required (one that often involves interaction with students), the importance of adequate school time to develop, implement, assess, share, and support others is obvious and must be provided.

The exploration and use of authentic and portfolio assessment as these relate to writing to learn and traditional writing tasks creates many exciting implications and possibilities. Those who are beginning to explore writing to learn strategies and those who have already begun to use these strategies should include the study of authentic and portfolio assessment in their research and implementation.

As a way of ending this chapter, I want to share a common occurrence in my in-service work. I am often asked what is the one key element in successfully implementing writing to learn activities, and I used to answer "courage." However, I now answer "time." Time to help students improve their educational experiences through writing to learn strategies, time to explore, time to develop, time to implement for both staff and students, time to assess, time to share, and most important, time to support these efforts must be provided. Writing to learn activities will change the role of the teacher, the structure of the classroom, and the experiences of students, but more than that, writing to learn strategies will help change students into active, competent, and confident lifelong learners.

Description of Programs

Name of School/District/Region: Arizona Department of Education
Address: 1535 W. Jefferson, Phoenix, AZ 85007
Contact Person: Muriel Rosman or Lois Easton
Phone Number/FAX/E-mail: (602) 542−3537 (Rossman); (602) 577−5080 (Easton)
Public/Private: Public   **Grades:** Pre-K−12
When and How Program Began: The Goals for Educational Excellence program was legislated in 1987; the ASAP was legislated in 1990. The curriculum is being implemented by districts according to a four-year, phase-in plan.
Funding: State funding formerly used for extensive norm-referenced testing
Collaborative Partners (colleges, businesses, networks, etc.): The Legislature and Department of Education were the fundamental partners in this endeavor. The Arizona Education Association and Arizona School Boards were also involved in passing the bill mandating the ASAP.
Description of Program: The basis of the ASAP in English is the state curriculum framework, Language Arts Essential Skills, which establishes guidelines for English K−12.
Special Features of Program: The guidelines describe processes and whole products or outcomes at grades three, eight, and twelve and leave to local control curriculum decisions at other grades. The guidelines establish not only integrated language arts but also language across the curriculum.

Name of School/District/Region: Baltimore County Public Schools
Address: 6901 North Charles Street, Towson, MD 21204
Contact Person: Marcella Emberger
Phone Number/FAX/E-mail: (301) 887—2328, FAX (301) 887—5811
Public/Private: Public   **Grades:**   Pre-K—12
Enrollment: 85,000
When and How Program Began: The program began in 1984 with a summer study committee composed of teachers and administrators across grade and content areas.
Funding: Baltimore County Public Schools funds, Conrad-Hilton grant, federal block grants
Collaborative Partners (colleges, businesses, networks, etc.):   Maryland Writing Project
Description of Program: Staff development program that supports teachers and school leaders as they initiate, implement, and institutionalize WAC
Special Features of Program: Effectiveness of on-site staff development (see *Journal of Staff Development*, "School-Site Support in a WAC Project," Spring 1989)
Future Plans: To explore the relationships among WAC theory and practices and other effective instructional practices that promote and assess thinking in all disciplines
Please list any sources you have found helpful in designing, establishing, and maintaining your program:
    National Writing Project model and research
    Bruce Joyce's research on coaching
    Marion Mohr, et al., teacher-researcher concepts
    Larry Lazotte, et al., effective schools research
    ASCD materials (*Educational Leadership*, yearbooks, etc.)

Name of School/District/Region: Berkshire School
Address: Sheffield, MA 01257
Contact Person: Anna Romano, director, International Student Program
Phone Number/FAX/E-mail: (413) 229–8511, ext. 609, FAX (413) 229–3178
Public/Private: Private/boarding   **Grades:**   9–12
Enrollment: 425
When and How Program Began: In 1983, TWAC began meeting on inter-disciplinary issues and writing as a vehicle for learning. In 1990, the Writing Center opened.
Funding: TWAC funded by faculty enrichment budget; Writing Center funded by capital funds/operating funds
Collaborative Partners (colleges, businesses, networks, etc.):   No formal alliance, only informal ones with other independent schools
Description of Program: TWAC voluntary membership of faculty from each discipline to discuss interdisciplinary issues and to implement WAC
Special Features of Program: 1984, 1987, *A Writer's Handbook* published for faculty/students; September 1990, Writing Center opened
Future Plans: To expand our interdisciplinary senior project and to develop/increase size/outreach of the Writing Center
Please list any sources you have found helpful in designing, establishing, and maintaining your program:
Farrell, Pamela B. 1989. *The High School Writing Center: Establishing and Maintaining One.* Urbana, IL: National Council of Teachers of English.

Name of School/District/Region: Burlington Community High School, "The Write Place"
Address: 421 Terrace Drive, Burlington, IA 52601
Contact Person: James K. Upton
Phone Number/FAX/E-mail: (319) 753–2211
Public/Private: Public   **Grades:**   9–12
Enrollment: 1,600
When and How Program Began: One of the initial goals of Writing/Learning Center
Funding: Volunteers
Description of Program: Based in Writing Center with a proactive staff
Special Features of Program: Extra events for staff and students include study-skills night, faculty coffees.
Future Plans: Hope to fund with state "Excellence" money and expand awareness/use of authentic and portfolio assessment
Please list any sources you have found helpful in designing, establishing, and maintaining your program:
Roots in the Sawdust
Writing to Learn/Learning to Write
Iowa Writing Project

Name of School/District/Region: Detroit Public Schools/University of Michigan Collaboration
Address: English Composition Board, 1025 Angell Hall, University of Michigan, Ann Arbor, MI 48109
Contact Person: Barbra S. Morris or George Cooper
Phone Number/FAX/E-mail: (313) 764–0429
Public/Private: Public   **Grades:** K–12
Enrollment: Fifteen teachers from eight schools (one elementary, two middle, five high school)
When and How Program Began: In 1980 Detroit Public Schools and the university cofounded it and published joint writing to learn manual.
Funding: Jointly/teachers' tuitions paid by Detroit schools
Collaborative Partners (colleges, businesses, networks, etc.): Detroit Public Schools/University of Michigan
Description of Program: In 1985, a collaboration between Mackenzie High School and the university began. Its success led to the course.
Special Features of Program: The course relies upon the continuing satisfaction of collaborative partners.
Future Plans: Now we are planning the course for alternate years with intermediate years used for follow-up in the schools to support the teachers.
Please list any sources you have found helpful in designing, establishing, and maintaining your program:
Many of our ideas have grown out of discussions and an attempt to meet actual classroom needs of teachers. We have attempted to keep all parties apprised of our progress over the years, thereby helping, we hope, to create a climate for open dialogue, evaluation, and planning in the schools.

Name of School/District/Region: Edwards Junior High, Pickens County School District
Address: 1157 Madden Bridge Road, Central, SC 29630
Contact Person: Nancy L. Linvill
Phone Number/FAX/E-mail: (803) 654–1400, CUFAN NTNLNVL
Public/Private: Public **Grades:** 7,8,9
Enrollment: 750
When and How Program Began: Program began when it was funded by a $90,000 Target 2000 South Carolina grant
Funding: South Carolina State Department of Education and a local Rotary Club
Collaborative Partners (colleges, businesses, networks, etc.): Dr. Chris Peters, Clemson University education professor, consultant; an advisory committee composed of parents, teachers, and businesses
Description of Program: Students use Macintosh computers and HyperCard to design computerized term papers. Their projects include written information, pictures, animation, and sound. The students present these to classes in the school.
Special Features of Program: The program is for bright students not meeting their academic potential.
Future Plans: The funding will end at the end of the school year, but we hope to continue the program.

Name of School/District/Region: Elk Grove High School in High School District 214 (northwest suburbs of Chicago)
Address: 500 W. Elk Grove Blvd., Elk Grove, IL 60007
Contact Person: Barry Gadlin, English teacher
Phone Number/FAX/E-mail: (708) 439-4800
Public/Private: Public   **Grades:** 9-12
Enrollment: 1,600 students
When and How Program Began: August 1990 at Dr. Jack Elliott's initiative (Elliott is presently assistant principal)
Funding: No extra funding needed
Description of Program: 105 high school students assigned to a team of six teachers for two years
Special Features of Program: Teachers in program have common planning periods; counselors are part of the team.
Future Plans: Proposal for all freshmen to be involved in a three- or four-teacher block; combinations of disciplines may vary

Name of School/District/Region: J. P. McCaskey High School, School District of Lancaster, southeastern Pennsylvania
Address: 445 North Reservoir Street, P.O. Box 150, Lancaster, PA 17602
Contact Person: Betty Beck, director, Writing Center
Phone Number/FAX/E-mail: (717) 291—6211, FAX (717) 396—6825
Public/Private: Public   **Grades:**   10—12
Enrollment: 1,606 from 12 countries: 45 percent white; 55 percent minority
When and How Program Began: In 1983 in response to low student test scores on statewide test, faculty and administration targeted writing and requested a writing center.
Funding: School board approved and funded the project.
Description of Program: A schoolwide, interdisciplinary, process-oriented program based on collaborative writing using word processing
Special Features of Program: A writing center with desktop publishing and two 20-PC LAN networks in adjoining classrooms
Future Plans: Involvement in Sizer's Coalition of Essential Schools requires performance assessment; thus, students will create exhibitions using HyperCard. Currently, a learning across the curriculum center with Millersville University as a collaborative partner supports the new tutoring program.
Please list any sources you have found helpful in designing, establishing, and maintaining your program:
Beverly Michalak, instructor, National Writing Project at Penn State Harrisburg
Lil Brannon, instructor, Northeastern summer seminars at Martha's Vineyard
IBM-sponsored network training program, Atlanta.

Name of School/District/Region: The McCallie School
Address: 2850 McCallie Avenue, Chattanooga, TN 37404
Contact Person: Pamela B. Farrell-Childers
Phone Number/FAX/E-mail: (615) 493–5849, FAX (615) 629–2852
Public/Private: Private (day/boarding)   **Grades:**   7–12
Enrollment: Over 700
When and How Program Began: Officially began in 1990 with appointment of endowed chair of composition whose duties included the establishment of a WAC program
Funding: Endowment and annual endowed budget
Collaborative Partners (colleges, businesses, networks, etc.):   All disciplines of school, Symposium for Educators (public and private schools), and University of Tennessee at Chattanooga
Description of Program: Based in the Writing Center, the WAC program involves all disciplines, all faculty, and all students in writing.
Special Features of Program: Collaborative teaching and writing workshops, faculty and student readings, guest artist program, WAC retreats
Future Plans: Continue WAC retreats, more writing workshops and presentations by faculty and students, continued publication including McCallie Press
Please list any sources you have found helpful in designing, establishing, and maintaining your program:

Clark, Beverly Lyons. 1985. *Talking about Writing*. Ann Arbor: University of Michigan Press.

Farrell, Pamela B. 1989. *The High School Writing Center: Establishing and Maintaining One*. Urbana, IL: National Council of Teachers of English.

Gere, Anne Ruggles, ed. 1985. *Roots in the Sawdust*. Urbana, IL: National Council of Teachers of English.

Harris, Muriel. 1986. *Teaching One-to-One: The Writing Conference*. Urbana, IL: National Council of Teachers of English.

Young, Art, and Toby Fulwiler, eds. 1986. *Writing Across the Disciplines: Research Into Practice*. Portsmouth, NH: Boynton/Cook.

Name of School/District/Region: Medgar Evers College, CUNY Humanities Division, Brooklyn, NY
Address: Thomas Jefferson High School, Social Studies Dept., Brooklyn, NY
Contact Person: Brenda Greene or Lorraine Kuziw, Medgar Evers College
Phone Number/FAX/E-mail: (718) 270–5055, FAX (718) 270–5126
Public/Private: Public   **Grades:**   High School–College
Enrollment: 350 high school students
When and How Program Began: Fall 1989, collaboration began between a high school administrator and a college faculty member to create a learning environment that would provide high school social studies students with language experiences to strengthen their social studies skills. It would also enable them to enhance their chances of going to college.
Funding: Medgar Evers College and Jefferson High School
Collaborative Partners (colleges, businesses, networks, etc.):   Medgar Evers College and Jefferson High School
Description of Program: Social studies teachers participated in WAC staff development, and students from their classes attended a social studies enrichment center three times a week. While in the center, students worked with a tutor who assisted them with miniprojects that incorporated WAC.
Special Features of Program: Improved scores on state Regents Competency Tests, access to telecommunications, tutorial instruction, use of student study groups and learning logs
Future Plans: Look of funding to reinstitute the project and start similar projects at other high schools

Name of School/District/Region: Merrimack High School, Merrimack Schools, Merrimack, New Hampshire
Address: 38 McElwain Street, Merrimack, NH 03054
Contact Person: Rae Bruce
Phone Number/FAX/E-mail: (603) 424−6204, FAX (603) 424−6230
Public/Private: Public   **Grades:**   9−12
Enrollment: Approximately 1,200
When and How Program Began: The program began three years ago over coffee and coincided with a new emphasis on interdisciplinary work.
Funding: Required extra funds, worked into existing funds
Collaborative Partners (colleges, businesses, networks, etc.):   Rodney Mansfield, science teacher; Rae Bruce, Write Room consultant
Description of Program: A series of writing activities designed to aid students in thinking about and learning environmental concepts
Special Features of Program: Writing to learn, science poems
Future Plans: At present, Rod's teaching assignment has been changed because of scheduling problems. Rae continues the program by collaborating with Marla Jones, who now teaches environmental science.
Please list any sources you have found helpful in designing, establishing, and maintaining your program:
Berthoff, Ann. 1981. *The Making of Meaning*. Portsmouth, NH: Heinemann.

Fulwiler, Toby, ed. 1987. *The Journal Book*. Portsmouth, NH: Boynton/ Cook.

Gere, Anne Ruggles, ed. 1985. *Roots in the Sawdust*. Urbana, IL: National Council of Teachers of English.

Worsley, Dale, and Bernadette Mayer. 1989. *The Art of Science Writing*. New York: Teachers and Writers Collaborative.

Name of School/District/Region: Morningside Middle School, Charleston County School District, Charleston, SC
Address: 1999 Singley Lane, North Charleston, SC 29405
Contact Person: Jeanne Sink
Phone Number/FAX/E-mail: (803) 745-7122, ntjsink@clust.1.clemson.edu
Public/Private: Public   **Grades:** 6-8
Enrollment: 850
When and How Program Began: The program began in July 1991 when we received a Target 2000 Innovation Grant from the SC State Dept.
Funding: SC Target 2000; REACH (Rockefeller Foundation)
Collaborative Partners (colleges, businesses, networks, etc.): College of Charleston, Westvaco Research, National Geographic KidsNet, Kidlink, FrEdMail.
Description of Program: Program uses technology as a catalyst for motivating teachers and students.
Special Features of Program: Students and teachers have become experts in telecomputing. For example, they were the first class in the U.S. to receive transmissions from South Africa through KIDS-92.
Future Plans: To continue to use technology in all content areas as an invitation to and tool for writing

Name of School/District/Region: Mt. Lebanon School District, Pittsburgh, PA
Address: 7 Horsman Drive, Pittsburgh, PA 15228
Contact Person: Dr. George D. Wilson
Phone Number/FAX/E-mail: (412) 344-2038, FAX (412) 344-2047
Public/Private: Public   **Grades:**   K-12
Enrollment: 5,000
When and How Program Began: In 1989-90 as an aspect of a districtwide WAC program
Funding: None required
Description of Program: Collaborations between teachers in different secondary disciplines
Special Features of Program: Team work, cross-discipline and cross-grade-level activities, telecommunications
Future Plans: Increased telecommunications networking

Name of School/District/Region: Northern Virginia Writing Project
Address: George Mason University, Fairfax, VA 22030
Contact Person: Donald Gallehr, director; Christopher Thaiss, associate director
Phone Number/FAX/E-mail: (703) 993−1168, FAX (703) 993−1161
Public/Private: Public   **Grades:**   7 through college
Enrollment: 400 teacher-consultants; 250 students in in-service courses per semester
When and How Program Began: The Language and Learning Program of the NVWP began with WAC workshops for college and high school faculties in 1978−79.
Funding: School districts contract for in-service courses, and individuals pay fees for conferences. The National Writing Project and the state of Virginia matched funds.
Collaborative Partners (colleges, businesses, networks, etc.):   George Mason University and Northern Virginia school districts
Description of Program: The program includes in-service courses in "Writing and Learning" for K−12 teachers, an annual full-day conference, WAC annual NVEP Summer Institute, and occasional workshops.
Special Features of Program: Follows NWP model of "Teachers teaching teachers"; classroom teachers coordinate in-service courses and annual conference; courses are writing/reading/speaking-intensive; emphasis on diverse language modes
Future Plans: NWP grant for an advanced "theory of writing and learning study group" and first "literature across the curriculum" summer institute

Name of School/District/Region: Philadelphia School District
Address: 21st Street and Parkway, Philadelphia, PA 19103
Contact Person: Judy Buchanan and Andrew Gelber
Phone Number/FAX/E-mail: (215) 299−7000
Public/Private: Public   **Grades:**   K−12
Enrollment: 200,000 students
When and How Program Began: 1984 — superintendent's reform agenda, support from area corporations, universities
Funding: Rockefeller Foundation (initial), School District of Philadelphia (since 1986)
Collaborative Partners (colleges, businesses, networks, etc.):   PATHS/PRISM: The Philadelphia Partnership for Education; PhilWP (the Philadelphia Partnership Writing Project)
Description of Program: Systemwide, school-based focus on uses of writing to learn and teach all subjects K−12
Special Features of Program: Teacher-consultant program and cross-visitation opportunities; school-level and "regional" program structure
Future Plans: To support district focus on (a) alternative assessment and (b) shared decision-making/school-based management

Name of School/District/Region: Puget Sound Literature Program of the Puget Sound Writing Program
Address: Dept. of English, GN-30, University of Washington, Seattle, WA 98195
Contact Person: Mary Kollar/Linda Clifton
Phone Number/FAX/E-mail: (206) 543−0141, FAX (206) 685−2673
Public/Private: Public   **Grades:**   K−University
Enrollment: Average 18 per class
When and How Program Began: 1986−87 began collaboration between Dr. Eugene Smith of PSWP and Robynn Anderson, then Lake Washington School District
Funding: Summer tuition and planning time as part of regular PSWP staff work funded by the English Department
Collaborative Partners (colleges, businesses, networks, etc.):   Informal collaboration of University of Washington and, first, Lake Washington and, more recently, Northshore School District
Description of Program: Collaborative teaching by a K−12 teacher of literature and a university English department faculty member.
Special Features of Program: The K−12 teacher is hired as summer faculty in University of Washington English department. The program offers credit toward teacher placement degrees for those enrolled in the class.
Future Plans: We have added PSWP Shakespeare, a second collaborative class, and will explore other such possibilities focusing on other specific subject areas. We plan to look at applying for NEH support.
Please list any sources you have found helpful in designing, establishing, and maintaining your program:
The most valuable supportive sources have been the teaching experience of the university professor and the classroom teachers from the public schools. We have extended our notion of literature to include film and art, and so have received support from art historians and film libraries.

Name of School/District/Region: Saluda High School
Address: 400 W. Butler Avenue, Saluda, SC 29138
Contact Person: William A. Whitfield
Phone Number/FAX/E-mail: (803) 445–2564
Public/Private: Public   **Grades:**   9–12
Enrollment: 560 students
When and How Program Began: Fall 1989 as school response to declining writing scores on state exit exam
Funding: Local school funds; consultant fees and in-kind services by Writing Improvement Network; $3,000 REACH grant
Collaborative Partners (colleges, businesses, networks, etc.):   Writing Improvement Network (USC); REACH (Clemson)
Description of Program: In-service training, classroom demonstrations, school planning committee, publication of student writing, schoolwide free-writing period daily, collaboration with support agencies
Future Plans: Continuation of existing program with ongoing review, assessment, and modifications as necessary

Name of School/District/Region: Shorewood High School, Shoreline School District, Seattle, Washington
Address: 17300 Fremont Avenue North, Seattle, WA 98133
Contact Person: Steve Pearse
Phone Number/FAX/E-mail: (206) 361-4372, FAX (206) 368-4711
Public/Private: Public   **Grades:** 9-12
Enrollment: Approximately 1,485
When and How Program Began: 1989, via selecting of building goals under the banner, "Success for Every Student"
Funding: None other than from individual teacher grants
Collaborative Partners (colleges, businesses, networks, etc.): None officially; ties with the Puget Sound Writing Program
Description of Program: A variety of integrative projects involving students more directly and personally in subject-matter learning
Special Features of Program: No true "program"; rather, teacher-leaders instigating change across the curriculum
Future Plans: To weave WAC throughout the high school, moving it beyond the teacher teams (and individuals) currently using writing as an exploration and learning tool

Name of School/District/Region: Tucson Unified School District (TUSD #1)
Address: 1010 E. 10th Street, District Headquarters, Tucson, AZ
Contact Person: Roger W. Shanley (high school coordinator)
Phone Number/FAX/E-mail: (602) 745−4740
Public/Private: Public   **Grades:**   9−12
Enrollment: 2,000 at Santa Rita High School
When and How Program Began: In August 1984, Pima Community College proposed a three-way partnership with local high schools and the University of Arizona.
Funding: The Fund for the Improvement of Post Secondary Education (FIPSE) for a three-year program
Collaborative Partners (colleges, businesses, networks, etc.):   Pima Community College, University of Arizona, and Tucson Unified School District
Description of Program: The program was designed to work with WAC programs at the three levels of high school, two-year community college, and four-year university. The program emphasized both speaking and writing across the curriculum.
Special Features of Program: Grant allowed stipends for ten individuals from each level to participate and develop activities or units for use in the classroom. Each semester (eighteen weeks) ten new members joined. At the end of three years, over fifty high school teachers had been involved.
Future Plans: Continued efforts of local teachers of English organizations (without a grant) to hold workshops and make presentations

Name of School/District/Region: Volusia County School District
Address: P.O. Box 2410, Daytona Beach, FL 32115
Contact Person: Nana E. Hilsenbeck
Phone Number/FAX/E-mail: (904) 255−6475 ext.2264, FAX (904) 238−7347
Public/Private: Public   **Grades:**   Preschool−12
Enrollment: 50,000 students
When and How Program Began: Writing across the disciplines began in 1981 with the support and vision of the assistant superintendent of instruction. Using the teachers teaching teachers model, it started from the top down and became a grassroots program.
Funding: District funding (no special grants)
Collaborative Partners (colleges, businesses, networks, etc.):   University of Central Florida and also Sylvan Learning (business partner)
Description of Program: K−12 grade students are expected to write and keep a writing folder. All subject areas are included.
Special Features of Program: Teachers were trained and became the consultants for their own schools to promote WAC. Computers were introduced in 1986.
Future Plans: Portfolio assessment with district support for more involvement with science and social studies
Please list any sources you have found helpful in designing, establishing, and maintaining your program:
In-service plan, which is ongoing; district support with teachers on assignment who are continuing to assist, coach, and provide in-service; assessment that is congruent with performance (writing)

Notes on Contributors

Linda Ashida has taught Spanish for six years at Elk Grove High School. She understands the value of writing in her classroom not only as a way for students to practice Spanish vocabulary but also as a way for them to think about cultural differences.

Betty Beck directs the Writing Center at McCaskey High School in Lancaster, PA.

Barry Brown is a school counselor at Elk Grove High. Having worked at the high school district's alternative school, he has spent much of his career focusing on students unable to cope in traditional high school settings. Barry's experience and belief in teacher-counselor teams helped the interdisciplinary pilot program for 105 students become accepted as a program for all 450 incoming freshmen two years later.

Rae Bruce, a member of the English department, founded the Write Room, an interdisciplinary writing center at Merrimack High School. In her role as Write Room consultant, she collaborates with teachers across the disciplines. Her collaborations include projects with teachers of social studies, art, science, and foreign language.

Judy Buchanan is a director of the Philadelphia Writing Project. A Philadelphia public school teacher for eighteen years, she is currently serving as a teacher on special assignment to the Writing Project. She has worked as a teacher-consultant, taught in-service courses, and is an active member of several teacher networks.

Gloria Caldwell is Media Specialist at Saluda (South Carolina) High School.

Constance Childress teaches social studies at Beaubien Middle School in the Detroit Public School System.

Elizabeth L. Clifford, English teacher at Ravenscroft, was hired to begin developing a cross-curricular writing program at Ravenscroft, including a computerized Writing Center. For fourteen years, 1978–1992, she taught English at Berkshire where she coordinated the TWAC committee, which developed the school's WAC program and a writing center.

Eve Coleman teaches in the School of Education at the College of Charleston in South Carolina.

George Cooper is a lecturer at the English Composition Board at the University of Michigan.

Mary Cox teaches English at Martin Luther King High School in the Detroit Public School System.

Melissa Deloach is an English and drama teacher at Saluda (SC) High School.

Lois E. Easton is Director of Re:Learning Systems at the Education Commission of the States, a partnership program with Brown University that focuses on school-level restructuring based on Ted Sizer's research into American high schools. Formerly she served the Arizona Department of Education as Writing Specialist, Director of Curriculum and Instruction, and Director of Curriculum and Assessment Planning.

Dean Ellerton is Assistant Director of the Writing Center at Berkshire. Dean teaches chemistry, coaches soccer, and is a member of the TWAC committee. Dean's work as computer specialist has been invaluable to the planning for and operation of the Writing Center.

Jack Elliott, who put the interdisciplinary program at Elk Grove into place, is now principal-elect at Rolling Meadows High School (in the same high school district) in Rolling Meadows, Illinois. His interest in writing comes from a belief that all disciplines need to include writing as a learning tool, and he urges parents to become part of the learning process.

Marcella Emberger is Innovative Program Manager for Baltimore County Public Schools (BCPS). She was an English teacher and English department Chair from 1970 to 1985. From 1985 through 1991, she directed the WAC project for BCPS, which won the Center of Excellence award from the National Council of Teachers of English. She coauthored "On-site Support in a Staff Development Project," *Journal of Staff Development*, May 1989, with Clare Kruft.

Edwin C. Epps works as a teacher-in-residence on loan from Spartanburg County (SC) School District Seven to the Writing Improvement Network.

Barry Gadlin teaches English at Elk Grove High School where he works with other teachers on ways they can use informal and formal writing activities in their classes.

Suellyn Gates, a Spanish teacher at Elk Grove High School, works with other teachers on using writing in a foreign language classroom for learning other than vocabulary practice.

Andrew Gelber is Director of School Programs for PATHS/PRISM: The Philadelphia Partnership for Education, an organization dedicated to improving public education for Philadelphia's students through supporting teacher professional development and school reform.

Bernadette Glaze teaches English at Thomas Jefferson High School in Fairfax County, Virginia.

Brenda Greene teaches basic writing, composition, and literature at Medgar Evers College, CUNY. She also chairs the Department of Language, Literature, Communication Skills, and Philosophy.

Nana E. Hilsenbeck is Coordinator of Writing for Volusia County School District in Daytona Beach, FL.

Bernie Kelly has taught math in High School District 214 in the northwest suburban Chicago area for twenty-three years. Presently he teaches at Elk Grove High School where he works to convince his colleagues of the value of writing and interdisciplinary learning.

Chris Kelly has taught math for seventeen years at Resurrection High School in Chicago. She also works with teachers of freshmen at Elk Grove High School to coordinate a study-skills program for the interdisciplinary program.

Mary Beth Khoury has taught biology and physical science to freshmen and sophomores at Elk Grove High School since 1986, and she requires many writing projects of her students.

Mary E. Kollar has taught English in public high schools for twenty-five years, during which time she has served as English department Chairperson and has participated in teacher training. In 1991 she left public schools to direct the Transition School of the Early Entrance Program, the Center for the Study of Capable Youth, at the University of Washington.

Robert Koralik spent fifteen years as a school librarian before coming to Elk Grove High School to teach world and U.S. history. Writing activities help his students learn about historical eras and philosophies instead of just memorizing facts.

Clare Kruft is an Assistant Principal at Bear Creek Elementary, Baltimore County Public Schools. Clare has worked as a trainer for many instructional programs, including Johns Hopkins Cooperative Learning project.

Lorraine Kuziw teaches English composition at Medgar Evers College, CUNY, and is currently the coordinator of English at MEC.

Peter LaRochelle teaches two levels of high school biology including a course for Honors students at the McCallie School. For the past two years the topical focus for the Honors course has been tropical rain forest ecology.

Nancy Linvill is a resource room teacher for learning disabled students at Edwards Junior High School in Clemson, South Carolina.

Rodney Mansfield served as a chairman of the committee that wrote a new Merrimack High School philosophy emphasizing interdisciplinary education. Currently, he holds a planning grant from the National Science Foundation for a collaborative project to improve the teaching of science in elementary and middle schools in southern New Hampshire.

Cissy May has been teaching chemistry for ten years at the McCallie School, where she is also an academic class dean, sponsor of the National Honor Society, and Science Bowl Competition Team.

Sally McNelis is English department Chairman at Eastern School of Technology in Baltimore County, and she has published several articles on WAC.

Barbra Morris is a lecturer in communications, the Residential College, and the English Composition Board at the University of Michigan.

Lyn Zalusky Mueller is Director of the Writing Improvement Network in the College of Education at the University of South Carolina in Columbia.

Catherine Neuhardt-Minor has taught, painted, and exhibited throughout the eastern seaboard, Ohio, and Texas. She has also painted and exhibited in England, France, Denmark, and Costa Rica. Ms. Neuhardt-Minor chairs the art department at the McCallie School.

Lance Nickel has been teaching at the McCallie School since 1974. He currently holds McCallie's Alumni Chair of Mathematics.

Steve Pearse has taught for nineteen years in the Shoreline School District just north of Seattle. As English department Chair at Shorewood High School, he has encouraged a process-to-product emphasis for student work and assessment, including a portfolio-based approach to writing instruction and practice.

David B. Perkinson teaches Applied Math, Algebra II, and Geometry at the McCallie School and has worked extensively on writing in math.

Chris Peters teaches instructional technology at Clemson University in South Carolina.

Heather Prescott is codirector of TWAC and Chair of the Professional Development Program at Berkshire. Heather teaches French and coaches girls' varsity soccer.

Sharon Robbins, currently Assistant Principal at Middle River Middle School, has been an educator for thirteen years.

Anna Romano is the current Director of the Writing Center and codirector of TWAC—along with Heather Prescott. As well, Anna is the Director of the International Student Program at Berkshire.

Marianne Rosenstein teaches math and geometry at Elk Grove High School. As a member of the first interdisciplinary team at the high school, Marianne expanded her use of writing in the classroom to include journal writing, admit slips, and exit slips to augment her use of writing as a critical thinking tool.

Hilary Russell is Chairman of the English department at Berkshire and a long-time member of the TWAC committee.

Roger Shanley teaches English at Rincon High School in Tucson, Arizona.

Jeanne C. Sink teaches English at Morningside Middle School in Charleston, South Carolina.

Christopher Thaiss teaches English at George Mason University where he also works with the Northern Virginia Writing Project. He coordinates the National Network of Writing Across the Curriculum Programs.

James K. Upton directs the Writing Center at Burlington High School in Burlington, Iowa, and works with the Iowa Writing Project. He is also a member of the Executive Board of the National Writing Centers Association.

Charles Widlowski had taught junior high school for three years before becoming a high school counselor for a little more than two decades, presently at Elk Grove High School. He has spent the last twenty-three years also as an Upward Bound instructor, taking groups of students into the Canadian wilderness to increase their self-confidence.

Patricia Williams teaches reading using a multisensory approach at Marshall Elementary School in the Detroit Public School System.

George D. Wilson serves as Director of Secondary Education for the Mt. Lebanon School District, Pittsburgh, PA. He acknowledges the outstanding work of Mrs. Marilyn Bates, Mrs. Cynthia Biery, Mr. Dale Cable, Mr. Brendan Fitzgerald, Mrs. Carol Hirsch, Ms. Virginia Nikolich, Mr. Mark Pelusi, and Mr. Ronald Schreiner. Without their initiative and creativity, these collaborations in service to students would not have occurred.

Odessa Wilson teaches at the Morningside School in Charleston, South Carolina.